'Sir BILL'

ABOUT THE AUTHORS

STEVE PERRYMAN MBE played more games for Tottenham Hotspur than any other player in history (854) and was selected for his debut at the age of 17 by Bill Nicholson. Nicknamed 'Skip', he went on to captain Spurs in back-to-back FA Cup finals when Bill Nick was Club President. He leans on his intimate inside knowledge of 'Sir Bill' to cover his personality, moods and perfectionism on and off the pitch. 'Bill,' declares Steve, 'was like a second father to me, and I am privileged to be able to help tell his incredible story.'

Steve's official website is steveperryman.com

NORMAN GILLER is a word master who has had more than 120 books published following a distinguished career as a Fleet Street football reporter and, for 14 years, a TV scriptwriter with the *This Is Your Life* team. He was a trusted confidant of Bill Nicholson for more than 40 years, and his closeness to Spurs includes a special relationship with the idolised Jimmy Greaves, delivering his epilogue on behalf of his many followers and team-mates. Norman's microscopic observations of the Nicholson/Greaves rapport makes fascinating reading in a book that belongs on every Tottenham followers' bookshelf.

Many of Norman's books are available from his website normangillerbooks.com
He can be found on X as @NormanGiller

MICHAEL GILLER, who at the age of eight used to go to bed wearing Steve Perryman's Spurs shirt, provides the extraordinary statistics that underline the fact that Bill Nicholson was a master manager after a hugely successful playing career with Tottenham.

'Sir BILL'

The Complete Bill Nicholson Story

**STEVE PERRYMAN
& NORMAN GILLER**

VSP

Published by Vision Sports Publishing in 2024

Vision Sports Publishing
19–23 High Street
Kingston upon Thames
Surrey
KT1 1LL
www.visionsp.co.uk

Copyright © Steve Perryman and Norman Giller, 2024
The moral rights of the authors have been asserted

Statistics: Michael Giller
Design: Doug Cheeseman
Typesetting: Paul Baillie-Lane
ISBN: 9781913412692

Every effort has been made to contact the copyright holders of the photographs used in this book. If there are any errors or omissions then the publishers will be pleased to receive this information.

All rights reserved. No part of this publication may be reproduced, stored in a retrieval system, or transmitted in any form or by any means, electronic, mechanical, photocopying, recording or otherwise, without the prior permission of the publishers except in the case of brief quotations embedded in critical articles or reviews.

This book is sold subject to the condition that it shall not, by way of trade or otherwise, be lent, re-sold, hired out, or otherwise circulated without the publisher's prior consent in any form of binding or cover other than that in which it is published and without a similar condition including this condition being imposed on the subsequent purchaser.
A CIP Catalogue record for this book is available from the British Library

Printed and bound in the UK by CPI Group

*In loving memory of
'Sir' Bill Nicholson
(1919–2004)*

CONTENTS

ACKNOWLEDGEMENTS IX

KICK OFF by STEVE PERRYMAN MBE 1
CHAPTER 1: LAST OF THE VICTORIANS 5
CHAPTER 2: OH! WHAT A LOVELY WAR 13
CHAPTER 3: THE 'PUSH AND RUN' DAYS 21
CHAPTER 4: A 90-MINUTE ENGLAND CAREER 27
CHAPTER 5: BOWING OUT TO BLANCHFLOWER 31
CHAPTER 6: SEEING OFF ALF RAMSEY 37
CHAPTER 7: STIFLING THE BOYS OF BRAZIL 45
CHAPTER 8: THE ASTONISHING 10-4 START 51
CHAPTER 9: THE DOUBLE 59
CHAPTER 10: SIGNING JIMMY GREAVES 77
CHAPTER 11: EUROPEAN CUP ROBBERY 85
CHAPTER 12: MAKING HISTORY IN ROTTERDAM 91
CHAPTER 13: THE DARKEST DAYS 97
CHAPTER 14: COMPLETING THE FA CUP HAT-TRICK .. 107
CHAPTER 15: A LEGEND DEPARTS 113

CHAPTER 16: A TALE OF TWO STRIKERS 127
CHAPTER 17: HAIR-RAISING FOR RALPH COATES 139
CHAPTER 18: NIGHTMARE IN ROTTERDAM 147
CHAPTER 19: ON THE DOLE 155
CHAPTER 20: BACK FROM THE WILDERNESS 161
CHAPTER 21: AT HOME WITH THE MASTER 169
CHAPTER 22: A FOND FINAL FAREWELL 185
CHAPTER 23: TEAM OF TEAMS 215

FINAL SHOTS by STEVE PERRYMAN MBE 231
EXTRA-TIME 241
THE NUMBERS GAME by MICHAEL GILLER 249
MAJOR SIGNINGS 270
TIMELINE 275
INDEX 281

ACKNOWLEDGEMENTS

Authors Steve Perryman and Norman Giller thank the skilled and knowledgeable Vision Sports Publishing team – in particular editorial staff Ed Davis and Paul Baillie-Lane, as well as chief motivator Toby Trotman – for helping to get this tribute book to 'Sir Bill' Nicholson off the launching pad.

Our thanks to the omniscient Spurs historian David Guthrie and statistician Michael Giller for their safety-net fact checking, to former Spurs press officer John 'Scoop' Fennelly for raiding his memory of 'Sir Bill' and to current Head of Publications Jon Rayner for his expert supervising on behalf of Tottenham Hotspur. We also acknowledge the encouragement of Tottenham executive director Donna-Maria Cullen.

Grateful acknowledgements also to two of my significant writing colleagues Brian Scovell and Harry Harris for priceless background details on 'Sir Bill'.

We have been expertly designed by Doug Cheeseman and Paul Baillie-Lane.

A special merit mention to Terry and Freda Baker, the promoters and entrepreneurs of A1 Sporting Speakers, whose brilliantly staged theatre shows have provided us with much background information.

There are repeated articles and comments from previous publications of ours for which we hold the copyright, and we thank the various publishers for permission to print them. And the authors dipped into the significant, official Bill Nicholson autobiography, ghosted by Brian Scovell and Harry Harris and published in 1984 by MacMillan.

We have been furnished with photographs by late, great Fleet Street cameramen such as Monte Fresco and Bob Stiggins, and some of their work features in the picture section.

'SIR BILL'

Our gratitude to Bill's daughters, Jean and Linda, and the Nicholson family for allowing Tottenham Hotspur to share the great man. As his late, wonderful wife Darkie once said: "He could have been accused of bigamy, because he was married to me and to the club."

We bow the knee to all Bill's former players and club colleagues, who willingly shared their memories. We just hope we have done the great man justice.

Thanks most of all to YOU for reading this book and keeping alive the memory of 'Sir Bill', the Master of White Hart Lane.

COYS!

KICK OFF

Steve Perryman MBE

I am sure that no two people can match the joint knowledge Norman Giller and I have of the life and times of Bill Nicholson, the subject of this special book which is dedicated to the memory of 'Mr Spurs'; or, as many with Tottenham blood think of him, 'Sir Bill'.

Norman, a doyen of the press box with a huge knowledge of the history of the 'Beautiful Game', used to watch Bill – then known as Billy – play at right-half in the famous 'Push and Run' Spurs side that won the Second and First Division titles in back-to-back seasons from 1949 to 1951. By the time Norm arrived in Fleet Street as a member of the *Daily Express* sports reporting team, Bill had established himself as the leading manager in the land and they started a long-running conversation that lasted more than 40 years. Every quote you are about to read from Bill was made either to Norman or me, and many are appearing in print for the first time.

Norman knows everything there is to know about 'Sir Bill' the man. My role as we paint the Bill Nicholson portrait together is to talk about Bill Nicholson the manager. I was just 17 when he threw me in at the deep end of the old First Division, a 1969 match against Sunderland at White Hart Lane that was the first of what would become a club record 854 appearances. We lost 1-0.

It was Bill who gave me my start – how could I ever forget that? This book is my thank you to the great man. A long campaign to get him a knighthood failed, but that has not stopped his many supporters still referring to him as 'Sir Bill'.

I looked on him as a second father, and there is nobody in my time who has got close to challenging his unofficial title as the 'Father of Spurs'. Club historians assure me that legendary figures like club pioneer Bobby Buckle, 1901 FA Cup-winning Scottish player-manager John Cameron, master tactician Peter – another Scot –

'SIR BILL'

McWilliam and 'Push and Run' genius Arthur Rowe are claimants for the crown, but none of them could touch Bill's trophy collection.

The back-to-back FA Cups that I collected as proud Spurs skipper came after Bill had given up the manager's baton, but he remained prominent in the background as Honorary Club President and we were still following his doctrine of skilled football at all times. 'Bill Nick', as he was known throughout the game, had Lilywhite corpuscles, and Norman and I are determined to give him the tribute book his memory deserves.

There have been millions of words written about Bill, several books and TV and video tributes, but nobody has shovelled as deep and personal as we are going in this microscopic look at his life, both in and out of football.

Now, here's Norman Giller to explain the running order and style of this unique book in which I am delighted to be adding my appreciation of the greatest servant Tottenham Hotspur have ever had...

Steve and I have known each other since the week he made his Tottenham debut in 1969, when I was chief football reporter for the *Daily Express*. Bill Nicholson called over this confident but never cocky, baby-faced kid to meet me during a session at Tottenham's then training ground at Cheshunt in Hertfordshire, just off the A10. 'I want you to meet Stephen Perryman,' he said in his precise North Yorkshire accent. 'He's a diamond of a prospect and we expect big things of him.'

As you will learn in the following pages, it was a rarity for Bill to make such glowing reference to any of his players, and it was years later when he confided: 'I knew I was asking a lot of young Steve at a difficult time for the team, so I wanted to boost his confidence and self-belief.'

Now here we are 55 years later singing Bill's praises, and also exposing the few warts of a man who went beyond the call of duty in his service to his beloved Spurs.

Steve and I will be telling his story in tandem, with the input from 'Skip' – as Steve is known by anyone with Spurs blood – clearly signposted. I am the conductor, and Steve the chief soloist. He saw him at work, but few of us saw Bill at play, because he was so rigid and disciplined with his life that he allowed little time for the trivia of pastimes and hobbies. Tottenham and football, in that order, always came first.

Throughout the book we drop in quotes from Bill made to either Steve or myself that give an insight to his personality and his life-long search for perfection. We are keeping it as conversational as possible and hope you feel as if you are sitting in with us on talks with the great man. Occasionally we go off on tangents with interludes in which we share anecdotes that add extra zing to our Bill Nicholson cocktail.

When interesting and informative enough, I occasionally repeat things that Steve and I have covered in previous books. We feel it important to include anything that helps make this a finished picture of the man I called – in the *Daily Express* back in the 1970s – 'The Master of White Hart Lane'. As the legendary Welsh wing wizard Cliff Jones has often said: "He was in charge from the boot room to the boardroom."

As well as copious quotes from Bill, we will be calling on old friends and colleagues – most, sadly, no longer with us – to help give an accurate portrayal of the man and the manager.

Bill's elegant wife, Grace – nicknamed 'Darkie' to identify her from her blonde twin sister – was a wonderful lady, who always gave her husband 'Willie' 100 per cent support. She once told me: 'Willie could be charged with bigamy. He is married to me and to Tottenham Hotspur.'

I along with many influential people in the game campaigned for many years from the 1970s for Bill to be recognised with a knighthood for his services to football, but we were always ignored by the myopic mandarins of Whitehall, who just about stretched to an OBE as reward for giving his life to Tottenham Hotspur in particular and the 'Beautiful Game' in general.

It is a call that is continued by many well-meaning Spurs supporters to this day, not realising that the Establishment never ever awards posthumous knighthoods.

Steve and I are doing our bit by calling this book 'Sir Bill'. Here comes his story…

COYS!

'SIR BILL'

Joint authors Steve Perryman and Norman Giller – mates for more than 50 years

CHAPTER 1

LAST OF THE VICTORIANS

Bill Nicholson was one of the last of the Victorians. Born in the seaside town of Scarborough in North Yorkshire on 26 January 1919 – two months following the First World War Armistice – he arrived on this mortal coil 18 years after the passing of Queen Victoria. He was the second youngest of nine children of Victorian-born parents, educated by Victorian-raised teachers and instilled with the iron discipline and strict morals of Victorian times. The 19th century influence never left him.

Bill was the most disciplined person I ever knew. He was a stickler for punctuality and God help any player who was late for training or, worse still, on match day. He was always first to arrive and last to leave for training sessions out at Cheshunt, and he would actually sulk with any players who got in after the call time. Describing him as the 'Last of the Victorians' is spot on.

Everything had to be spick and span, and he used to have perfectly trimmed short back and sides haircuts, trousers with creases that could cut your fingers, and you could see your face in his highly polished leather shoes. Bill was an immaculate man, old-fashioned with his dress sense but always military smart, and he expected his players to be just as particular about their appearance. 'You're representing Tottenham Hotspur,' he'd say. 'Smartness at all times, take your hands out of your pockets and no slouching.' He was happiest in a tracksuit and talking tactics, and he demanded discipline and dignity. Yes, Victorian captures him perfectly.

With hair that was ginger tinged, 'Billy' had a freckled face as a youngster and the sun used to burn him when he often accompanied his horse-groom father, Joe Nicholson, on Sunday hansom cab drives along Scarborough seafront, taking day trippers on sixpenny rides and families to church worship.

His dad walked with a heavy limp all his life and was unfit for service in the First World War. He continued to scrape a living with a horse-drawn cab in the immediate post-war years, and it was through his dad that the boy Billy developed a deep love of horses, but the growing dominance of the motor car ended early ambitions to become a horse groom. The rambling rented house at 15 Vine Street where he was born was an extension of the livery stables that employed his father, and the four bedrooms were shared by Billy's parents and his eight brothers and sisters.

The Nicholsons later moved to nearby 6 Quarry Mount where Bill became an enthusiastic and energetic member of a generation known as 'tanner ball players', thousands of young boys going everywhere with a small, rubber ball at their feet. It was a Woolworths bestseller and cost sixpence (2.5p)... here's Bill sharing thoughts with me about those early days:

"In later years 'tanner ball players' became a sneering, uncomplimentary description, but in the early days any boy who had the ball – which was the same size and weight as a tennis ball – learned tricks and flicks that called for skill and control. I got my first one at seven as a present from an uncle, and from not having shown any interest in football I suddenly became a fanatic. The ball went everywhere with me and became my best friend. From playing with the tanner ball, I progressed to the laced, leather-panelled balls of the time that were not water resistant. They could weigh twice as much at the end of the game, played on what were often mud heaps – there was rarely a flat pitch on the hills surrounding Scarborough and I got used to playing on slopes.

"When I won a scholarship to Scarborough High School at the age of eleven, I started to establish myself as a useful footballer, and I recall one of my teachers describing me as 'having talent and a good temperament'. I went straight into the Under-14 team as a centre-half and had a spring that enabled me to out jump much taller opponents.

LAST OF THE VICTORIANS

"I became self-sufficient by getting an early-morning paper round for six bob (30p) a week, and I bought my own pair of football boots that I used to repair myself on my dad's work bench. Nothing was ever handed to me on a plate, but I was never afraid of hard work and it shaped me for the rest of my life. I could forgive most things, but never lack of effort. It was a tough existence back in the '20s and '30s, but it prepared me to handle anything thrown at me in later life. I took after my mum, who did an office-cleaning job while running a spotless home for 11 of us. What an organiser that lady was.

"There was always something to do, like mucking out the stables, polishing the brass on the harnesses or oiling the hooves of the horses. My football developed when I started playing in a local league for the Young Liberals team. I had no interest in politics but they saw something in me and I became a sort of utility defender for them.

"Mum and Dad were too busy to take any real interest in my football, so it came as a surprise to them when they got a hand-written letter from Tottenham Hotspur scout Ben Ives inviting me to White Hart Lane for a month's trial. I'd never been outside Yorkshire, so it was as if I'd been invited to go to the moon.

"I had just got a job in the local Alexander laundry for £2 a week, supervising the giant washing machines. To be honest, I'd not given too much thought as to what to do and it came out of the blue that my future could be in football. Spurs had been tipped off by a Tottenham fan who worked for a dentist called Herbert Jones. He ran the Young Liberals team, and it was in that roundabout way I agreed to travel down to London for a trial. I knew little about Tottenham, just that they were a club in North London – where Arsenal were better known for what they had achieved under the management of another Yorkshireman called Herbert Chapman. Every schoolboy knew he had guided Huddersfield and then Arsenal to three successive league titles. It's a fact I don't like thinking about that Tottenham lived in their shadow, but that was the way it was back then."

So 17-year-old, raw, naive Billy Nicholson left behind the bubbling cauldron of washing machines and made his first visit to London by night train from York to King's Cross, took the Piccadilly Line to Manor House – deep in Arsenal territory – and then caught what was still called the omnibus to White Hart Lane. It was Monday 16 March in the momentous year of 1936 – remembered for having three monarchs (George V died, Edward VIII then abdicated, compelling George VI to assume the throne), the Berlin Olympics that served as a propaganda platform for Hitler's Nazis, the start of the Spanish Civil War, the Jarrow Hunger March, and the BBC making its first television broadcast – that Billy Nicholson joined Spurs, passing his month's trial thanks to his natural enthusiasm and driving energy, capturing the way he always played the game.

Spurs were then a struggling First Division club under the unconvincing management of Jack Tresadern, who was notoriously aloof from all but the club's first-team players. He showed little interest in the progress of the platoon of young, would-be professionals hoping to join a playing staff that numbered a huge 48. This was in the days of the £8 a week winter, £6 a week summer maximum football wage, and teams had to be fielded in League, Combination (reserve), Kent District, youth and 'A' team matches.

Back in 1982 I scripted an official Spurs centenary video (in Betamax rather than VHS format, which dates it…), and it was presented by a new-to-broadcasting chap called Jimmy Greaves. We started the video under the very Tottenham High Road lamppost where Bobby Buckle and his cricketing schoolboy pals decided to launch Hotspur Football Club in 1882. Steve Perryman, fresh from collecting the FA Cup for a second successive season, was just one of the Spurs legends we interviewed…

> *"Among the guests who came to White Hart Lane for the filming was Tottenham legend Ron Burgess. It was a privilege to meet him, and he told me that he and Bill had signed for Spurs on the same day in 1936. Ron had been a coal miner in South Wales and was spotted by a Tottenham scout, just as Bill was invited to come down from Yorkshire. They played together for Northfleet in Kent, Tottenham's feeder club. It was another world to what my generation was used to, and Ron told me their wage was £2 a week. He explained how he and Bill used to rake the pitch*

and paint the White Hart Lane stands in the summer months. Ron recalled that Bill was a good carpenter but suffered from vertigo and struggled to climb ladders – although he proved when he was manager that he actually had a head for heights!"

In charge of the nursery club – later known as Gravesend & Northfleet – was trainer and future first-team manager Jimmy Anderson, who had been a disciple of Peter McWilliam during his first spell as Spurs manager from 1912 to 1927, until being poached by Middlesbrough for a then record £1,500 a year. While playing for Newcastle United, McWilliam had been known as 'Peter the Great', with a left foot that was like a magic wand. He more than anybody introduced and popularised the Spurs-style 'Push and Run' method that was later passed on like a relay baton by one of his star players, Arthur Rowe.

"It's fitba' not heid ba'," McWilliam used to repeatedly preach as he encouraged Spurs to play the game on the ground the Scottish way rather than the common English system of pumping long balls upfield to be chased – a muscular style still occasionally seen today in the guise of Route One. In 1938 McWilliam, by then an Arsenal scout, returned to White Hart Lane in place of the disenchanted Tresadern, and among his pupils were Bill Nicholson and his best mate Ronnie Burgess.

Meantime, Rowe – along with the legendary 'Sheffield Stroller' Jimmy Hagan – had moved on to Hungary as a teacher sponsored by the Football Association, and he gave lectures to other coaches in the art of 'Push and Run'. Among those who got the message was a young player from Budapest called Ferenc Puskas, who later formed a prolific partnership at Real Madrid with Argentine ace Alfredo di Stefano. Puskas was the captain of the 'Magical Magyars' team that wrecked 'Old Masters' England 6-3 and 7-1 in 1953–54, and at the end of his distinguished playing career he toured the world as a coach and manager, spending much of his time in Greece with Panathinaikos and AEK Athens. His wind-down period came with South Melbourne in Australia, where his captain and interpreter was a Greek-born defender called Angelos Postecoglou – yes, the same Ange who brought Puskas-propelled front-foot football to Tottenham in 2023. The McWilliam/Rowe style of playing the game had gone full circle.

Also playing with Bill and coming under the influence of Rowe was a wing-half called Vic Buckingham, who had signed for Spurs a year ahead of Nicholson and Burgess. The three of them learned football the Spurs way from McWilliam and Rowe, and in 1954 Vic coached West Bromwich Albion to an FA Cup triumph before taking his 'Tottenham tactics' to Holland, where Vic passed on his knowledge to an Ajax team that included the young Johan Cruyff. With Rinus Michels as the main instigator, the Dutch masters created 'Total Football', based on the Tottenham 'Push and Run' style, which was later introduced to Barcelona (where Buckingham coached and was so close to Cruyff that he became godfather to one of his sons).

So the Spurs influence ran deep through European football, and Bill Nicholson was in on the ground floor learning the simple yet sophisticated technique and tactics of the give-it-and-go style. He also picked up and added to the vocabulary first inspired by McWilliam and which became unofficially known as Spurs talk. Steve Perryman is fluent in it…

> *"Bill – we called him that at his insistence rather than 'Boss' or 'Gaffer' like at most other clubs – had a language all his own, lots of little sayings that made the basics easy to remember. Things like, 'when not in possession, make sure you're in position'; 'never let the ball die, keep it alive'; 'make it quick, make it easy, make it accurate'; 'play the way you're facing'; 'one ball back, the next ball forward and through'; 'no spectating when you're playing. If you want to watch, pay your entrance fee and join the crowd'; 'the three As: accuracy, accuracy, accuracy'. These were all short, simple slogans that I passed on to all the players during my managing and coaching career, knowing I was using the words of the Master. If you're going to borrow, borrow from the best."*

Not yet 20, Bill made his league debut at Blackburn Rovers on 22 October 1938, selected by McWilliam because of injury problems in the first-team squad and Bill Whatley's call-up to the Wales side that beat England 4-2 at Ninian Park on the same day – as a consequence Nicholson filled in at left-back. It was not the start he had been dreaming of while lodging at 23 Farningham Road, Tottenham, with the Lawrence family, who treated him like a son. He finished the match limping on the wing as Spurs lost 3-1.

A few doors away, at 17 Farningham Road, lived Grace 'Darkie' Power, with her two sisters. Bill had already fallen in love and started a romance that lasted more than 60 years. Almost as appealing as Grace was the fact that at Number 17 her father had a billiards table, and Bill spent hours playing the game in the style of his hero, Joe Davis, who became the supreme world snooker champion for two decades. (I once boldly challenged Bill to a game of snooker at a hotel in Athens during an England Under-23 tour when he was manager... I broke off and then sat watching him clear the table. Stupid boy.)

Even while courting in the old-fashioned way, Bill's relationship with Grace had to take second place to football as he worked at earning a permanent place in McWilliam's first-team squad. Then, suddenly, all careers were put on hold. Adolf Hitler had marched his Nazi troops into Poland and war was declared on 3 September 1939.

The Football League programme was immediately cancelled and within a month 19-year-old W. E. (Edward) Nicholson was a member of His Majesty's Armed Forces.

"It was," Bill Nick later recalled, "the making of me."

CHAPTER 2

OH! WHAT A LOVELY WAR

Within a month of war being declared, Private W.E. Nicholson was doing his basic training with the Durham Light Infantry at Brancepeth, a village in North-East England 77 miles from where he had grown up in Scarborough. He then moved to a barracks at the nearby town of Spennymoor, where he was taught to load and dismantle guns at speed and to shoot straight, but not with a football. Bill tackled soldiering with the same enthusiasm and energy that he poured into his football and quickly became a lance corporal and later a sergeant as he developed into a formidable instructor in the Army Physical Training Corps.

The once shy former laundry worker grew in confidence and stature as he lectured platoons on fitness and discipline, and it was during the war – after marrying Grace in 1942 – that his interest in coaching approached fanaticism. He made brief wartime guest appearances with Newcastle United, Darlington, Sunderland, Hartlepool, Middlesbrough, Fulham and a rare home match at Tottenham. It was when he was posted to Italy in 1945 to work on the fitness of the British troops that he decided that his future lay in coaching once his playing career was over.

> "I went into the Army a boy and came out a man, and my world changed when I met a chap who inspired me to think not just of playing football but of the physical and tactical side of the game. His name was Geoff Dyson, a major in charge of the Army fitness programme in Italy. I'd never met such a motivational and organised man, and he more than anybody opened

my eyes and mind to the possibilities of what could be achieved by proper planning and the right physical input. 'Fitness of mind and body is everything', he used to say, and then showing in an intelligent, common-sense way how they could be combined, whether you were playing sport or soldiering. He was a genius of a coordinator and a master of communication, who later became chief athletics coach of the Amateur Athletic Association and was a powerhouse as a lecturer and teacher. He married our top Olympic hurdler, Maureen Gardner, who was also an expert at forward planning. I could not believe it when the Establishment allowed them to emigrate to Canada to spread the gospel of properly organised training schedules and facilities. Madness. He was needed in British sport.

"When I was demobbed, I found somebody as inspirational as Dyson in Walter Winterbottom. He was the driving force behind the introduction of a series of coaching courses while also successfully managing the England football team, despite the interference of amateur selectors. I got my coaching certificate at the first attempt at Birmingham University and later took on the part-time job of coaching the Cambridge University team. My rival at Oxford was my Spurs teammate and good friend Vic Buckingham. These were the days when we had a sort of football brains trust at Tottenham, with Alf Ramsey, Eddie Baily, Vic, Ronnie Burgess and, of course, Arthur Rowe pitching in ideas. Alf was nicknamed 'The General' but, in truth, we were all Montgomerys, planning and plotting. We would talk football tactics and theories morning, noon and night.

"Something I learned from the coaching experience at Cambridge is that being an intellectual does not make you bright on the football pitch. I would much rather have my footballers with their brains in their feet. Being academically brainy does not translate to having a football brain. The greatest footballers are born with natural gifts. Regardless of how intelligent you are, you cannot be taught ball control and tactical understanding. I find that, generally speaking, those players clever at things other than football do not give the game the 100 per cent concentration that it requires. Of course, there are some who prove me wrong, like Danny Blanchflower. He had a brain the

size of Mars and all his outside interests did not interfere with his play. But on the whole I wanted my players committed to the one subject, and that was football."

It was in the Army that Bill got the confidence to address large audiences, and under Dyson's influence he developed into a lecturer who could command attention and concentration. A million miles from his sheltered, speak-when-you're-spoken-to Victorian upbringing at Scarborough. Most of his military service was in Britain and he always looked on the experience as educational and enlightening. He developed as a footballer as well as a man, and his midfield marking and motivational work was noted to the point where he was selected to represent Northern Command, one step away from the full England team. With Neil Franklin established at centre-half, Bill wore the number four shirt and played an anchorman's role in midfield, winning the ball and then passing it precisely to the likes of Tommy Lawton and Nat Lofthouse in attack.

He had an eventful war but nowhere near as adventurous and remarkable as that of his Spurs club-mate Eddie Baily, who became his right-hand man and coach in his later managing days.

"Bill rarely mentioned that he was in the Army but Eddie never let us forget that he had a war to remember. He would often shout in that Cockney voice of his just as we were preparing to leave the dressing-room for the kick-off: "Fix bayonets, lads, we're going over the top!" I've left out the f-words. I can lord mayor with the best of them, but Eddie was the king of the swear words, a habit he said he'd picked up – quoting him – "while fighting the f—ing Jerries!" I sat down with him one day and found out just what an incredible war he had.

"A sort of Alf Garnett soundalike, he served with the Royal Scots Fusiliers by some freak clerical error and survived full-on battles right across Europe. One day he was posted as 'missing in action' and Spurs scrubbed him off their list of players. He had been an outstanding amateur on their books before the war. It was, of course, a mistake and when Spurs did not get in touch after VE Day he signed

for Chelsea. He went to White Hart Lane to collect his boots and they thought they were seeing a ghost. The misunderstanding was sorted out and Chelsea conceded that he was still officially a Tottenham player. Just as well, because he became the vital cog in the 'Push and Run' team and later – let's say – an aggressive coach alongside Bill Nick. He gave me a few tongue-lashings, but I can honestly say I was a better player for his influence. Eddie knew the game inside out."

Back to the Bill Nick story. Bill and Grace – she preferred to be called 'Darkie' – lived in cramped loft rooms in Farningham Road when they first married, and then after the war moved to a house in the adjoining Commonwealth Road, residing next door to Tottenham goalkeeper Ted Ditchburn. He was a larger-than-life character who drove around in a huge American car that they nicknamed 'Dillinger', after the infamous US gangster. Ted often gave Bill lifts to and from training sessions in the days before Nick eventually bought a second-hand Morris Eight in the 1950s. Bill used to describe being a passenger alongside Ted at the wheel as "hair-raising", and it was years later that he learned that the happy-go-lucky goalkeeper had never had a driving lesson in his life and had not passed his driving test!

Bill lived to tell the tale and he and Darkie settled down to a family life in the immediate post-war years of ration books and of London being rebuilt after the Blitz. Their two charming daughters, Linda and Jean, were born before a move to an end-of-terrace club house at 71 Creighton Road that was in sight and sound of White Hart Lane. They lived there for 25 shillings (£1 10p) a week, until buying the house from Tottenham for a nominal £2,000. It was, with several extensions added, their home for the next 50 years.

People could never understand why Bill remained in such a modest house, even at the peak of his success. It was Darkie who explained it best: "[It] was a joint decision to remain there. I knew that if we lived farther away from the ground I would never see Willie. At least with the club just a stroll away he could pop home between his managerial duties. I used to tease him and say that perhaps he should have a bed in his office. He always liked to be on top of things."

Being a Tottenham girl, Darkie was a Spurs fan before falling for

Bill, but after she had once seen him lose early in their relationship she was considered a jinx by superstitious Bill and banned from attending matches. She used to have the kitchen window open and listen to the roar of the crowd to judge how the match was going.

> "They say behind every successful man is a good woman, and Darkie was exactly that. We used to meet her at club functions but never at matches, because Bill said she'd once watched him play and they had lost. The only other way Bill showed the superstitious side that most footballers have is if anybody in his company wore red – that was strictly a no-go. Arsenal red was to him like a red rag to a bull. And none of the players under him dared buy a red car. You'd never hear the end of it.
>
> "Darkie was a delightful lady, and their two daughters, Linda and Jean, were brought up in her image. They were sophisticated but down to earth, easy and comfortable to chat to. The three of them were so proud of Bill and always spoiled him at home, where he famously insisted on doing the washing up after meals. Darkie was a wonderful character, who used to cycle everywhere with a wicker shopping basket on the front of the handlebars. It was like watching a Miss Marple type out of an Agatha Christie novel. She was very well respected and taught dressmaking and arts and crafts at the local school. Bill used to call her 'the perfect football manager's wife, always encouraging and never interfering, and knew when best not to say a dickie bird'. They were a very special couple.
>
> "Darkie would always happily wave and smile if she ever passed you when she was out on her faithful bike. She was never the type to be interested in flash cars. It was all part of the Nicholson normality – just 'getting on' with life and not considering themselves special despite being Bill's immediate family. Living by White Hart Lane just added to the feeling that this was the place to work, rest and play while pushing on with your life experiences.
>
> "I recall meeting Jean and her husband in the White Hart Lane boardroom before one home game and both she and I

had the same thoughts of Bill – me as a young player and she as his daughter. Each of us had such respect for him that we could never do anything, be it in life, football or school, that could be seen to let him down in any possible way. That was the effect Bill had on people. He inspired loyalty.

"From my perspective I always thought about how Bill would be feeling, especially after a defeat, and what I personally needed to improve to rid myself of that 'letting him down' feeling.

"If you were part of not living up to the trust that he'd had in your being selected, then, of course, that led to being aware of the same with the paying customers and the whole club. It was always Bill first, truly first in your thoughts! You just dared not let down Bill or the supporters. It was Bill who set the agenda and his main priority was always Spurs. Don't let the club down.

"His strict discipline and timekeeping stretched to his family life. Jean related a story to me about going on a school trip by minibus to spend a day at the Wimbledon tennis tournament. The whole group were warned that they should meet up in a certain place at such a time, and that anyone not adhering to the instruction would be left behind and had to find their own way home.

"Jean's small group of friends had been inhibited by unusually large crowds and missed the pick-up, so not only missed the bus but arrived home late. A worried Darkie agreed with Jean that the teacher had been a little harsh.

"Bill listened to all the reasoning, how lucky it was that between Jean's group they'd rustled up enough money to get train and bus tickets, while Darkie was getting more and more critical of the teacher's lack of care and understanding.

"Eventually, an exasperated Bill put paid to any more such discussion by announcing strongly: 'She [Jean] knew the rules and for whatever reason didn't react to these, WAS late and therefore had to suffer the consequences and possibly this is a great lesson for later life! End of excuses.'

OH! WHAT A LOVELY WAR

"Yes, Bill was hard but always balanced. And Linda, Jean and, of course, Darkie loved him to bits."

With the war over and Bill back to his playing career, he brought home lots of win bonuses to his beloved Darkie – as much as £2 a time! – as he settled into a successful playing routine after Hitler and the evil of Nazism had been defeated.

CHAPTER 3

THE 'PUSH AND RUN' DAYS

When Bill resumed his professional playing career after the war he found former Arsenal and England winger Joe Hulme in charge at a White Hart Lane that was being shared every other week with the Gunners – Highbury was still operating as an Air Raid Precautions Centre at the time.

There was not the hatred between the two clubs that clouds today's North London Derbies, and for many years there was a plaque in the Tottenham boardroom from the Arsenal directors thanking Spurs for ground-sharing and being so hospitable during the war.

Bill Nick was a makeshift centre-half and then an industrious right-half in the Spurs team that Hulme steered to the 1948 FA Cup semi-final, where they were beaten at Villa Park by a Stanley Matthews-inspired Blackpool. But red-blooded Joe was never totally accepted by the old enemy, and when he moved on in 1949 to a distinguished career in journalism, it was a Spurs-through-and-through-man – Arthur Rowe – who took over as manager, with Tottenham down in the Second Division.

I became friends with Arthur in my *Daily Express* reporting days when he was curator of the short-lived PFA-supported Football Hall of Fame in Oxford Street in the early 1970s (a venture that quickly died because of lack of public interest before being revived in Manchester many years later).

A gentle, kindly man, Arthur was easy to talk to and we had many long conversations about his career in the game in general and his management of Spurs in particular. He revealed that the art of 'Push and Run' football – the signature style of Spurs – was born against the walls of North London. Tottenham-born Arthur, the chief architect of the meticulous method, remembered playing with a tennis ball against the wall as an Edmonton schoolboy and suddenly thinking to himself: "That's how easy and simple the game should be!" Wall passes became a key ingredient in his revolutionary style of play.

I caught Arthur in reflective mood 20 years after he had entered the land of football legend by steering Spurs to back-to-back Second and First Division titles. Speaking quietly, with a discernible Cockney accent, he told me:

> "My philosophy was that the easier you made the game the easier it was to play it, so I used to tell the players to push the ball to a team-mate and then run into space to take the instant return pass. It was making the most of the 'wall pass' or the 'one-two'. Make it simple, make it quick. It was easier said than done, of course, but I got together a squad of players with the football intelligence to make it work. We used to operate in triangles, with Eddie Baily, Ronnie Burgess and Les Medley particularly brilliant at the concept out on the left. It was amazing to watch as they took defenders out of the game with simple, straightforward passes and then getting into position to receive the return. Over on the right Alf Ramsey, Billy Nicholson and Sonny Walters were equally adept at keeping possession while making progress with simple passes. It was very similar to the style I introduced while coaching in Hungary, where I was preparing to take the job of national coach before the declaration of war put the kibosh on that. Sheffield United's great inside-forward Jimmy Hagan and I were ambassadors for the Football Association, and I think we made our mark on the Hungarian game before that Hitler went and destroyed everything."

The cynics described Tottenham's style on the way to the Second Division title in 1949/50 as 'school playground' football and most prophesied that they would be found out in the First Division. Instead, at the first time of asking, they strolled to the First Division Championship, comfortably beating Matt Busby's Manchester United to the title by four points in the days of two points for a win.

THE 'PUSH AND RUN' DAYS

I got Bill reminiscing on the 'Push and Run' days in his first full season as Tottenham manager and before 'The Double' and the abolition of the maximum wage:

"Arthur Rowe was the architect of the system. Remember that he won the Second and First Division Championships in back-to-back seasons with virtually the same players he had inherited from Joe Hulme. That was down to Arthur's organisational and coaching skills. He believed, like me, in keeping things simple. Make it simple, make it quick. When not in possession, get into position. Give it and go. Arthur was full of these sort of easy-to-remember instructions, and I use many of them with my players today. It was all stuff we learned in our formative days at Northfleet. When I think back on the football education I got there, it was better than going to university.

"Most of us came through the Northfleet ranks to form the nucleus of the 'Push and Run' side. It was hammered home to us that there is no 'I' in team We were very much a collective and we had no prima donnas or selfish individualists. Our motto was the same as that of the Four Musketeers, all for one and one for all.

"I doubt if we could have been so successful without the measured passes of Eddie Baily, but for me the player who had the biggest influence was our skipper Ronnie Burgess. We joined Spurs on the same day in the 1930s and grew up together with identical team-first standards and discipline.

"He was a powerhouse of a player who could be driving the attack forward one minute and then back clearing and tackling in defence the next. Ron made the rest of us lift our game and our energy to try to keep up with him.

"If I could turn back the clock, the forward I would have most wanted from that team would be the Duke, Len Duquemin. He was raw when he first arrived from the Channel Islands but developed a good positional sense and had a cannonball shot. Len was lucky to be served by two outstanding wingers in Sonny Walters and Les Medley, and he and Les Bennett struck up a radar-like understanding of where to be to get the best out of each other. They were a real handful in our Championship season.

'SIR BILL'

"People often ask me if I was disappointed not to get more than the one England cap, while Alf Ramsey got 32. The plain and simple truth is that Billy Wright played in my position and was a better player. Simple as that. I used to pull Alf's leg and tell him that he got so many caps because of all the running I did to cover for him. He was a magnificent defender with great vision. His distribution was an important part of our success. He is now a fine manager with Ipswich Town. They will be worth watching because Alf has got a lot of good ideas that, like me, he picked up under Arthur Rowe. He is very inventive with his tactical ideas. That's why we used to call him 'The General'.

"Supporters sometimes ask why the 'Push and Run' era was over so quickly. I like to think we're continuing it. Our style is not dissimilar to how we used to play under Arthur. A bit quicker, but the principles are the same. You have to remember that most of the 'Push and Run' players came through wartime military service, which robbed us of five or more years. Many of us were past our peak by the time we won the Championship. Now my hope is to be able to put together a team that is every bit as good.

"I see the players' union is pressing for the abolition of the maximum wage. That would in my opinion be a bad thing for the game and would encourage greed and selfishness. If you can't live on £20 a week there's something wrong with your housekeeping.

"Money should never be the motivation for players. The thing that should drive them is pride in their performances and a love for the game. I would willingly have played for nothing, just as long as I was enjoying my football. Too much money in the game will just cause problems. That's my view. But I don't suppose too many players will agree with me. I don't like greed in any shape or form."

That quote – "If you can't live on £20 a week there's something wrong with your housekeeping" – will astonish some of today's footballers who consider themselves underpaid if they are not on at least 60 grand. The superstars collect as much as £600,000. I honestly don't know how Bill could handle that. He was never ever money-orientated and it used to annoy his players that he thought they should share his 'love of the game' attitude. He would willingly have played for nothing, and Steve and I used to take every opportunity to encourage him to talk about his footballing career, never ever in a boastful way but with pride and passion that he later passed on as a manager.

"I used to love listening to Bill and Eddie speaking about the 'Push and Run' days. It was as if they were talking about a foreign land. They were getting £11 a week when winning the League Championship. Wonder what today's millionaire footballers would make of that?

"Bill took the standards that were set under Arthur Rowe into management and demanded we do everything with style, and God help anybody giving less than 100 per cent. The 'Push and Run' heroes had all come through a war and so football was no sweat. They were all weaned on hard work, and both Bill and Eddie encouraged us to roll up our sleeves and get the job done. There was no room for slackers.

"What Bill had to say about the maximum wage will strike a chord, or, more appropriately, a bum note with a lot of my old team-mates. He was always miserly with the club's money. Goodness knows how he would get on with today's players earning thousands a week. Getting a rise from Bill was like getting blood out of a stone. Oops, better not say blood because that's red. Let's just say he didn't like parting with the club's money. Anybody would have thought it was his own dosh. That's about the only moan I had about Bill, and I was quite muted with my criticism, because I considered him a very fair man, treating us all alike.

"Eddie Baily was famously a star in the 'Push and Run' side, and used to show his incredible skill in our gymnasium workouts. Even well into middle age, Eddie could strike the ball beautifully with either foot and his accuracy was uncanny. He could be very cutting with his tongue if any player showed less than perfect skill and technique on the ball. It all came so naturally to him and he had little patience with those who had not been blessed with his sort of talent. I liked Eddie a lot but he could be a pain in the bum with his demands and commands that were never issued without several swear words thrown in. What a character!

"He used to get grumpy because he never won an FA Cup winners' medal, which was rated the absolute pinnacle in his day, even more so than winning the league. He used to tell us how Alf Ramsey of all people cost them a place in the 1953 final. Spurs were playing Blackpool in an FA Cup semi-final at Villa Park in 1953, and Alf gave Blackpool a winning goal on a plate with a back pass that he hit straight into the path of a Blackpool player. That was the year of the famous Stanley Matthews final, and Eddie used to say it would never have happened but for Alf gift wrapping them a goal.

"I won't repeat the language he used to describe Alf, who all the old-timers used to say was one of England's greatest-ever right-backs. When that take was mentioned in Eddie's hearing, he used to say: 'Bill Nick made him twice the player by covering for him. He was Bill's legs because Alf turned slower than milk.'

Club always came before country for Bill, but he was a willing member of the England squad even though he rarely got a game. He learned to live in the shadow of the first man in the world ever to win 100 caps for his country, the legendary Billy Wright.

CHAPTER 4

A 90-MINUTE ENGLAND CAREER

Bill travelled thousands of miles with England as understudy to skipper Billy Wright, setting a record of 22 squad selections without getting a game. When an injury to the Wolves maestro caused him to miss a match against Portugal at Goodison Park in 1951, Bill marked his one international appearance with a goal from his first kick after just 20 seconds. He never got to play for England again.

He made a point of sitting at Walter Winterbottom's side on the many tours he went on, never once complaining at his lack of action and taking every opportunity to pick the England manager's brains. I wrote the official biography of Billy Wright, who said of Nicholson:

"If there was anybody who was going to make it as a manager after he had finished playing it was Bill. He always had an appetite for football knowledge and on our tours was inseparable from Walter Winterbottom. I had never known anybody as inquisitive as he was when it came to football tactics. He wanted to know every reason for Walter making tweaks to the team and would often offer opinions of his own about how players should be used.

"I would guess he must have made 20 trips with us without getting a game, but never once did he moan or complain. He was there on the sidelines encouraging us at every step, showing as much if not more enthusiasm than those of us lucky to be wearing the white shirt of England. I used to joke that Bill had the England badge tattooed on his heart. What a loyal and likeable man.

"Bill rarely got involved in conversations outside of football. He had tunnel vision for the game and nobody who knew him was surprised when he enjoyed such success as a manager at Tottenham.

'SIR BILL'

"We became rival managers when I took over at Highbury, but we remained firm friends. He was not the sort of man who took rivalry beyond the bounds of good sportsmanship, and win or lose he would be sincere with his praise for the opposition. He was what I like to think of as a proper football man. The game always came first and he had no time for gimmicks or showboating."

Bill became the perpetual reserve and was like part of the furniture on the England bench, but all the time he was listening, learning and preparing himself for a new future as a coach. He accepted his role as understudy to the great Billy Wright with grace, and he and the England captain became close, lifetime friends.

"I was honoured to be selected so many times for the England squad, and it meant I was able to travel the world while learning as much as I could about football coaching and tactics. I would have paid to sit alongside Walter Winterbottom, listening to his views on strategy and fitness. But I always considered my first responsibility was to Tottenham Hotspur, who paid my wages.

"To sit and listen to the likes of Stanley Matthews, Tom Finney and Billy Wright talking football was a fantastic bonus, and for me there has never been a coach quite as intelligent and innovative as Walter. He was the father of coaching in Britain and the game owed him a lot. It was Walter who set up the nationwide coaching schools and all this on top of his duties as England manager. He was the target for a lot of unfair criticism from the newspaper reporters who did not have a tenth of his knowledge of the game. But he took it all in his stride and got on with his job of improving facilities and the performances of individual players.

"Throughout most of his career as England manager he was anchored by a committee of well-meaning but often nincompoop amateur selectors, who were too often interested in pushing the case for their own club players to be picked for England.

"Walter would sit patiently listening to their biased arguments but – usually in a good-mannered way – get the team he wanted. He often had to appease people who, frankly, did not know what they were talking about. I sometimes sat in on the selection meetings and used to quietly think to myself that I

would not touch the England job with a bargepole. Walter was a thorough gentleman, almost headmaster-ish in his manner, and was far too polite to tell the selectors where to shove their opinions.

"The most excited I got in all my times sitting on the touchline bench watching England was when we played Italy in Turin in May 1948. It was my first international call-up and I saw close-up the two Stanleys (Matthews and Mortensen), Wilf Mannion, Tommy Lawton and Tom Finney destroy the Italian defence and silence a fanatical crowd of 75,000 Italian spectators. We won 4-0 and it was the greatest performance I ever saw from an England team. I was rarely a demonstrative man but that day I was leaping from the touchline bench like a demented fan.

"The lowest point was when I sat helpless on the bench watching England lose 1-0 to the part-timers of the United States in the 1950 World Cup finals in Belo Horizonte. That was a freak result and threw a dark shadow over our international game for a long time. If we had won 9-1 it would have been a fair reflection of the play, but that result was written in the stars. It continues to hurt to this day, and I was just a spectator.

"When Alf took over from Walter as England manager in 1962, he insisted that he would only do the job if the selection committee was abandoned. Even then I would not have taken on the responsibility. I was a Spurs man, full stop."

Steve Perryman knew exactly what Bill meant ...

"I had similar international experiences to Bill. I set some sort of record by playing in 17 England Under-23 matches and got called up to the first team for just the one game, against Iceland in 1982. I did not even have the satisfaction of celebrating my debut cap because the game was originally filed as an England 'B' match but was later upgraded to a full international. Yipee. But believe me, I am so honoured to have that cap. Like Bill, I am a very proud Englishman and I grew taller with every one of my Under-23 appearances.

> "Bill's reaction to serving his country as a faithful understudy to Billy Wright captured the man's loyalty and unselfish approach to football and life.
>
> "'It's Spurs who pay your wages' was a favourite saying of his. He was mean with his praise because he thought whatever you did out on the pitch was merely what you were paid to do. He used to say, 'Get out there and give those spectators the entertainment they deserve. It's the supporters who pay their hard-earned money so that you lot can live a life of luxury. Without them, you're nothing. The supporters are the most important people of all. Bring some light into their lives. Get out there and give it your all. I don't want any player coming back into this dressing room with a dry shirt. Then Eddie would add: 'Fix your bayonets, lads, we're going over the top!'
>
> "What I would give to have those days back. Another of Bill's sayings was: 'A footballer's life is a short one, enjoy every moment because it is all over in the blink of an eye.'
>
> "He was so right. I don't know one of my peers who does not ache to play again, particularly when you see the billiard-top pitches they play on now... oh yes, and the money they earn. But Bill Nick would have done it all for nothing."

A recurring knee injury forced Bill's retirement from playing at the age of 34 in 1955. Waiting to fill his No.4 shirt was an Irishman called Danny Blanchflower.

CHAPTER 5

BOWING OUT TO BLANCHFLOWER

An interlude in our Bill Nicholson narrative here while we introduce one of the most gifted, garrulous, persuasive and accomplished people ever to step into the Tottenham history books. Enter Danny Blanchflower, who played a huge part in the 'Sir Bill' story.

Bill, being the brutally honest man that he was, tipped off manager Arthur Rowe that he was running on empty at the end of the 1953/54 season and that a troublesome knee was handicapping him. "It's time to be thinking of my replacement," he told Arthur, with the candour that marked everything he did in football and in life.

Rowe started his search for a successor in the number four shirt, and he zeroed in on Danny boy, who was parading his skills with Aston Villa in the Midlands and, at 29, was considered to be still at the top of his game. The Spurs manager had been impressed by his performances as captain of Northern Ireland, for whom he shared midfield playmaker duties with skilful Burnley schemer Jimmy McIlroy. He persuaded the Tottenham directors that Danny was the perfect man to not only fill Bill Nicholson's shirt but also lead the club into the future with his motivational powers as skipper.

Both Steve (who was later to show those same Blanchflower-esque leadership qualities) and I agreed that we just had to include the following anecdote in this Bill Nicholson adventure story ...

Danny let it be known through his Birmingham evening paper column that he detested the apathy that dogged the Villa boardroom and dressing room, and in September 1954 he submitted a transfer request in writing. He could not find anybody who would accept it.

Manager Eric Houghton pushed it back at him, and the club secretary deliberately made himself scarce. Danny finally handed it to an assistant secretary, who with fear and trembling took it to the boardroom for the attention of the dictatorial Villa chairman, Fred Normansell. The single-minded Irishman had secretly made up his mind to get himself a London-based club, mainly because he wanted to be near what he considered his spiritual home of Fleet Street. He had already made up his mind that on retirement he would take up full-time his first love of journalism, and he had been cutting his teeth with a series of hard-hitting written articles in the provincial newspapers.

It was weeks before Danny was summoned to a board meeting, as the chairman had been taken ill. This was when the transfer saga developed into French farce. Tom Lyons, the old-school sports reporter with the *Daily Mirror*, ate out for years on this story:

"I had chased all over Birmingham trying to track down Danny for quotes on the transfer rumours, and then as a last resort decided to try Villa Park, even though it was late in the evening. I noticed there were lights on and the entrance door to the administrative block was open. I let myself into the annexe to the boardroom and found Danny sitting all alone.

"I told him how I had been looking for him everywhere to see what the situation was with his move. He said he knew as much or as little as me, and that he was waiting to be called in to talk to the directors.

"We chatted for a few minutes when he excused himself to go to the toilet. He had just disappeared from view when the boardroom door opened and the club secretary came out, peered at me over the top of his glasses and said: 'The chairman and directors will see you now. Please come in.'

"I followed him and found myself facing the directors in a darkened room. 'We have decided we would like you to stay,' the chairman said, then doing a double take as he realised I was not Danny.

"'Who the hell are you?' he asked.

"'Tom Lyons, of the *Daily Mirror*,' I said. 'I'm here to ask if you have made a decision on Danny Blanchflower's transfer request.'

"The old boy nearly blew a gasket as he told me: 'Get out and send Blanchflower in.'

"Danny was back sitting in his chair as I came out of the boardroom, and he fell about laughing when I told him what had happened."

BOWING OUT TO BLANCHFLOWER

The Villa board failed in their bid to talk Danny into changing his mind and put him on the transfer list at a then-British record fee of £40,000 – knowing full well that no club would pay such a deliberately prohibitive sum. Three clubs, Tottenham, Arsenal and Wolves, were initially interested but none would meet the excessive asking fee. That number dropped to two after a five-week delay caused by Danny damaging knee ligaments playing for Northern Ireland against Scotland at Hampden Park.

Arsenal manager Tom Whittaker talked to Danny four times and stressed that he was determined to get him. The Gunners were roasting-hot favourites to complete the deal, but much to Whittaker's frustration the Highbury directors refused to go above £28,500.

Can you imagine the difference it would have made to Tottenham's history if Blanchflower had gone to N5 rather than N17? Neither can I.

Danny was being kept in the dark by Villa, and one afternoon in December 1954 he walked into a London hotel to join the Northern Ireland squad when his brother, Jackie, shouted across the foyer.

"Hey kid, well done. You're joining Tottenham."

"How the heck do you know?" Danny replied.

"Eric Houghton just told me on the blower," Jackie explained with a big grin. "There was an announcement that there was a telephone call for Mr Blanchflower, and I took it. 'Eric here,' the caller said. 'We've agreed to sell you to Tottenham, and Arthur Rowe will be getting in touch.' You could say he was not best pleased when he realised he had the wrong Blanchflower!"

Arthur Rowe had spoken to Danny twice on visits to Birmingham, and they had struck up an instant rapport. Danny recalled:

"Of all the teams Villa had played, Tottenham was the one that impressed me most. They had a grace about them that appealed to me, and you could tell the Arthur Rowe coaching influence.

"He came across as a quiet, likeable and very modest man. But what he couldn't hide was his enthusiasm for football, the way the game should be played. He did not try to buy me with baubles but with his exciting ideas of how good Tottenham could become with my contribution added to what he considered a team ready to repeat the success of the 'Push and Run' champions.

"I was more than happy to hitch my wagon to his star. He was travelling in the right direction. I was ready to go to the moon with him and with Tottenham Hotspur."

Spurs won the transfer race with a club-record bid of £30,000. Danny signed, dare I say, at the double. It had to be written into his contract that any written articles for newspapers would have to be vetted by the club's board before publication. The directors were already petrified of his ability to stir up a hornets' nest with his explosive opinions.

Steve Perryman was just three years old when all this was happening on 8 December 1954. He got to distantly know Danny while repeating his experience of collecting back-to-back FA Cups as Spurs captain at Wembley...

"I remember seeing Danny described as 'donnish', and I had to look it up to see that it meant 'like a university tutor'. Well that description can never be aimed at me, or few ex-footballers! He truly was the brains of that great Tottenham Double team of 1960/61, which is one of the first things you learn about the club's trophy-winning history.

"The year before I joined the club I watched Danny when he appeared as a pundit on the BBC's 1966 World Cup panel. I could not believe the way he pulled the England team apart at every opportunity, and he kept taking swipes at Alf Ramsey as if he was an enemy rather than a former team-mate at Tottenham – in fact he took over as Spurs captain from Alf.

"I'm told the England players jeered when watching him on the TV at their Hendon Hall hotel headquarters when he said it would be a defeat for football if England won the World Cup with Alf's wingless team.

"He had equally strong opinions in his newspaper columns about the Spurs side I was proud to lead to two FA Cup finals, and I respected him for his straight-to-the-point views.

"Bill Nick used to tell us that Danny was the most intelligent footballer he'd ever known but that he could start an argument in a cemetery with his contentious beliefs.

Jimmy Greaves was his big mate – his oldest son Danny is named after him.

"Greavsie said that Danny – Blanchflower that is – could make you feel ten-foot tall with his pre-match dressing room talks. He was a completely different leader to me. Jim said he would get through a game with as little physical effort as possible, which was an accusation often made about Greavsie. He had dodgy knees and would rarely tackle, preferring to corral opponents like a sheepdog with his intelligent positioning, leaving the heavy tackles to team-mates like Dave Mackay and Maurice Norman.

"Danny was a penalty specialist and slotted home 11 spot-kicks for Spurs, the most crucial in the 1962 FA Cup final against Burnley at Wembley. Jimmy often told the story of how – as Danny placed the ball for the kick – his Northern Ireland team-mate and best pal Jimmy McIlroy sidled up to him and said: 'Bet you miss.'

Danny duly deposited the ball into the net with his usual deadly accuracy and then, running back past McIlroy, said out of the side of his mouth: "Bet I don't."

He is rightly a legend at Tottenham because of his achievements, and will always be remembered for his famous quote: 'The great fallacy is that the game is first and last about winning. It's nothing of the kind. The game is about glory. It is about doing things in style, with a flourish, about going out and beating the other lot, not waiting for them to die of boredom.'

"Couldn't have put it better myself!"

CHAPTER 6

SEEING OFF ALF RAMSEY

While Tottenham's battle to sign Danny Blanchflower ahead of deadly rivals Arsenal was claiming the headlines, Bill Nicholson was quietly plotting his switch from playing to coaching. He had an ambitious rival in Alf Ramsey, the England international right-back and the player for whom he had been covering for several seasons. They both had an eye on the job of Tottenham coach.

Bill had a major advantage over Alf. He got on with Jimmy Anderson, who had been his manager back in the pre-war Gravesend & Northfleet days. Alf, who had joined Spurs from Southampton in 1949, did not always agree with Jimmy's tactics and there was little warmth between the two cautious men. When Danny took over from Bill at right-half it was soon obvious he and Alf could not fit together in the jigsaw because both needed the sort of support player that Bill Nick had always been. It was Ramsey who was dropped.

This all coincided with Arthur Rowe suffering a nervous breakdown following a catastrophic third-round FA Cup defeat at York City, and it was the veteran Anderson who was promoted to manager. He selected Nicholson as his coach...

> "I never made a secret of the fact that I wanted to coach. It was something that came naturally to me. They say of schoolteachers that they have a calling to educate, and I guess that was how I felt about football. I had learned so much about coaching from giants like Arthur Rowe, Geoff Dyson and Walter Winterbottom, and now I wanted to pass it on. Football management was not in my thoughts.

> "When Jimmy Anderson asked me to be his coach I could not have been happier, working with players I knew well and for a club with which I had such a strong bond. Yes, I admit to wondering whether I would get the Spurs job ahead of Alf Ramsey, but he preferred to take up what looked a tough challenge at Ipswich down in the Third Division. What he achieved there was pretty close to miraculous. Like me, he was a believer in good, strong organisation and with an emphasis on fitness and doing the basic things well. Once you've laid that foundation you can start introducing the more intricate things that can make a good team great and a great team exceptional. But the basics must be observed.
>
> "I was fully in support of Danny Blanchflower taking over my job in the Tottenham midfield. We were poles apart as players, Danny very creative and imaginative while I liked to consider myself a worker who made the team tick. He was a true artist of a footballer, while I was a grafter who left the clever stuff to more gifted players."

Jimmy Anderson found his promotion to manager a burden rather than a blessing. He filled in as emergency manager when Arthur Rowe became unwell and was then given the job permanently in July 1955. After years of playing second fiddle, he suddenly found himself conducting the orchestra, and he just could not get the rhythm right.

A man of few words, Anderson would not have lasted five minutes in today's world in which Premier League managers are expected to give regular one-on-one interviews and press conferences. They have to know how to please and satisfy not only newspaper reporters but television, radio, internet, bloggers, vloggers and social media interrogators. Jimmy was from the Victorian school philosophy: speak only when spoken to and treat the press like you would treat the police. He considered reporters a pain in the derriere (which Steve says I always was in my sniffing-for-stories days… I think he's joking).

Anderson, who seemed stuck in the 1930s both in his style of dress and his demeanour, said in a prepared statement following his promotion from the back room to the top job: "Spurs have been my life virtually since I left school, and I will do my best to meet the standards that Arthur Rowe set in his Championship-winning season. All

I ask from the players and supporters is patience while I settle into the job. I have inherited a talented team that is a little lacking in confidence. We must all pull together to get back into a winning groove. I ask the press to leave me to get on with the job without unnecessary interference. Matters of club business will be dealt with by our secretary. My one priority will be dealing with the players and getting things right on the pitch."

There were encouraging signs that Anderson was starting to get it right when Tottenham reached the FA Cup semi-final in 1956, going down 1-0 to a Don Revie-inspired Manchester City, again at Villa Park, where Ramsey had made his suicidal back pass in 1953. But it was another false dawn, and suddenly all the media attention centred on an earthquaking bust-up between Anderson and his outspoken skipper Danny Blanchflower...

> *"I felt a bit like a piggy in the middle because I could see both sides of the argument. It reached the point where Danny was telling the newspapers how Spurs should be playing the game and how the club should be managed. That was out of order. It all came to a head when Jimmy blamed Danny for the FA Cup semi-final defeat by City because he made tactical changes during the game without even a glance in the direction of the manager or me, the coach.*
>
> *"I looked on in the dressing room immediately after the semi-final as they went for each other. Jimmy was extremely angry as he said to Danny, 'You have made me look a fool in front of the directors. I'm manager of this club, not you. In future don't make any tactical changes without my say-so.'*
>
> *"Danny, never one to take a verbal volley without retaliating, replied: 'I'm as disappointed as you and the directors. I tried to win the game by taking a gamble. You think I made a mistake. I think it's better to make a mistake trying something than to accept things and do nothing.'*
>
> *"Blanchflower had still not taken his boots off and was fuming that Anderson had gone for him so soon after the final whistle and the disappointment of defeat. From then on they were daggers drawn. As coach I felt my loyalty had to be with the manager. Danny was far too headstrong and not willing*

to listen to reasoned argument. The atmosphere was as bad as I had ever known it."

Anderson always cut something of a comic figure because he used to wear his trousers with the bottoms tucked into socks, like golfing plus-fours. But there was nothing amusing about his conflict with Blanchflower, and he stripped him of the captaincy after a row during which he accused Danny of trying to knife him in the back.

According to Danny, he was innocent of any wrongdoing. It kicked off when he telephoned the *London Evening News* to discuss an article that he was due to write for football editor JG ('Jack') Orange. He had been left out of the team to play in a crucial relegation match at Cardiff, and Anderson had told Orange earlier in the day that it was because of an injury, which led the early editions.

I was working at the *News* as a sports room assistant and took the call. Danny asked for Orange, and I told him he was out of the office. I passed the telephone to his deputy Vic Railton, who was establishing himself as one of the hungriest news gatherers in Fleet Street sports history.

Vic asked Danny about his injury, being polite rather than seeking a story. Danny was puzzled and answered truthfully: "Injury? What injury? I'm in fine shape. I've just been left out."

The *Evening News* ran a "Blanchflower dropped" exclusive under Vic's byline in the last edition, and Anderson went ballistic, accusing Danny of trying to undermine him and stir up trouble. Ironically, the next day the veteran, bowler-hatted Orange accused Railton of trying to steal his job by making him look a fool by rewriting his story. It's a funny old world.

It became the talk of football and the Tottenham board of directors had to choose between the manager they had just put in charge or the articulate but prickly Blanchflower, who had arrived from Aston Villa in 1954 in the Arthur Rowe era for a then-club record £30,000, with promises of putting himself and Spurs on top of the tree.

The directors told Danny to button his lip, which was like asking a chaffinch not to chirp. The garrulous Irishman had a perfect understanding with Arthur Rowe, but when Anderson took over he just could not get on the same wavelength. This was old school meeting new school, and a collision of ideals, ideas and personalities.

The articulate, atomic-tongued Irishman did not hold back with his two-barrelled attack on Anderson despite boardroom warnings, and he described him as being out of his depth and living in the past. He was stripped of the club captaincy and went on the transfer list.

Danny and I later became good pals when we were both writing for Express Newspapers and during our many one-sided conversations (when I listened and Danny talked) he told me:

"My dispute was not so much with Jimmy as with the directors, who were guilty of massive interference. They got it wrong in the first place by promoting a man beyond his capabilities. He was a fine backroom worker, but was just not cut out for managing, and he had never played at the top level.

"It made no sense that he was managing a major club. You don't put an able seaman in charge of the ship. That way you will eventually hit the rocks.

"The Hungarians and Brazilians had recently shown we were light years behind with our methods, and it was so obvious that Jimmy Anderson was still living in the Ark.

"Jimmy never forgave me for sending Maurice Norman up from defence to lead the attack when we were battling to pull back the Manchester City lead in the FA Cup semi-final. I could not be one of those captains who just spun the coin. I saw it as my duty to make changes in the heat of battle rather than save it for the after-match inquest.

"Sadly, my argument with Jimmy dragged our then coach Bill Nicholson in, and for a while I was at loggerheads with a man for whom I had utmost respect. I went on the transfer list, and when Bill finally took over from Jimmy he played me in the reserves. That hurt like hell. It all came right in the end, but I was never on Jimmy Anderson's Christmas card list."

In fairness to Anderson, he should not be judged on his managing stint at Spurs. Let's remember that his great service to Spurs included playing a vital part in the foundation building of the 'Push and Run' side while in charge of the Northfleet nursery team from 1934 to the outbreak of war. This meant he was effectively the Tottenham youth-team manager and brought along the likes of Ted Ditchburn, Ron Burgess, Les Bennett, Les Medley and, of course, our hero Bill Nicholson.

Jimmy also set up the deal with Southampton for Alf Ramsey in March 1949, but never managed to pierce the shield of suspicion with which Alf protected himself throughout his playing and managerial career. I got closer than most to Alf in the days when he reluctantly had to talk to the press, but – always called Alfred by his wife Victoria – I could not claim to have really known him, because he was continually guarded about his past. In his boots, I would have been shouting about what I had achieved from a background of poverty, but Alf was ashamed rather than proud of where he had come from. But I digress...

There were signs of better things to come at Tottenham when big Maurice 'The Ox' Norman signed from Norwich as reinforcement for a creaking defence, and another beefy player – Bobby Smith – arrived from Chelsea to help power Tottenham to the runners-up spot in the 1956/57 title race. By then, super coach Bill Nicholson was virtually running the show, as Anderson – in his mid-sixties – battled with what had all the signs of the sort of nervous illness that had ended Arthur Rowe's reign.

Jimmy was finally beaten by his health issues, and his long-anticipated resignation was announced in October 1958. He had just celebrated 50 years with the club, loyalty beyond the call of duty. But he was not cut out to be a manager. And, just like Arthur Rowe, he caved in to the enormous pressures and stress of the job. (Billy Minter, the Harry Kane of his time as a Spurs player, had suffered a similar fate when holding the managerial reins in the late 1920s.) It makes you wonder how modern managers, in the days of social media, cope with the pressure of it all...

> *"I must own up to being more a reader than a participant in this book so far. My turn will come! I love learning the club history, and that Jimmy Anderson period is fascinating. His battles with Danny Blanchflower must have been incredible to observe. The nearest I saw to it were the stand-up rows between Martin Chivers and Bill Nick and, much noisier, his assistant Eddie Baily.*
>
> *"They used to scorch the dressing room ceiling with their disputes, usually over the big man's attitude. He could be very stubborn and wanted to play the game his*

way, not be told how to do it, particularly by Eddie. They were sometimes like sworn enemies rather than colleagues. It must have been like that between Danny and Jimmy Anderson. Can you imagine that in today's game? An agent would be called in to sort out the issue. It's a whole new ball game."

The man who took Anderson's place was to become, without argument, the greatest and most successful manager in Tottenham's history. For me, the appointment remains the most momentous and significant event in my near 75 years of watching Spurs.

Enter as Spurs manager 'Sir' Bill Nicholson ... but first he had a job to do for his country.

CHAPTER 7

STIFLING THE BOYS OF BRAZIL

Before landing the role of manager of Spurs, Bill had cemented his reputation as an outstanding coach who was admired by his peers in what is the small world of football. He was a student of the game and made such an impression with his knowledge and ability to put over his ideas that England manager Walter Winterbottom selected him as his right-hand man for the World Cup challenge in Sweden in the summer of 1958.

The tournament was staged in the dark shadow of the Munich air crash on 6 February 1958 that cost the lives of eight Manchester United players and nine travelling journalists. I was among those football reporters who moved up a rung following the disaster. What a way to get promotion.

It is part of the Nicholson legend how Bill was given a brief in Sweden to watch eventual champions Brazil play, and he came up with the tactics that produced a creditable goalless draw against the Pelé-propelled team that was slaughtering all opposition.

This is what Winterbottom, literally a gentleman and a scholar, a former schoolteacher and a one-time Manchester United centre-half, told me: "I had my hands full with our match against Russia, and so I asked Bill to check out Brazil against Austria in their group match that the Brazilians won 3-0. He came back with a notebook full of assessments of every player, their overall tactics and just about everything you could possibly want to know about a team. It was remarkable in its thoroughness and observation.

"Working to Bill's analysis, we staged a practice match with Bill and I joining in as pretend Brazilians against our first-choice team.

We demonstrated the positions they took at set pieces, and Bill gave concise instructions as to how to cramp the space of their forwards.

"I wish I had saved the notes as an example of the perfect in-depth reconnaissance. That goalless draw against the magnificent Brazilians was one of the highlights of my career as England team manager, and there is no question that Bill Nicholson should take much of the credit."

I tried hard to draw Bill into commenting on his part in that plotting against Brazil, arguably the greatest international team of all time. But he would shrug and only say:

"I just did my job. It was a privilege to help Walter, one of the finest coaches there has ever been. Until he arrived on the scene and got things organised, clubs did not employ coaches as such, just trainers who concentrated on the fitness of players rather than showing them how they could improve their game and fit into team plans and formations. Walter opened eyes and doors. Including for me."

That was typical Bill, shifting the praise to somebody else. There were times when I wanted to kick him for not taking his deserved role at centre stage, but then it would not have been the Bill Nick we all grew to admire, respect and – yes – love.

Bill started to regularly take charge of the England Under-23 team, and showed he was not frightened to make tough decisions when he axed leading goalscorer Brian Clough because he considered him a lazy trainer. "If he shows the same attitude on the pitch, he will be letting the side down," he said. "I don't care what he has achieved at club level with Middlesbrough. I want him to be hungry for that England shirt. This will teach him a lesson and one day he will thank me for it."

He never did get that 'thank you' call and headstrong Cloughie held the humiliation of being dropped against him for many years.

Bill was one of the few football people whose autograph I ever requested. I asked him to sign the photograph featured on this page and scanned from my cuttings book.

Bill Nick pictured towards the end of his playing career, and the author's treasured autograph.

Bill winced when he saw the photograph. "Ouch!" he said, pulling a face. "That brings back painful memories. I was having awful problems with my right knee at the time. You can see I have an elastic bandage on it. I might look in complete command there but even posing for that photograph sent a pain shooting through my knee. Shortly after that it seized up altogether, and I had to have an operation and was hobbling on sticks for quite a while. It made me realise that I was never going to get back to my peak form and fitness, and I decided it was best for the club and the team if I retired. I conveyed my thoughts to our manager Arthur Rowe, who had gone through a similar crisis with his knee back in the 1930s. That all led to the arrival of Danny and what followed. It's a compelling story."

The 'Push and Run' team was breaking up, most of them Second World War veterans who had seen the best years of their careers lost to six years of conflict. Bill recalled while studying the cuttings book picture:

"Eddie Baily, Alf Ramsey and I were all photographed that day. It was for a coaching book that had the blessing of the FA. But by the time the book was published, not one of us was playing for Spurs anymore. Alf had moved on to Ipswich, Eddie to Port Vale and me into coaching. It was also about that time that Arthur Rowe had health problems and had to stand down.

"Jimmy Anderson took over in a caretaker role and invited me to be his coach. Then Arthur came back for a short while until he could not carry on anymore, and Jimmy was then officially manager. Arthur Rowe's 'Push and Run' era was over. They were great days, in many ways the best of my life. You can't beat playing. But then I poured myself into coaching, and trying to pass on to players all the good habits I had learned with Arthur and Walter. I had no designs on the manager's job. I just wanted to coach. It was what I liked doing best.

"What hurt me deeply was that Jimmy Anderson and my successor in the No.4 shirt, Danny, just could not see eye to eye. It was painful to watch and their differences became public because of Danny's links with Fleet Street. No player can ever be bigger than the club, and the board – rightly in my opinion – came down on Jimmy's side. It was a situation that made my early days in coaching very difficult. I liked Danny a lot as a person but he could be a difficult handful when he felt he was being treated less than fairly. He was openly contemptuous of Jimmy, who, admittedly, was quite old-fashioned in his approach to the game. But you couldn't have one player dictating

how the club should be run. As the coach, I found it an extremely concerning period. I only wanted what was best for the team and the club, and so that meant I had to condone it when Anderson decided to drop the man who was really our best player. They were worrying times."

There would have been even more worrying times if Bill had taken a job he was offered at the end of the 1958 Word Cup, when his ability as a coach was being internationally recognised. Sheffield Wednesday general manager Eric Taylor was so impressed that he told him: "We want you to come back to Yorkshire and manage Wednesday."

"I discussed it with Darkie," Bill told me, "and we decided we'd rather stay where we were. We had a young family and I was happy coaching at the club to which I had given my soul. Little did I know that a few months later I would be Spurs manager! The Hillsborough job went to Harry Catterick, who became my big rival with both Wednesday and then Everton over the following few years."

"That's an incredible fact about Bill almost becoming manager of Sheffield Wednesday. I just cannot imagine Tottenham without Bill in charge. I had a lot of tasty offers to join other clubs when I left school but Spurs representative Charlie Faulkner and chief scout Dickie Walker persuaded my very protective Dad that I should meet Bill before making any decision. Also heavily involved in any of my future plans was my older brother, Ted, who looked after my interests and watched my back like – well, like a brother. Both wanted what was best for me, and thought it was Spurs who were most likely to give me a guaranteed future in the game, although at one stage Ted was favouring West Ham because of the marvellous job Ron Greenwood had done in turning their great trio Bobby Moore, Geoff Hurst and Martin Peters into household names. Then we met Bill Nicholson and Ted, thank goodness, changed his mind.

"Dad, Ted and I were immediately impressed by Bill's straightforward, honest attitude. He volunteered nothing under the counter or any of the sort of inducements I know

other young talented footballers were getting to sign for this or that club. Bill just offered a proper education in the right way to play the game and a promise that I would 'get a fair crack of the whip'. That was Bill. As honest as the day is long – it was an approach I found appealing. And it was because of Bill that this West London schoolboy decided to make the daily trek across the capital to North London. Bill was worth the journey."

Steve had been just starting out on his football career as a seven-year-old schoolboy at Northolt, Middlesex, when Bill Nick was appointed manager of Tottenham on 11 October 1958. And what an extraordinary day that was.

CHAPTER 8

THE ASTONISHING 10-4 START

Anybody with Spurs in their soul will know of Bill Nicholson's first game officially in charge of Tottenham. Few managers in the history of the Beautiful Game have had such a startling start to a career, a 10-4 victory over Everton in a mad match that could have come out of the imagination of a Hollywood scriptwriter.

There was a blizzard of gossip about things happening behind the scenes at White Hart Lane, but this was in the pre-social media days. Few facts spilled out from clubs shy of publicity and contemptuous of nose-ointment reporters like me. Fleet Street and football were not on good terms.

Bill was never one to boast or make any sort of fuss, and I had to work hard on him over many interview sessions to get his memories of a day that was like no other...

> *"Yes, I suppose it was a pretty extraordinary day. I had been summoned to see vice-chairman Fred Wale at his tool-making premises in Tottenham earlier in the week, and he told me Jimmy Anderson was standing down because of illness. He wanted to know whether I was interested in taking over as manager. As I had been sort of acting manager for much of the season it seemed the natural thing to accept. We shook hands, and that was it.*
>
> *"We did not talk terms or a contract, and indeed I did not have a contract throughout my managerial career at Spurs. My thinking was, 'If they want me out, a piece of paper is not going to save me.' It honestly did not bother me. I've never been much of a businessman. My business is football, period.*

'SIR BILL'

"They kept back the announcement of me taking over from Jimmy until midday on the Saturday, and my wife was a bit peeved that she had to hear it on the wireless. I did not want to make a big deal of it, otherwise I would have been risking getting myself in the same state as Arthur Rowe and Jimmy Anderson. It was not pleasant watching them suffering with their health because of the pressures of the job. I was determined to take it all in my stride. The only pressure came from people like you with your nosey questions! Tell you what, the hardest thing about the job was being told how to do it by people who could not trap a bag of cement. But I bit my tongue, said nowt and got on with managing to the best of my ability.

"Anyway, the game against Everton was like nothing I've seen before or since. For purists, it was an awful game to watch, with both defences making elementary mistakes that made coaches like me want to tear our hair out. I honestly did not know whether to laugh or cry. Yes, I wanted to start with a victory – I always want to win – but this was just ridiculous.

"Cheeky Tommy Harmer had the game of a lifetime and told me as he came off, 'Don't expect 10 goals every week, Boss.' Danny Blanchflower summed it up with one of his Irishisms: 'It can only get worse.'"

But what appalled the perfectionist in Nicholson thrilled the Tottenham faithful as his team treated them to a banquet that left even the hungriest spectators completely gorged. Providing the opposition were an Everton side struggling three from the bottom of the First Division, a point behind 16th-placed Spurs.

Selecting the side earlier in the week in consultation with the ailing Anderson, Nicholson made the decision to recall Tottenham's impish inside-forward Tommy Harmer, known to the White Hart Lane fans as 'Harmer the Charmer'. But that afternoon Everton found him more like 'The Harmer' as he pulled them apart with an astounding individual performance after four weeks sulking in the reserves. He had a hand – or rather a well-directed foot – in nine goals and scored one himself as Everton were sunk without trace under a flood of goals. The final scoreline was 10-4. It could just easily have been 15-8!

THE ASTONISHING 10-4 START

Harmer was the Tom Thumb character of football. He stood just 5ft 5in tall and was a chain-smoking bantamweight who looked as if he could be blown away by a strong wind. But he had mesmeric control of the ball and when conditions suited him could dominate a match with his passing and dribbling.

Born in Hackney on 2 February 1928, he joined Tottenham from amateur club Finchley in 1951, and over the next eight years played 205 league games and scored 47 goals and created many more.

For the record, Bill Nicholson's first selection as Spurs manager was:

Hollowbread
Baker   Ryden   Hopkins
Blanchflower   Harmer   Iley
Medwin   Smith (capt)   Stokes   Robb

The match facts: There was a hint of what was to come in the opening moments when Spurs took the lead through Alfie Stokes after an inch-perfect diagonal pass from Harmer had split the Everton defence. The Merseysiders steadied themselves and equalised eight minutes later when Jimmy Harris side-footed in a Dave Hickson centre.

The unfortunate Albert Dunlop, deputising in goal for the injured first-choice keeper Jimmy O'Neill, then suffered a nightmare 30 minutes as Spurs ruthlessly smashed five goals past him through skipper Bobby Smith (two), schoolmaster, part-time pro George Robb, Stokes again and Terry Medwin.

The foundation for all the goals was being laid in midfield, where Harmer and Danny Blanchflower, both masters of ball control, were in complete command.

Jimmy Harris gave Everton fleeting hope of a revival with a headed goal to make it 6-2 just after half-time, but bulldozing Bobby Smith took his personal haul to four and the irrepressible Harmer helped himself to a goal that was as spectacular as any scored during this gourmet feast.

Bobby Collins lost possession just outside the penalty area, and the ball bobbled in front of Harmer. He struck it on the half-volley from 20 yards and watched almost in disbelief as the ball rocketed into the roof of the net. It was the first time Tommy had scored a league goal from outside the penalty area.

Everton refused to surrender and the industrious Harris completed his hat-trick from a centre by dashing centre-forward Dave Hickson. Then the wee Scot Bobby Collins, two inches shorter than Harmer, showed that this was a magical match for the little people when he hammered in a 25-yard drive as both teams crazily pushed everybody forward. It was like watching two heavyweight boxers with fragile chins slugging it out.

All the goals were scored by forwards until Spurs centre-half John Ryden, limping on the wing, scrambled in Tottenham's 10th goal – the fourteenth of the match – in the closing minutes. It was sheer bedlam... and the crowd loved every second, while newly installed manager Bill Nicholson wondered if he was dreaming it all.

There is nobody with knowledge of Tottenham's history who has not heard of that 10-4 match. It is one of the best-known results in football, but Bill always played it down. I often used to try to get him talking about the game but he seemed almost embarrassed by it. He was such a perfectionist that he could only recall the mistakes rather than the goals. This is not a criticism of Bill but more a comment on the fact that he was rarely satisfied in victory. He could always see what was wrong rather than right with a goal or a team performance.

"Old-time supporters still talk in awe of Tommy Harmer's performance in that match. Everybody tells me he was a real box of tricks, and when I arrived at Tottenham to start my career he was a regular visitor to White Hart Lane and I don't think I ever saw him without a lit cigarette in his hand or mouth.

"He famously told Bill Nick as he came off the pitch at the end of the 10-4 rout, 'Don't expect 10 goals every week, Boss.' A few years later he scored the winning goal that took Chelsea to promotion, the ball going into the net off his groin. He quipped, 'I got really cocky over that goal.' What a character."

Bill Nick still had the nagging problem of Danny Blanchflower to overcome as he started out on his managing journey. The enigmatic

THE ASTONISHING 10-4 START

Irishman remained on the transfer list, and the rookie boss let him kick his heels in the reserves for a couple of weeks. Then, after a quiet and private hatchet-burying talk before a crucial match against champions Wolves at Molineux in March 1959, it was announced that Blanchflower was being reinstated as club captain. Blanchflower took over from Bobby Smith, who was rarely on good terms with the new manager because of a gambling habit that was foreign to Nicholson's life code.

"Thank goodness for that," Bobby said when relieved of the captaincy. "The responsibility was getting me down. Danny's welcome to it. There's nobody better for the job."

Just before Easter that year Bill had bought Dave Mackay from Hearts. Cliff Jones had arrived from Swansea in February 1958, and in October 1959 John White was imported from Falkirk. The 'Double' side was taking shape.

Blanchflower – rejuvenated after his thinking time in the reserves – got on famously with Nicholson after the fog of misunderstanding had been cleared, and they started to bounce off each other with their tactical ideas and theories. He came off the transfer list and White Hart Lane was suddenly buzzing with ambition and hope after Bill's dodgy first season, when Spurs had finished just out of the relegation zone despite the emphatic 10-4 victory that had launched the Nicholson era. In this day of social media blitzing, the keyboard warriors would have hounded Nicholson out of his new job, but people back then were much more patient and loyal. A 13-2 FA Cup fourth-round replay victory over Crewe Alexandra at White Hart Lane in February 1960 served as further notice that Spurs were developing into a goal machine.

After a promising third-place finish in the 1959/60 season – just two points behind champions Burnley – Danny started to quietly tell anybody who would listen: "We can do the Double."

"Most people looked at him as if he was a crackpot. Back then the Double was considered the 'Impossible Dream'. No club in the 20th century had managed it.

Danny later told me:

"When I predicted to our veteran chairman Fred Bearman before the start of the 1960/61 season that we would achieve the Double, I said it quietly and confidently... but not confidentially, because I wanted to get the message out. It was not a boast but a belief. I am a great believer that confidence, like fear, can be contagious, and I wanted our players to catch my belief. It was a question of making everybody at the club think not 'we may' but 'we can'. It was positive thinking to go with our positive play.

"I was impressed by the individual ability running through our squad, also its teamwork, and its whole personality. You could say we were one of the last of the good teams in which players were allowed to do things their own way, without restrictions from the coaching manual. Bill Nicholson deserves enormous respect and praise for the way he ran our ship. He was a captain who knew when to stay on the bridge, but also when to come and mix with the men and inspire and motivate them with good common-sense tactics. He is an absolute master of a coach who knows how to get his ideas across without being confusing or complicated. Football is basically a simple game that is sometimes made more complicated than it need be by the people doing the coaching. Bill Nicholson made us do the basics well but gave the freedom to think for ourselves.

"I sensed people grew to like us because we were a cosmopolitan team as well as a very good one. We had Englishmen, Welshmen, Scots and Irishmen, big guys, little guys, fat men and thin men. Also, we scored goals in so many different ways. I know if I had been a spectator I would have wanted to watch us. We were exciting, explosive and – virtually throughout the season – exceptional.

"There was, of course, the little matter of luck that we needed on our side. It was important that we avoided serious injuries, but there was a depth to our squad that convinced me that we could overcome most things.

"When I mentioned the possibility of doing the Double to Bill, he considered it in his usual cautious manner, and seemed at first to think I was being my usual romantic and fanciful self. Then, almost in a whisper, he confided: 'Yes, I think it can be done too.'"

Danny and Bill were football's Odd Couple, who could not have been more opposite in personality and presence. Bill was a blunt, sometimes stubborn, no-nonsense, say-it-as-you-see-it, almost stereotypical dour Yorkshireman. Danny was a romantic, occasionally a fantasist, always artistic, articulate and a born charmer, yet often argumentative. Bill's only reading was football manuals; Danny

THE ASTONISHING 10-4 START

usually had his head buried in classic novels. Danny went to work on an ego, Bill on an egg.

But they were both perfectionists who agreed on how the game of football should be played and plotted, and in the unforgettable season of 1960/61 they found the keys to paradise.

Danny, naturally, found his own way of describing their relationship:

"Bill and I were as far apart as you could be in our tastes and habits. It's fair to say that socially we had little in common. But we could both look at an empty football canvas and see the finished picture. He would not claim to have been the best educated of men, but when it came to matters of football he was something of an intellectual. He and I balanced each other perfectly. Bill always talked common sense and had his feet firmly on the ground, while I had an imagination that could send me flying up to the heavens. In that Double season, we often met in the middle."

Bill said of Danny:

"There were times when I had to pull Danny back because his optimism could get out of control. It put extra pressure on us because virtually every preview of any match in the newspapers and on TV and radio mentioned the Double. Confidence is good, but over-confidence can be dangerous and draining."

The Double was on the horizon.

CHAPTER 9

THE DOUBLE

The unforgettable 1960/61 Double season dawned with Bill Nicholson having to dowse the flames of optimism being lit by his chatterbox captain, Danny Blanchflower. But even this cautious, 41-year-old footballing perfectionist had to accept the confidence was justified when Spurs started the season with a record 11 successive victories. Eleven! The First Division had never known anything like it, and by Christmas the league title was virtually in the bag. Now for the FA Cup to become the first club of the 20th century to capture English football's two major trophies in the same season.

Maybe the modern football fan will wonder what all the fuss was about. After all, Manchester United, Liverpool and Manchester City have since completed Trebles. A Double? Big deal. But what the younger supporter has to realise is the huge psychological barrier that had to be surmounted. The Double was the equivalent of Everest (not conquered until Hillary and Tenzing in 1953) and the first four-minute mile (not broken until Roger Bannister's historic run of 1954).

Many clubs had got within shooting distance of the Double and then fallen, often at the final hurdle. It was usually the FA Cup that tripped them up, with the large element of luck involved in the draw and smaller clubs playing above themselves for what in those days was considered the main prize.

That opening blitz of 11 victories proved beyond doubt that Bill Nick had pieced together one of the most formidable teams ever to grace the playing fields of England. This was what Bill told me about that Double team in a moment of fond reflection in the autumn of his years:

"Everything was right. The balance of the team. The attitude of the players. We managed to find the perfect blend and

everybody gave 100 per cent in effort and enthusiasm. We had the sort of understanding and cohesion that you find in only the finest teams, and we tried to keep our football as simple as possible – imaginative but simple. I kept pushing an old theory: When you're not in possession, get into position. The man without the ball was important, because he could make things happen by getting into the right place at the right time. Running off the ball was as vital as running with it. The secret is finding space and using it.

"I was so fortunate to have been influenced by great thinkers like Peter McWilliam, Arthur Rowe and Walter Winterbottom. All shared my belief that the important thing is getting the basics right and then building on that. The first thing a footballer must have, even the naturally skilled ones, is physical fitness. It was no secret that I worked the players very hard in pre-season training, to the point where they found 90 minutes of football almost a relief. They moaned when being pushed through pain barriers but were grateful when they found themselves getting comfortably through a gruelling game. Fitness is the most vital of all ingredients. You can be the most skilful footballer in the world but you are useless to the team if you're having to look to take a breather after just a couple of runs.

"Do you know who are the fittest athletes in the world? Ballet dancers! Yes, they are supreme athletes. I remember once on a pre-season club tour of Russia in 1959 we went to the Bolshoi Ballet in Moscow. Most of the lads grumbled when I told them what we were going to see, but they came away astonished at the fitness and stamina of those dancers.

"I got our interpreter to ask questions backstage and I found they did lots of weight training for muscle development and stamina, and so I invited an Olympic weightlifter called Bill Watson to introduce weight training into our fitness programme. It made a huge difference to our fitness levels, which were a major reason why we dominated in that Double year. The players got to appreciate and understand why I preached the three Fs: Fitness, Fitness, Fitness."

Over to Steve:

"Only Bill could have sat watching the Bolshoi and seen athletes rather than ballet dancers! But the revolutionary weight training he introduced set the fitness standards for what is taken for granted by clubs today. It was Bill Watson, working to plans drawn up by Bill Nick, who was a pioneer of the weight-training programme that most clubs now employ. Remember, this was not weight lifting but weight training, and our faithful trainers – Cecil Poynton and Johnny Wallis – helped supervise the Watson routine with light-ish weights. We were not looking to become Mr Universe contestants or the next Arnold Schwarzenegger. Muscle-bound footballers are the last thing a club needs. It is on the training pitch and in the gymnasium where players get the necessary strength and stamina to go with the skill factor. And it all started with Bill's visit to the ballet!

"The achievements of that Double side are, of course, written into football legend and they set the benchmark for all the teams that followed them. I think it fair and reasonable to say that long-suffering Spurs fans are still waiting for a modern side to get anywhere near their standards and consistency.

"The Double era was already a memory by the time I joined the club, and there was nobody left in the team from those giddy days when I made my debut against Sunderland at White Hart Lane on 27 September 1969, a date carved on my heart. Just for a matter of record, my team-mates that day were Pat Jennings, Phil Beal, Cyril Knowles, Alan Mullery, Mike England, Peter Collins, Jimmy Pearce, Dennis Bond, Alan Gilzean and the one and only Jimmy Greaves, who had joined Tottenham the season after the Double. John Pratt was the non-playing substitute. Everything we did was compared with that Double team that still stood large in the memories of Spurs fans. They had been spoiled!"

On the way to the title, all five of Tottenham's first-choice goal-hunting forwards reached double figures: Bobby Smith (28), Les Allen (23), Cliff Jones (15), John White (13) and Terry Dyson (12).

Between them they scored 115 First Division goals. It was mind-blowing, even mine-blowing, stuff.

These were the 12 men who carried off the League Championship and FA Cup trophies in a style that was almost poetical:

> *Brown, Baker, Henry – They roll off the tongue like old friends – Blanchflower, Norman, Mackay – Creating a legend that never ends – Jones, White, Smith – They played the game with style and flair – Allen, Dyson, Medwin – And were – at the double – beyond compare...*

For those not lucky to have been around to witness the feats of those Double heroes (my writing partner Steve was only nine at the time, for example), let me revisit an earlier summary of mine of that magical season. For a start, Nicholson's Double team was never defence-minded as is revealed by the fact that they conceded 50 league goals on their way to the First Division Championship. But they were sufficiently steady at the back to allow heavy concentration on attack.

Bill Brown, one of the more efficient Scottish goalkeepers, had excellent reactions and a safe pair of hands, which made up for his occasional positioning misjudgement. He forged an excellent rapport with the 6ft 1in Norfolk-born colossus Maurice Norman, a dominating centre-half who won 23 England caps (anybody over six foot back in those days was categorised as a giant).

'Big Mo' – or 'Monty' as he was known in the dressing room – was flanked in a fluid 3-3-4 formation by full-backs Peter Baker and Ron Henry, both of whom were disciplined and determined and had unyielding, competitive attitudes.

Dave Mackay was always quick to take up a defensive position alongside Norman when needed and his tackles were like a clap of thunder. They used to say in the game that anybody who felt the full weight of a Mackay challenge would go home feeling as if he was still with them. Meanwhile, Danny Blanchflower was not noted for his tackling but was a shrewd enough positional player to manage to get himself between the opponent in possession and the goal. His impact on a match was more cerebral than crushing.

The Tottenham attacking movements in that Double year were full of fluency and fire, a blaze lit in midfield by three of the greatest players to come together in one club team (up there with Best-Law-Charlton, Kendall-Ball-Harvey, Bremner-Giles-Hunter, Moore-Hurst-Peters). Blanchflower, an inspiring skipper for Northern Ireland as well as Tottenham, was the brains of the team and had an instinctive feel for the game and an ability to lift the players around him with measured passes and intelligent tactical commands. One of the best things Bill Nick ever did was taking him off the transfer list. It is difficult to imagine Spurs of those early 1960s being nearly so successful without Danny's motivational contribution.

Mackay, the Scot with an in-built swagger and a he-man's barrel chest, was the heart of the side, always playing with enormous enthusiasm, power and panache.

John White, an artist of an inside-forward in the best traditions of purist Scottish football, was the eyes of the team, seeing openings that escaped the vision of lesser players and dismantling defences with precision passes and blind-side runs that earned him the nickname, 'The Ghost of White Hart Lane'. This talented trio were essentially buccaneering, forward-propelling players, but were sufficiently geared to team discipline to help out in defence when necessary.

Spearheading the attack in that memorable start to the Swinging Sixties was burly, bulldozing centre-forward Bobby Smith, a 15-cap England centre-forward who mixed subtle skill with awesome strength. He was the main marksman in the Double year with 33 league and FA Cup goals. The mighty Smith was in harness with Les Allen, father of future Spurs hero Clive. He was a clever and underrated player who was the odd man out when Jimmy Greaves arrived the following season. Les contributed 23 goals to the Championship season. Smith, Allen and Greaves all started their careers with Chelsea.

Out on the wings Spurs had Terry Dyson, tiny, quick and taunting, the son of a Yorkshire jockey, and the marvellous Cliff Jones, one of the Untouchables of Welsh international football, who could take the tightest defences apart with his fast, diagonal runs. He was essentially right-footed but was at his most dangerous when raiding from the left with the speed of an Olympic sprinter and the heart of a lion. What a player! He was the best winger I ever saw in a Spurs shirt... until Gareth Bale arrived on the scene five decades later. Cliff was big enough and honest enough to describe Gareth as the greatest of all Welsh wingers, but I promise there was not a lot between them.

'SIR BILL'

It was the Bill Nicholson ensemble, with the redoubtable Danny Blanchflower an extension of his manager on the pitch.

In reserve Spurs had players of the calibre of the beautifully composed Welsh method player Terry Medwin, fearless Frank Saul, cultured wing-half Tony Marchi and the utility player and ex-Hammer John Smith, all of whom made occasional appearances during that golden season.

When Spurs set that new First Division record by winning their opening 11 matches on the trot (or, perhaps, at a smooth canter...), Blanchflower found his was no longer a voice in the wilderness. Good judges began to wonder if – as Danny had been insisting from day one – this could be the year for the Double. Spurs were looking that good.

Aston Villa were crushed by six goals, Manchester United by four, and mighty Wolves were hammered by four goals on their own territory at Molineux. They were victories that brought gasps of astonishment and admiration right around the country, because Manchester United and Wolves were still living on their reputations of the previous decade of being the kings of English football.

It was records all the way as Tottenham romped to the League Championship with eight points to spare over runners-up Sheffield Wednesday. Their 31 victories constituted a league record, as did their total of 16 away wins. The 66 points collected with style and flamboyance equalled the First Division record set by Herbert Chapman's Arsenal in 1930/31.

While winning the First Division marathon, Bill Nick's team also managed to survive in the minefield of the FA Cup, getting a scare in the sixth round at Sunderland, but winning the replay 5-0 at White Hart Lane.

The final against a Leicester City team handicapped by injury problems was something of an anti-climax, but Spurs managed to win 2-0 to prove Danny Blanchflower as good a prophet as he was a footballing captain. Bobby Smith and Terry Dyson scored the victory-clinching goals past the goalkeeper who was to become a legend – Gordon Banks.

Leicester were handicapped by an injury to full-back Len Chalmers, and the Foxes, reduced to virtually 10 men, managed to upset the rhythm of Spurs to such an extent that Bill Nick described it as one of Tottenham's worst performances of the season. For the rest of his life, it niggled and gnawed at the supreme idealist that Spurs had not performed to anything like their best on that historic Double-clinching day at Wembley.

How lucky was I to get to talk one-on-one to the architect of that wonderful 1960/61 League and Cup triumph for the official centenary video of Tottenham's first hundred years in 1982? This was how the great 'Sir Bill' assessed each of the Double heroes...

BILL BROWN
Born: Arbroath, 8 October 1931
Died: Ontario, 30 November 2004
Tottenham's goalkeeper in 222 league matches between 1959 and 1965 after joining them from Dundee, his local club, during Bill Nicholson's first season as manager. He was capped 28 times by Scotland, and wound down his league career with Northampton Town. Throughout his career he worked part-time on building up a printing business, eventually emigrating to Canada where he went into real estate after briefly playing for Toronto Falcons. Bill died after a long battle with cancer in 2004.

BILL NICK ASSESSMENT: *"I was faced with the huge problem of finding a successor to Ted Ditchburn, who had been one of the finest goalkeepers in the country while playing for us. My Scottish contacts tipped me off that Dundee were willing to listen to offers for Bill, who was the current Scotland goalkeeper, and I jumped on the overnight train to Dundee in the 1959 close season and snapped him up for £16,500. He had a good pair of hands, was very agile, and stood his ground when aggressive forwards tried to unsettle him. He quickly established a good rapport with centre-half Maurice Norman, and between them they usually managed to clear any danger. There were sometimes questions about his ability to deal with crosses, but he rarely let Spurs down. I would rate him one of my most important and successful signings, and he continued to do a fine job for us while we waited for Pat Jennings to settle."*

PETER BAKER

Born: Hampstead, London, 10 December 1931
Died: Hampstead 27 January 2016
Played 299 league games for Spurs, and scored three goals. Signed for Tottenham from Enfield in 1952 – at the age of 20 – during the Arthur Rowe era and served the club for nearly 14 years. After eventually losing his place in defence to Cyril Knowles (who was more comfortable on the left), he wound down his career in South Africa with Durban City, where he coached and then ran a furniture business. Educated in Arsenal territory at Southgate County School, he was the only player in the Double defence not to win an international cap.

BILL NICK ASSESSMENT: *"Peter was an established member of the staff when I took over, and I had great confidence in him because he was an excellent all-round sportsman with good stamina and an impressive fitness level. His hard, uncompromising style balanced perfectly with the more skilled approach of his partner, Ron Henry. I can never recall a winger giving him a roasting, and this was in an era when every team played two who stayed out wide on the flanks. He could be tough to the point of brutal when necessary and many is the time he ended dangerous raids with perfectly timed tackles. He was steady and reliable, just what you want from a full-back. It is not a position for Fancy Dans. Our supporters sometimes gave him a tough time for being caught out of position, but they lost sight of the fact that he was often covering for Danny, who was not the greatest defensive player in the world!"*

RON HENRY

Born: Shoreditch, 17 August 1934
Died: Harpenden, 27 December 2014
Played 247 league matches for Tottenham between 1954 and 1965 before becoming a highly regarded youth coach. He was at left-back in all 42 of Tottenham's league matches during the 1960/61 season. Early in his career with Redbourn he had been a skilful winger, then switched to wing-half and later, on turning professional with Tottenham, settled down at left-back. He made his league debut at centre-half against Huddersfield in 1955, but it was not until the 1959/60

season that he took over the No.3 shirt from Welsh international Mel Hopkins. Capped once, in Alf Ramsey's first match as the England manager – against France in 1963. England were beaten 5-2 and Ron did not get another chance. He ran a successful market garden in the fields adjoining his home in Redbourn, Hertfordshire, and continued to coach Tottenham youth team players into his old age and was Lilywhite through and through, right up to his passing at the age of 80.

BILL NICK ASSESSMENT: *"I had the difficult decision of choosing between Ron and Welsh international Mel Hopkins at left-back. In fact, it was not until Mel was sidelined by a broken nose that Ron became the automatic choice, and in that Double season he proved he was well worthy of his place. He was an ever-present along with Blanchflower, White and Allen, and seemed to grow with every game. He was brilliant at making sliding tackles, looked composed on the ball, and was clever at jockeying wingers until they ran out of space. As with any player brought up to think 'the Spurs way', Ron could play the ball out of defence with accuracy and in a positive manner. Like me, he won just one England cap. He deserved more."*

DANNY BLANCHFLOWER
Born: Belfast, 10 February 1926
Died: London, 9 December 1993
Played 337 league games for Tottenham between 1954 and 1963 after service with Glentoran, Barnsley and Aston Villa. One of the most creative and authoritative players ever to set foot on a football pitch, he was a born leader who, as well as skippering Spurs through their 'Glory Glory' years, also captained the Northern Ireland team that reached the quarter-finals of the 1958 World Cup. His younger brother, Jack, was a prominent centre-half who never played again after surviving the Manchester United air crash at Munich in 1958. Danny was twice voted the Footballer of the Year before a recurring knee injury forced his retirement in 1963. He had mixed fortune as manager of Northern Ireland and then a disastrous spell in charge of Chelsea before returning to his career as a journalist.

BILL NICK ASSESSMENT: *"Danny had a spell on the transfer list in my early days as coach, but I had no intention of letting him go. I knew how important he was to the club as a born leader on and off the pitch. He was a captain in every sense of the word, inspiring the players around him with his highly skilled performances and lifting them with words of wisdom. His contribution went much farther and deeper than his performances on the playing field. He was a great reader of the game, and had an in-built radar system that guided him to the right places at the right times. His weakness was that he put so much thought into attacking play that he sometimes forgot his defensive responsibilities. He was a true master of the footballing arts and an inspiring leader on and off the pitch."*

MAURICE NORMAN

Born: Mulbarton, Norfolk, 8 May 1934
Died: Trimley St Martin, East Suffolk, 27 November 2022
Played 357 league matches for Spurs between 1955 and 1965, following one full season with his local club, Norwich City. He was England's centre-half in 23 international matches and was shortlisted for World Cup duty in 1966, before his career was effectively finished by a broken leg received in a Spurs friendly against the Hungarian national team in November 1965. At 6ft 1in and 13 stone, he stood like an immovable mountain in the middle of the Spurs defence. 'Monty' was a former farmer's boy and one of the greatest footballers ever to come out of Norfolk. Norman had joined Tottenham as a full-back, but it was his switch to centre-half following the retirement of Harry Clarke that established him as one of the most reliable defenders in the league.

BILL NICK ASSESSMENT: *"Maurice was an ox of a man. Big in build, big in heart and big in personality. Strangely enough he was not that commanding in the air, but he was so tall that he usually got to the high balls before rival forwards had started jumping. He helped make goalkeeper Bill Brown's job easier with his expert covering and support play. On those occasions when the usually dependable Brown made a mess of a cross, you would usually find Maurice thumping the ball away. He would not claim to have been* *the most skilful centre-half, but he had immense strength and was reliable and a totally committed competitor. But for tragically breaking a leg I am sure he would have been England's other centre-half in the 1966 World Cup finals [alongside Bobby Moore] and Jack Charlton might never have got his chance. That's football for you. Full of cruel and unexpected twists."*

DAVE MACKAY

Born: Edinburgh, 14 November 1934
Died: Nottingham, 2 March 2015
Scored 42 goals in 268 league appearances for Tottenham after joining them from Hearts for £30,000 in March 1959. While with Hearts he won Scottish League Cup, Scottish Cup and Scottish League Championship medals; then with Spurs he collected three FA Cup winners' medals, a League Championship medal and a European Cup Winners' Cup medal, although he missed the final because of injury. Later, he skippered Derby County to a Second Division Championship medal; and as manager he steered Derby to the First Division title in 1974/75. He also managed Swindon, Nottingham Forest and Walsall before coaching in the Middle East. He twice made comebacks after breaking a leg. He shared the Footballer of the Year award with Tony Book in 1969, and in total won 22 Scottish caps.

BILL NICK ASSESSMENT: *"I've often gone on record as saying that Dave Mackay was my best signing. I did not just get a player from Hearts, I got a motivator. He could bring the best out of his teammates by his effort and enthusiasm, not only during matches but also on the training pitch. Dave gave 100 per cent every time he played and was the heart and soul of the team. He had an incredible will to win and this rubbed off on every player in the side. While he was a powerful man with a shuddering tackle, he also had delicate skill and an educated left foot. He came out top in most of the gymnasium skill challenges. It was remarkable the way he came back as a vital force after twice breaking a leg. He was a manager's dream."*

'SIR BILL'

TERRY DYSON
Born: Malton, North Yorkshire, 29 November 1934
Played 184 league games for Spurs and scored 41 goals. The son of famous jockey Ginger Dyson, he came to White Hart Lane from non-league Scarborough in 1955. He was a member of the first-team squad until 1965 when he moved on to Fulham, and then Colchester and Guildford City. A regular in the Double-winning side, he scored two goals that clinched victory in the European Cup Winners' Cup final in 1963. In 1961 he became the first Spurs player to score a hat-trick in the derby against Arsenal (Spurs won the match 4-3). He later became an assessor of schoolboy footballers for the Football Association.

BILL NICK ASSESSMENT: *"Terry was a determined competitor who never let the side down. His grit and whole-hearted endeavour just gave him the edge over 'the other Terry' – Medwin – who was desperately unlucky with injuries. 'Terry D.' would run his legs off for the team, and often popped up with vital winning goals. He, of course, had the most memorable match of his career in the European Cup Winners' Cup final. He continually had the Atletico Madrid defence in trouble with his thrusting runs, and his two goals turned the match. He was big enough to admit he did not have the skill of some of those tremendous players around him, but he more than made up for it with his effort. Terry's enthusiasm was infectious and you could always count on him to run himself into the ground for the team."*

JOHN WHITE
Born: Musselburgh, Lothian, 28 April 1937
Died: Crews Hill Golf Course, Middlesex, 21 July 1964
Scored 40 goals in 183 league games for Spurs after joining them from Falkirk in 1959 for the bargain price of £20,000. He was capped 22 times by Scotland and was an ever-present for Spurs during the Double season. In his youth he had been turned down by both Glasgow Rangers and Middlesbrough for being too small, but he quickly showed that his frail appearance was misleading when starting his career with Alloa Athletic and then Falkirk. Bill Nicholson bought him on the advice of both Dave Mackay and Danny Blanchflower,

who had seen him in action for Scotland. The year after helping Spurs capture the European Cup Winners' Cup in 1963 he was struck down and killed by a bolt of lightning while sheltering under a tree during a solo round of golf.

BILL NICK ASSESSMENT: *"I still get very emotional when I think of the cruel way John was taken from us. He was a great player when he died, and I am convinced he was going to get better. He was so aptly nicknamed 'The Ghost of White Hart Lane'. It was his ability off the ball that made him such a phenomenal player. He would pop up from out of nowhere just when he was needed most to make a pass or collect the ball. Like Danny Blanchflower, he had the gift of being able to give the exact weight to a pass. John was a former cross-country runner who had the energy to run all day and could cut a defence in half with just one cunningly placed ball. With White, Blanchflower and Mackay operating together in midfield, we just could not go wrong."*

BOBBY SMITH
Born: Lingdale, North Yorkshire, 22 February 1933
Died: Enfield, 18 September 2010
Scored 176 goals in 271 league matches for Spurs after joining them from Chelsea in 1955. Wound down his league career with Brighton, his 18 goals in 31 matches helping them win the Fourth Division Championship in 1965. He later briefly played with Hastings. He scored 13 goals in 15 appearances as England centre-forward, all but one of them in partnership with Jimmy Greaves. In the Double season he was top First Division marksman for Spurs with 28 goals, and he netted in each of the successive FA Cup final victories. He and Les Allen were lethal together in 1960/61, continuing a double act that had started at Stamford Bridge.

BILL NICK ASSESSMENT: *"Because he could be a battering-ram style of centre-forward, Bobby was rarely given the credit he deserved for his high level of skill. People seemed to think he was all brute force. Strength certainly played an important part in his game, and he used to make full use of his heavyweight physique. But he also had subtle touches and could lay off delicate passes. He was the perfect partner* *for Les Allen and later Jimmy Greaves, and he assisted in many of their goals. Bobby used to win the ball for Les and Jimmy in the air, removing a defender or two with the sheer force of his challenge. Foreign goalkeepers used to be petrified of him in the days when players were allowed to let them know they were around. He was magnificent in that Double season, and when he had to miss a few games because of injury, young Frank Saul did an excellent stand-in job for us. I did not approve of Bobby's gambling lifestyle, but I never had any complaints about his input on the pitch."*

LES ALLEN
Born: Dagenham, Essex, 4 September 1937
Scored 47 goals in 119 league matches for Spurs. Started his career as an amateur with Briggs Sports while working as an apprentice with the local Ford factory. Signed for Chelsea in 1954 and netted 11 goals in 44 league appearances before joining Tottenham in December 1959 in a straight swap for Johnny Brooks. Making way for the arrival of Jimmy Greaves, he joined Queens Park Rangers and helped them become the first Third Division side to win the League Cup at Wembley – in the same 1966/67 season that they were promoted. He scored 55 goals in 128 league games for QPR before starting a management career during which he was in charge at Loftus Road and at Swindon, and then in Salonika, Greece. He later became a skilled model maker, and in retirement shared his time between his homes in Essex and Cyprus. From a famous football family, his brother Dennis, sons Clive and Bradley, and nephews Martin and Paul all made an impact as professionals.

BILL NICK ASSESSMENT: *"A much-underrated player, Les had a prolific partnership with Bobby Smith, and together they played a major part in clinching the Double. Les was a neat, constructive centre-forward or inside-forward, with a fine turn of speed, an accurate right-foot shot, and excellent positional sense. He was unlucky not to get international recognition. I got him in a swap deal for Johnny Brooks when Les was languishing in Chelsea reserves, and I definitely got the better of the deal. He did a superb job for us and I felt sorry for him when he lost his place to Greavsie. But these things happen in football. Nobody's place is guaranteed."*

CLIFF JONES

Born: Swansea 7 February 1935

Scored 135 goals in 318 league matches for Spurs after joining them from Swansea for £35,000 in February 1958. He won 59 Welsh international caps and had the final shots of his career with Fulham, for whom he signed in 1968 after collecting a string of honours with Spurs. He stood 5ft 7in tall, weighed just over 10 stone, and moved like a whippet along either wing for Spurs and Wales. He was the son of pre-war Welsh international Ivor Jones, and the nephew of former Arsenal and Wales inside-forward Bryn, and the brother of long-serving league professional Bryn Jnr. His cousin, Ken Jones, was an ex-professional who became one of the country's leading sports columnists (and the father of that brilliant writer and biographer Lesley-Ann Jones... what a family!).

BILL NICK ASSESSMENT: *"The remarkable thing about Cliff was that he was a right-footed player, yet had his best moments on the left wing. At his peak, he was without question one of the world's greatest wingers. When he was in full flight I doubt if there was a more dangerous forward on the ball. He used to run with the pace, determination and bravery of a Welsh wing three-quarter. He was brave to the point of madness in the penalty area. It was a common sight to see Cliff rising like a salmon at the far post to head spectacular goals that were amazing when you realise he was a smallish bloke with a slim frame. When you talk about great wingers like Matthews, Finney and Best, you can mention Jonesie in the same breath. He was as effective as any of them, and on either wing."*

These, then, were the players who collectively achieved the greatest season in Tottenham's history. Yet at the end of it, ultra-perfectionist Bill Nicholson was dissatisfied. "We just did not perform in the final against Leicester," he groaned for years afterwards. 'The eyes of the nation were on us and I wanted us to win in true Spurs style. Our victory left me feeling flat and frustrated."

"I was coming up 10 when Spurs did the Double in 1960/61, and to this day it remains the most successful season in the club's history, but the enormity of it did not strike me

at the time because I was too busy growing up and falling in love with the Beautiful Game. Back in those days, I was playing three or four matches every week at schools, youth team and kick-about level. I was only happy with a ball at my feet and – with big brother Ted always encouraging me – I used to run everywhere, including the three miles to and from school. Come to think of it, I can't remember a time in my young life when I was standing still except when I was sleeping. A bundle of energy and action, and that was how I played my football. Mr Perpetual Motion. In those early days you would have put your money on me joining a west London club, like Brentford or QPR, so it was only later when I was lucky enough to become a professional footballer with Spurs that the full impact of what that Double team achieved hit me.

"For starters, they won every one of their first 11 matches of that season and then drew the twelfth. That is extraordinary. To this day, more than 60 years later, it remains a record.

"Whenever I tried to get Bill reminiscing he would dismiss the feat as if it was just another day at the office. He made no secret of the fact that he was desperately disappointed by the FA Cup final, when his wonder team clinched the Double by beating Leicester City. Bill only liked to win if it was done in style. He was like an eccentric artist who wanted to destroy the canvas if he was not happy with the painting.

"He used to say how the injury to Len Chalmers not only upset the Leicester plans but also wrecked the Tottenham rhythm. 'We had played some magnificent football during the season,' he said, 'but we were way below our best at Wembley.'

"Obviously Bill was proud that Spurs had become the first team of the century to win the Double; it was a remarkable achievement. Yet for him it all fell flat because of a final wrecked by injury. If only substitutes had been allowed..."

THE DOUBLE

But there were a lot of golden moments still to come to cheer Bill up and satisfy even his high standards, and he gave all we Tottenham disciples the gift of a lifetime when he went to Italy and bought The One and Only Jimmy Greaves ...

CHAPTER 10

SIGNING JIMMY GREAVES

It took Bill Nicholson six years to bring Jimmy Greaves to the club he was originally scheduled to join back in 1955, and it cost him £99,999 rather than the £10 signing-on fee that Spurs would eventually have had to pay if – as arranged – he had joined them straight from school at 15.

Most people know the tantalising tale of how Chelsea stole 'Boy Wonder' Jimmy from under the noses of Tottenham Hotspur, but it is worth repeating because – for many – the purchase of Greavsie was the most significant signing in Spurs history and it helps put flesh on the Bill Nicholson story.

Manager Arthur Rowe was relaxed and confident he had the agreement of Jimmy's father – Jim senior, a London tube train driver – that his son was joining Spurs on his departure from Kingswood Secondary Modern School in Dagenham. But while Arthur was at home recovering from illness, Jimmy was poached by a Chelsea scout masquerading as 'Mr Pope'. In actual fact the man responsible was Jimmy Thompson, who netted a shoal of Essex schoolboys over the course of his career – including Jimmy, Terry Venables, Peter Brabrook, Les Allen and Ken Shellito – using the 'Mr Pope' pseudonym, which stopped West Ham and Tottenham from reporting him to the Football Association for plundering young players from their territory.

Jimmy came back to haunt Tottenham on his league debut for Chelsea at White Hart Lane in August 1957, conjuring a magical goal that left half of the Spurs defenders on their backsides as he nonchalantly slipped the ball into the net. "The best debut goal I never saw," was how Spurs skipper Danny Blanchflower put it after he had been one of those outwitted by the lightning-quick teenager.

Bill Nicholson, then Tottenham's coach, was among those looking on in a mixture of anguish and admiration at the demolition work of this cheeky whiz kid...

"That young rascal scored the sort of goal that almost made we Tottenham people weep, because it could so easily have been for rather than against us. I had first seen him playing for London schools in a representative match at White Hart Lane and he was one of the most natural goalscorers I had ever clapped eyes on. Arthur Rowe was convinced he was coming to Spurs, and we were devastated when Chelsea announced he'd signed for them. I've seen hundreds of promising schoolboys looking the part and then drifting into oblivion, but I knew Jimmy was the real deal and kept a close eye on his progress.

"As I expected, he went on to score many great goals for Chelsea and I admit to being jealous when AC Milan got him in the days just before the maximum wage was kicked out. Nobody could then compete with what the Italians were offering.

"I met Jimmy in the toilet at an end-of-season football awards show at the Café Royal in London where Danny was being presented with a trophy. He had just signed for Milan and I wished him luck, adding that I would have preferred it if he'd been signing for Tottenham. 'That will be my next move if you'll still have me,' he said. I thought he was joking but he really did mean it.

"As we know, it all quickly went pear-shaped for him in Italy and I was alerted that he was for sale. I couldn't wait to get out to Milan to try and sign him. They messed me about something rotten and we started having meetings with their officials both in Milan and London. Then, just as I thought I had it wrapped up for us to buy him for £92,000 – a huge profit on the £80,000 Milan had paid for him just four months earlier – they said another club had come in for him.

"I knew on the grapevine that it was Chelsea, and I agreed in confidence with their representative John Battersby, the club secretary, that we would both put in an identical offer of £96,000 and then let Jimmy decide which club he wanted to join. We were both determined not to let Milan turn it into a bidding war.

"John sat Jimmy down and told him the terms Chelsea were ready to offer for his return to Stamford Bridge. I offered less but Jimmy was desperate to appear with that great Double side that he had played against the previous season. He chose Tottenham.

"Milan then tried to push me up to a world-record £100,000, but I held out for one pound less. I just wanted to save Jimmy from being burdened with the label of football's first £100,000 player. Sounds silly now, but that was a mind-blowing sum at the time, yet I still thought Spurs had got a bargain, and I have never had reason to change my mind.

"He never gave me a spot of trouble, you know. Even when it came time for us to part company he knew in his heart he'd lost his appetite for the game. I could hardly make it public but I knew West Ham were getting a shadow of the great Jimmy Greaves.

"People who didn't know what they were talking about sometimes described him as a bit of a faint-heart, but in all the years I watched him I never ever saw him shirk a tackle. And I'll tell you what, there were at least 10 goals that should have been added to his career total. Time and again he would be flagged offside simply because his movement was too quick for the eye of the linesman.

"The hardest of all to take was in the 1962 European Cup semi-final against Benfica at White Hart Lane, when he scored a perfectly good goal that was ruled offside. That broke all our hearts. We might have beaten Jock [Stein] and his great Celtic side to become the first British team to win the European Cup.

"Jimmy had two great partnerships for us – first with Bobby Smith, who provided lots of muscle in making openings for Jimmy, and then with Alan Gilzean, one of the most elegant forwards you could wish to see. Greavsie and Gilly together were like poetry in motion. I was hoping for a third one when I put Jim together with Martin Chivers, but by then he was only giving half his attention to the game. He was quite the businessman off the pitch, and that took the edge off his appetite for football.

"But even with half his concentration he was still twice as good as any other goal-scoring forward. It hurt like hell the day I decided to let him go in part-exchange for Martin Peters. But as a manager you often had to do things that hurt you inside but were necessary for the team and the club. There is no room for sentiment in football management. You would get eaten alive.

"Martin was another wonderfully gifted footballer, but completely different to Jim. Alf [Ramsey] described him as being 10 years ahead of his time, and I knew exactly what he meant. He was an exceptional reader of the game, a bit like Danny and dear John White, and knew where to be before anybody else had spotted the gap.

"Nothing's changed. The game is still all about positioning. If you're not in the right place, then you're not going to be able to do the right thing. Positioning, positioning, positioning. The three Ps.

"Jimmy always knew where to be to make the most of a goal-scoring opportunity. It came naturally to him. You couldn't teach it. Quite a few of his goals were tap-ins, and people said he was lucky. He made his own luck by being in the right place at the right time.

"He was not the best tackler in the world and his effort in training left a lot to be desired. But as he often said to me, 'You have bought me to score goals, not stop them.' And he scored goals by the bucketful. And he used to practise his goal finishing like a golf professional working on his swing, steering the ball into the net with both his left and right foot. It was uncanny to see the number of times he hit the target.

"Jimmy was the greatest scorer of them all. I've never seen a player get near him for putting the vital finishing touch. While others were still thinking about what to do, whoosh, he would just get on and do it. He would have the ball into the net in the blink of an eye and then amble back to the centre-circle as casually as if he'd just swatted a fly. A genius.

"He was a cheeky Cockney sod who always had the last word. I admired him as a bloke and as a player. If there has been a better goalscorer, then I've not seen him."

SIGNING JIMMY GREAVES

When it comes to Jimmy, I am slightly biased. We were close mates from when we were both 17, him starting out on his glittering football career while I was serving my apprenticeship in word accumulation, articulation and alliteration. I was privileged to share the eulogy duties at his funeral... and I can think of nobody more gifted across the board than our Jim – footballer extraordinaire, television personality, stage performer and stand-up comedian, husband, family man (and he wouldn't mind me adding, recovered alcoholic). What a man: The Great Entertainer. We wrote 20 books together, and I can never remember Jimmy having a bad word to say about Bill Nick. Here he is talking about his relationship with 'Sir Bill' at the time of Nicholson's first testimonial match:

"You won't catch me saying a bad thing about Bill, even though he nearly broke my heart when he let me go to West Ham. He could see through me and knew I'd lost my appetite for the game. Back in those days, I was more interested in boozing, my businesses and my rally driving. When you analyse it, no wonder he wanted to get rid of me, but I'm sure I could have given more to Spurs if he'd been willing to give me a gee-up and get me playing again. But I blame myself more than Bill. He'd got the best out of me, and there's never allowances for loyalty in football.

"I can clearly remember punching the air in delight when I knew Spurs were in for me during that best-forgotten experience with Milan. Again, it was not the Italians at fault as much as me. No sooner had I got out there than I wanted to come home. I didn't give it a fair whack, but never once did I regret my decision to join Bill and that wonderful Tottenham team that he'd built.

"Bill could talk the hind legs off a donkey, but his knowledge of football and its tactics were second to none. I often said to Bill with tongue in cheek that we could do without his lectures. It was all to wind him up, but he knew I respected him and I like to think the feeling was mutual. Any player who spent time listening to him was a better footballer for the experience. He knew the game inside out and back to front and had a photographic memory of every player he had ever seen – he would know their strengths and weaknesses and develop ways to nullify any team we might meet.

"I was never a fan of coaching because I was lucky to be blessed with a natural gift for the game, but Bill had a way of putting his ideas and theories across that were easy to understand and implement.

"He was not the sort of bloke you would choose as a companion for a good night out. He was too stiff and disciplined for that social side of things. But as a football coach, he was second to none and could strengthen any team with his wise words and deep knowledge of football.

"Bill always set his standards high and only wanted to win with panache. He could be a miserable git if things were not going to plan, but was always fair, balanced and honest in a lovely old-fashioned way. While he could be a dull, dour man he was a contradiction in that he always looked to produce exciting and entertaining football teams. His favourite mantra was 'Go out and entertain the fans... they pay your wages.'

"He detested cheating of any kind, and brown envelopes and under the counter deals were completely foreign to him. In a way he belonged in the past, yet he had great vision when it came to football and he always came alive when the first whistle blew.

"He was a unique mixture of a man, shy and retiring until preparing his football team for combat. Then he would become Churchillian and demanding, calling for superhuman effort and heaven help any player who slacked. As well as team tactics, he made sure every player knew what was expected of him as an individual, and we were given full details of our opposite number. He left no stone unturned and would read his instructions from plans prepared in beautiful copperplate handwriting. He had won handwriting prizes at school and it showed in the neatness of his note making.

"Bill and Alf [Ramsey] were alike in many ways, both perfectionists and with a tunnel vision that allowed only football as a topic. I was a bit too much of a maverick for each of them, but they never got anything less than my full respect... yes, even after Alf had left me out of the '66 World Cup-winning team and Bill had told me to bugger off to West Ham.

"Both Alf and Bill had in common the strong belief that the team must always come first. They were born organisers and English football was greatly improved thanks to their input.

"I liked to think of Bill as a friend as well as manager. Above all, he was a good man."

SIGNING JIMMY GREAVES

Steve came into the Tottenham team close to the end of Jimmy's time at White Hart Lane...

"Jim was a legend at the club, a legend in football and one of the reasons I wanted to play for Spurs. As I was dreaming of becoming a professional footballer, Jimmy was a national treasure – I couldn't believe it when Alf left him out of the 1966 World Cup final team. Even though he had superstar status, Jim was friendly and encouraging to me from day one and never ever came 'the big I am'. By the time I got into the first team in 1969 – I was 17, the same as he had been when making his bow for Chelsea – he was struggling to give full commitment to a game that had been his life since he was eight years old. Bill sussed that he had lost his appetite and decided to use him to hook the vastly talented Martin Peters.

"It was terrific to get Martin in our squad but we were all stunned that Jimmy had been used as a makeweight in the transfer. I have often wondered what part our coach Eddie Baily played in getting Jimmy out. There was a lot of tension between the two of them in Jimmy's last season and I used to watch it close up as they swapped verbal digs that went deeper than the usual banter. Eddie always felt Bill was too soft on Jim because he was not exactly the hardest of trainers, and I sensed that eventually it was Eddie who persuaded Bill that it would be a good thing for the team to let him go. On social media even to this day Bill gets heavily criticised for parting with Jimmy, but I think Eddie played a big part in the controversial decision. I was too young to poke my nose in, but there is no way I would have let Greavsie go. He was still a giant of the game in my eyes.

"I used to watch Jimmy and Alan Gilzean playing together and wondered at their artistry and devilment. Imagine the thrill and honour it was for me to start my league career with these two masters. Bill made tongues wag when he put me under Gilly's wing, given he was a renowned man about town. I room-shared with him on all away trips and he used to tell me wonderful stories about

the things he and Greavsie got up to on and off the pitch. They were very special footballers. Goodness knows what they would have achieved on today's billiard table-style pitches.

"When Bill became our club president he lost a lot of his stiffness and was relaxed and happy to chat about his days as one of the all-time great managers, and he would get particularly sentimental when recalling the performances of Jimmy. He described him as the greatest goal-scoring footballer the English game had ever known, and he warmed himself on memories of his performances.

"I became very close to Jim in his later years and often guested on his travelling road show with his manager Terry Baker. Jim always talked of Bill with fondness and summed him up as being the most dedicated manager there had ever been. It's difficult to argue with that assessment."

'Sir Bill' was now into his paradise of European football... "If you're not in Europe," he would often say, "you're nothing."

CHAPTER 11

EUROPEAN CUP ROBBERY

A t his most bullish, Bill liked nothing better than the challenge of pitting his tactical wits against the best coaches on the European circuit, and in 1961/62 he went so close to lifting the treasured European Cup at his one and only attempt. It was Tottenham's reward for winning the League Championship, and this was how in happy retirement Bill recalled a season that veteran eye-witnesses remember as the most exciting in all their years watching the mighty Spurs...

> "Anybody who was at White Hart Lane for the European Cup nights will confirm I'm not exaggerating when I say there's never been an atmosphere to match it. The floodlights picking out our players in their all-white kit and the 'Glory Glory Hallelujah' singing of the fans made every European night special.
>
> "But it was almost a disaster when we went four goals down in our preliminary opening tie against Gornik Zabrze in Poland. You wouldn't have bet a penny on us surviving to the first round proper until late in the game when the inspiring Dave Mackay created goals for Cliff Jones and then Terry Dyson to give us a fighting chance in the second leg at White Hart Lane. Gornik were a hard, hard team of real men, all former coal miners who saw football as a release from their stark lives. They came to London determined to finish the job they had started in Chorzow.
>
> "Our support in the return was unbelievable, with the noise from the crowd deafening and so intimidating that Gornik just

collapsed under our barrage of attacks. Before the game the Poles had complained about our tackling in the first leg, and claimed that we 'were no angels'. A handful of our witty supporters responded by coming to the match dressed as angels, and they kept up their heavenly chorus right through the rest of our run to the semi-finals.

"Our proud and talented players reached down into their boots to win the match 8-1 and the tie a remarkable 10-5 on aggregate. I have always been hard to please but this was just sensational. I'll be honest and admit I was in something of a daze at the end of it all. I'd never known anything like it in my football career.

"Cliff Jones with a hat-trick and two-goal Bobby Smith were too much of a handful for the Poles that night, but I have to admit the real stars were our fans. They made more noise than I'd ever heard in all my years at Tottenham. The crowd was like a twelfth man – amazing.

"In the next round we faced Feyenoord, who had beaten their all-star rivals Ajax to the Dutch Championship. I had to play young Frank Saul in the away leg in Rotterdam because of an injury to Bobby Smith, and he came up trumps with two goals to help us to a useful 3-1 victory in a match strewn with mistakes that left me fuming. The victory was sweet but the overall performance far from satisfactory, and I feared for our chances in the return match at the Lane.

"To our surprise, Feyenoord abandoned their fine, composed football and played a very physical game in London. Our key man, Dave Mackay, was knocked unconscious but insisted on going back on and played a storming part in our 1-1 draw to clinch a quarter-final place. Dave always seemed to grow six inches when the chips were down. I told the players they were going to have improve a hell of a lot, and then got on with the business of bringing Jimmy Greaves to Tottenham."

Jimmy, newly arrived from Milan, had to sit out the two legs of the quarter-final against the Czech army side Dukla Prague while his £99,999 transfer was investigated to make sure there had been no under-the-counter payments. There was no way in a million years that the almost Corinthian Bill Nicholson would have got involved in anything illegal.

Greavsie was in Prague as a spectator and was relieved not to be playing because it was freezing brass monkeys weather. The pitch was a skating rink and everybody had trouble keeping their feet. There was one hilarious moment when Bobby Smith got so fed up being kicked up in the air that he threw a snowball at his opponent after his name had gone into the referee's book.

Dukla managed a 1-0 win, but it could have been worse if goalkeeper Bill Brown had not been in brilliant form. There were also Artic conditions for the return leg when Bobby Smith and Dave Mackay grabbed two goals each for an emphatic 4-2 victory on aggregate, which set up a semi-final against reigning kings of Europe, Benfica. Bill Nicholson quietly admitted that he would have preferred legendary former champions Real Madrid 'because they are showing signs of being over the hill'.

The two games against Benfica were monumental. The Portuguese champions were driven in midfield by the masterly Mario Coluna, and scorching in a striking role was Eusebio, arguably the greatest player ever to have been born in Africa. It's a match that remained burned in the memory of Jimmy Greaves for the rest of his life. He told me with real vehemence:

"The referee is six foot under so he would have to dig himself out to sue me. But I know in my heart that I scored a perfectly good goal in the second leg and he called it offside. Bobby Smith got the same treatment after I had made a pass to him that was played with both of us unquestionably onside. It stank. They were the most diabolical decisions I ever saw in a match and came in the most vital game in Tottenham's history. We should have at least gone to extra-time in that second leg. I have never felt so crushed by a referee. I can honestly say the two calls gave me the most agonising moments of my life and they were the only footballing incidents I carried into retirement like a nagging toothache that wouldn't go away. People always wanted to talk about me missing the 1966 World Cup final, but that didn't hurt me nearly as much as those disallowed goals. The refereeing was scandalous."

Steve and I got a technician to give Jimmy's 'goal' the modern VAR treatment, and the verdict was "certainly a goal"... but with the added rider that there were not enough camera angles to give a definite VAR-varnished judgement. We could find only two angles of the disallowed goal, both showing Jimmy onside as he slotted the ball home. The VAR technicians have half a dozen views and this is why it often takes so much time to make a decision, which sucks the immediacy out of modern football.

So it was that Benfica – 4-3 winners on aggregate – went to the final in Amsterdam and beat the old masters Real Madrid to retain the European Cup. Bill Nicholson looked on in anguish because he knew that it 'coulda, shoulda' been Tottenham skipper Danny Blanchflower lifting the European Cup. What made it even harder to swallow is that Spurs had narrowly lost out on a historic Treble. They retained the FA Cup with a 3-1 victory over Burnley, including a magical third-minute goal from Greavsie when he simply rolled the ball through a forest of legs from 15 yards.

For the record, the Spurs team that beat Burnley was:

Brown
Baker   Norman   Henry
Blanchflower (capt)   White   Mackay
Medwin   Smith   Greaves   Jones

This was nearly identical to the team that clinched the Double a year earlier, apart from Greavsie for Les Allen and Terry Medwin in place of Terry Dyson.

But a major disappointment for our hero Bill is that Tottenham agonisingly tossed away the chance of winning a second successive League Championship because of home and away defeats plotted by Bill's old nemesis, Ipswich Town manager and his former Spurs team-mate Alf Ramsey. He had studied the revolutionary Ipswich formation in which Alf played winger Jimmy Leadbetter as a withdrawn midfield schemer, and he drew up plans for defensive measures to stifle the skilled Scot. 'Stop Leadbetter and you stop Ipswich,' was the way he read it. But Danny Blanchflower and Dave Mackay liked the way they had been playing and talked him out of his imaginative but cautious plan. Bill proved he was a democratic manager by agreeing to bow to what in later years would have been described as player power.

Ipswich went on to win the Championship with Spurs in third place, the four points difference in their final totals exactly mirroring the points that they had dropped to the Suffolk club. When the Tottenham players finally agreed to Bill's defensive stranglehold on Leadbetter for the FA Charity Shield match at Portman Road in the summer of 1962, Spurs won 5-1. Never boastful, Bill quietly muttered: "I told them so. Stop Leadbetter and you stop Ipswich." Alf later adopted his withdrawn wingers tactic with England and was rewarded with the 1966 World Cup! All because of a craggy, canny Scotsman called Leadbetter.

"In his later years, Bill would get a sort of glazed look in his eyes when recalling that 1961/62 season. He reckoned the European Cup ties were among the greatest matches he was ever involved in, and like Greavsie felt they had been robbed by dubious refereeing decisions in the semi-final against Benfica. But he wasn't as strong as Jimmy in his criticism. Jim had a load of goals turned down during his career, but that was the only one he constantly moaned about. He felt Spurs had been cheated.

"Bill seemed begrudging in his praise of Alf, who gave me the first of my 17 England Under-23 caps. I think there was a sort of jealous rivalry between the two of them, and our veteran trainer Cecil Poynton reckoned Arthur Rowe was ready to offer Alf a coaching job ahead of Bill when he became ill. Those two defeats by Ipswich in 1961/62 stopped Bill getting back-to-back League Championships, which would have meant two successive Doubles! I can almost hear Jimmy saying, 'It's a funny old game.'"

Quickly getting over the bitter disappointment of the defeat by Benfica, it was 'Sir Bill' who showed British clubs how to win silverware in Europe...

CHAPTER 12

MAKING HISTORY IN ROTTERDAM

The victory over Burnley at Wembley earned Tottenham a place in the European Cup Winners' Cup, and the "Glory Glory" chanting supporters – bringing new sights and sounds to the playing fields of Europe – roared them into the final. There was quite a kerfuffle on the way, when Jimmy Greaves was sent off in the semi-final first leg against OFK Belgrade in what was then communist Yugoslavia.

Jimmy at first refused to walk when the referee pointed to the dressing room. He had retaliated with an angry, out-of-character kick after being ruthlessly tackled off the ball. Tony Marchi, playing in place of injured skipper Danny Blanchflower, became the diplomat as he persuaded Greavsie to leave the field while warring players swapped insults and a few punches. It was the first time he had ever been given marching orders. Jimmy recalled:

"Cliff Jones had been sitting on the bench and came and put a protective arm around me as we walked the 100 yards to the dressing room, with a hostile crowd shouting insults and throwing coins and rubbish at us. The warrior came out in Cliffie, all nine stone of him, and he was challenging the spectators to take him on. 'For gawd's sake, Jonesie,' I pleaded, 'you'll get us lynched.' His eyes were ablaze and he loved it, while I just wanted to get to the shelter of the dressing room. The choker for me was that I failed to connect with my attempt at a kick against an opponent who had been out to really damage me.

"After the match our centuries-old trainer Cec Poynton went for me. 'You've disgraced the club,' he said in his distinctive East Midlands accent. 'I hope you're suitably ashamed. You're only the second Spurs

'SIR BILL'

player sent off since 1928.' I played along with him and asked: 'Who was the first?' 'T'were me,' confessed Cec with a cackling laugh. He was a likeable bloke whose solution to every on-field injury was to come on and squeeze a spongeful of cold water on our meat and two veg. Yet most times it seemed to do the trick and we recovered to play on. We all loved Cec."

No British team had won a major trophy in Europe when Spurs travelled to Rotterdam for the final, having comfortably accounted for Glasgow Rangers in the 'Battle of Britain' (8-4 on aggregate), Slovan Bratislava (6-2) and OFK Belgrade (5-2). Hopes that Tottenham could break the duck were suddenly diminished when their main motivator, Dave Mackay, failed a fitness test on the day of the final. The absence of Mackay was a devastating blow because he had been a major force in Tottenham's magnificent success over the previous two seasons. As it sank in that they would have to perform without his battering ram backing, a blanket of gloom dropped on the Spurs camp.

Despite an airlift of 4,000 fanatical Spurs fans and thousands more by ferry, Atletico were suddenly considered by neutrals to be warm favourites to retain the trophy they had won in impressive style the previous year, when they mastered a high-quality Fiorentina side.

Mackay's absence plunged Bill into a morose mood, and he added to the air of pessimism when he ran through the strengths of the opposition during a tactical team talk. He made Atletico sound like the greatest team ever to run on to a football pitch, and he bruised rather than boosted the confidence of his players. This was when skipper Danny Blanchflower, promoted to 'assistant to the manager', showed both his qualities as a leader and as an orator. After Bill had frightened the life out of his players, Danny told his team-mates:

"Just think of what's being said in their dressing-room: 'They've got this centre-half Maurice Norman, built like a man mountain and so ugly with his teeth out that he will frighten us to death. They've got quick players like that Welsh flier Cliff Jones, who is fast enough to catch pigeons. They have hard men like Bobby Smith who can run through walls, and that little genius Jimmy Greaves can score goals from out of nowhere. Goalkeeper Bill Brown has the safest hands in football, they tackle like demons and John White can ghost through any defence. Their manager Bill Nicholson is a world-renowned coaching master who will have the tactics to beat us.' Come on lads, heads up and go out there and play with a swagger. Let them worry about *US*! We are Super Spurs, and this is going to be our finest hour..."

Yes, it was Churchillian stuff.

This was how Tottenham lined up for the game of their lives, with Tony Marchi stepping into Dave Mackay's place in a flexible 3-3-4 formation:

Brown

Baker   Norman   Henry

Blanchflower   White   Marchi

Jones   Smith   Greaves   Dyson

The match stayed etched in Bill's memory, and this is how he recalled it many years later:

"There has been a load of nonsense written about my brief to the players before the final against Atletico. I had watched them and knew their every strength and weakness, and I gave a full breakdown to our players, knowing that Danny would then follow me with his usual upbeat call to arms. He did not have a negative bone in his body. It was a worry to me that we had lost Dave with a stomach muscle injury and Danny was playing on one knee. If Mackay had been fit, Blanchflower would have stood down. That was the sort of team-first man that he was.

"I quietly told Cliff Jones and Terry Dyson that this could be their night because I knew both Atletico full-backs would struggle against their pace. I also told Greavsie that they were slow to clear their lines and that he should stay on their shoulders. He followed instructions and was there to meet a Jonesie cross and give us a vital early lead. It was a typical pickpocket goal from Jim.

"It was on the wings that I knew we would monopolise the match, with Cliff and Terry Dyson running the Spanish full-backs into dizzy disorder. Atletico, strangely enough, also had a winger called Jones, but he was not in the same class as our Welsh wizard.

"It was Dyson and Jones who combined to set up goal number two in the 35th minute, exchanging passes before releasing

the ball to Bobby Smith, who laid it back for John White to rifle a low shot into the net. This was a rare but crucial goal for White, who had made his reputation as a creator rather than taker of goals. I always told him he should be hungrier for goals and this was his reward. His signature was stamped on most of our attacks as he prised open the Atletico defence with beautifully weighted passes. He was a class act and the Spaniards did not know how to cope with him.

"John, Danny and the stately Marchi were working like Trojans in midfield to make up for the absence of the mighty Dave Mackay. At most clubs, Tony would have been an automatic choice for the first team, and he played with such skill and determination that his contribution was in the Mackay class. I can give him no higher praise.

"Atletico revived their hopes in the first minute of the second-half when Collar scored from the penalty spot after Ron Henry had fisted the ball off the goal-line. It was the worst possible start and for 20 minutes there was a danger that we could lose our way as the cup-holders forced a series of corner-kicks, but our defence managed to survive the Spanish storm.

"Goalkeeper Bill Brown took his life in his hands as he threw himself courageously at the feet of Mendonca to snatch the ball off the forward's toes. Chuzo broke free and we along with our wonderful fans sighed with relief as he shot the wrong side of the post; then Ramiro drove the ball just off target. This was when I admit to beginning to wonder and worry whether we were going to get by without the great Mackay, who in a situation like this would have been breaking Spanish hearts with his thundering tackles and brandishing a fist in a demand for extra effort from all his team-mates.

"It was 'Dynamo' Dyson, having the game of a lifetime, who ended the Atletico comeback when his hanging cross was fumbled into the net by goalkeeper Madinabeytia, who had one eye on the menacing presence of our burly Bobby Smith. This was in an era when goalkeepers could still be barged provided it was shoulder to shoulder. Nobody was better or more determined at the tactic than Bobby, who was a real warrior of a centre-forward.

MAKING HISTORY IN ROTTERDAM

"Dyson became a man inspired and laid on a second goal for Greavsie, before putting the seal on a memorable performance with a scorching shot at the end of a weaving 30-yard run. His first goal was something of a fluke, but the second was a masterpiece.

"As our triumphant players paraded the cup in front of Tottenham's ecstatic travelling army of fans, Bobby shouted at Dyson in his typically blunt way: 'If I were you, mate, I'd hang up my boots. There's no way you can top that. You were out of this world.'

"While all this celebrating was going on, I saw out of the corner of my eye Jimmy Greaves hugging Dave Mackay. The toughest man I'd ever seen in a Spurs shirt was crying his eyes out. He was happy for everybody but so sorry for himself. We would never have made it to the final without him. The greatest of all competitors.

"It was one of the most satisfying nights in my career, and I was always proud to say that it was Tottenham that showed our fellow British clubs how to win trophies in Europe. I just wish it had been the European Cup the year before..."

Watching the Tottenham triumph at home on black and white television in Middlesex was 13-year-old schoolboy Steve Perryman...

"By then I was convinced that my future lay in the game, and I was filled with pride as I watched Tottenham become pioneers, the first British club ever to win a major European trophy. I had no idea then that I was going to become a Spur, but they had awoken in me – in all starry-eyed young footballers of the time – a confidence that we could rule the world. Jimmy Greaves told me many years later that it was the icing on the cake of his football career, and while it was Terry Dyson who got the man of the match acknowledgement, we all knew that Spurs could not have done it so emphatically without Jimmy's skilled input.

"There was always a question and answer session in the Greavsie road shows Terry Baker used to promote, with me joining Jimmy on stage. Time and again he singled out

that victory in Rotterdam as the pinnacle of his club career.

"He privately told me that he and Bill exchanged handshakes and hugs at the end of the game, both of them too choked to talk. All that Bill had promised during the drawn-out transfer negotiations in Italy had come true, first the FA Cup and now the European Cup Winners' Cup.

"This was the night both Jim and Bill knew for certain they had made the right decisions in Milan."

Everything was set for the Spurs to go marching on to more glory, but cruel fate was waiting to crush the mood of optimism and rain on Bill Nicholson's parade.

CHAPTER 13

THE DARKEST DAYS

The demise of the Double team started with two broken legs – waltzing Welsh winger Terry Medwin having his career virtually finished on a pre-season tour of South Africa in the summer of 1963, and then the indomitable Dave Mackay coming second best in a fierce challenge for the ball with Manchester United skipper Noel Cantwell at Old Trafford in the winter of 1963.

A controversial tackle? Let's put it this way, for ever after Dave always referred to the Irishman as "Cant", making it sound as close as possible to a particularly crude swear word.

Now was the winter of Bill Nicholson's discontent as he measured the loss of Mackay following the second leg of their first European Cup Winners' Cup defence – which Tottenham lost 4-1 and 4-3 on aggregate after a 2-0 victory over United in the home leg at White Hart Lane.

Dave was still in the early stages of recovery from his broken leg when Danny Blanchflower surrendered to his continuing knee problems and announced his retirement at the age of 38. The brains and heart of the team had gone.

Then, on 21 July 1964, Bill took a telephone call that you would not wish on your worst enemy...

"I was sitting at home that afternoon in the off-season when the phone rang and a man's grave voice said: 'This is Tottenham police station. I'm sorry to have to tell you that John White has been killed by lightning while playing golf.' Instead of feeling shock, I lost my temper. John was a born prankster but now I thought he'd gone too far. Just that previous week I'd taken two hoax calls

telling me Jimmy Greaves had been killed in a car crash, plus my two daughters had been pestered with obscene calls. I decided to call his bluff: 'Give me your phone number, and I'll ring you back.'

"Tragically, it turned out to be true and I took Cec Poynton with me to the morgue at the Prince of Wales hospital in Tottenham to make the official identification. Most difficult thing I ever did in my life. I called a team meeting at Cheshunt to try to lift everybody but I couldn't get the words out and had to go to the dressing rooms and have a quiet cry all by myself.

"John was taken from us at the very peak of his career. I had told him just a few days before his awful death that I was ready to rebuild the team around him. He had the passing accuracy, positional sense, stamina, and football intelligence to carry it off. John was very excited at the prospect. He had really grown up and was ready to take the responsibility.

"I lose sleep thinking about the way we as a club handled it all. We managed to raise about £15,000 for his wife, Sandra, and their two children. But we should have done a lot more. I had my hands full with worrying club matters so was unable to give it the time and thought it deserved. The family were just recovering from losing Sandra's dad, Harry Evans, to cancer. He was my assistant and had taken John into his home rather than have him live in a hotel when he joined us after his National Service. John and Sandra fell in love and got married... and now this. It was a horrible, horrible time."

It was particularly terrible for John's widow, Sandra, who was still grieving the loss of her father and was now left to bring up their two children, Rob and Mandy. I am a witness that photographer Rob and the lovely Mandy have grown into wonderful adults thanks to Sandra's discipline and encouragement. (There is a book I highly recommend by distinguished writer and Spurs historian Julie Welch in harness with Rob, called *The Ghost of White Hart Lane: In Search of My Father the Football Legend*).

So from the Double side Bill had, in a short span of time, lost Danny Blanchflower's brains, Dave Mackay's heart and John White's vision. And the following year, 1965, Maurice Norman's career came to a painful halt when he shattered a leg in a meaningless friendly against a Hungarian XI warming up for the 1966 World Cup in England, a tournament in which Big Mo would have almost definitely played, or at least been in Alf Ramsey's squad. It was the same week that Jimmy Greaves went into hospital suffering from hepatitis.

A concerned Bill Nick got busy in the transfer market and bought Alan Mullery from Fulham, Laurie Brown from Arsenal (much to the consternation of some supporters), Cyril Knowles from Middlesbrough, Pat Jennings from Watford, Jimmy Robertson from St Mirren, and Alan Gilzean from Dundee. He took a breather, and then went shopping again, this time buying centre-half Mike England from Blackburn and Terry Venables from Chelsea.

Clearly, Bill was trying to build another 'Super Spurs'. He never quite made it. The new Tottenham team had some memorable moments together in the mid-Sixties, but they never touched the peak performances of the Blanchflower-White-Mackay era. Bill was like a man who had been in love with the most beautiful girl in the world and spent the rest of his time as manager looking for her twin sister.

Another of the Double heroes – top marksman Bobby Smith – helped hurry Bill's once gingery hair to grey. As I chronicled when ghosting an autobiography for Bobby before his sudden death in 2010, he had a falling out with Bill Nick that could have been measured on the Richter scale.

A notorious gambler, Bobby ran up debts to such an extent that he had a real fear that he could get kneecapped by some of his less sympathetic bookmakers, who did not take kindly to him placing bets and then not paying up when his horses or dogs lost.

He got the reputation for being a 'welsher', somebody who does not pay his betting debts, and he was banned from attending racecourses by the racing authorities.

Bobby insisted after all the shooting and shouting was over: "It was all a misunderstanding and I was the innocent party, although nobody would believe me. One of my club-mates was putting on losing bets using my account. Terry Dyson also used the account, but he was decent enough to pay up when he had a losing streak, while the other chap – who I refuse to identify – left the club, leaving me with his debts in my name.

"Somehow it leaked to the newspapers that I was having problems with the bookmakers. But I was not nearly as black as painted. One of my bookmakers rang me at home and told me in very plain language that he wanted me to pay up, but I said I was not going to settle somebody else's debts. He put it about that I had welshed, but I had always paid off my personal debts in the past even though it often left me skint."

Bill Nicholson did not approve of Smith's betting habit but considered it a private matter for him and did not try to interfere. It was one of football's buried secrets that Bobby and Nick didn't get along. They managed to keep it hidden from press and public, but barely acknowledged each other apart from when talking tactics.

"It was a clash of personalities," Bobby told me long after he had hung up his boots. "Maybe it was because we were both stubborn Yorkshiremen. I found him a miserable bastard and when I once told him that to his face he hardly ever talked to me again unless it was something to do with how he wanted me to play."

Their silent feud surfaced in the 1963/64 season when Bobby hit a bad patch of form. It all came to a head on the Thursday before the North London Derby when Spurs were at the top of the table but had hit a worrying run with only one goal in three games and a spirit-shattering exit from the FA Cup at the hands of Chelsea. Nicholson summoned Bobby to his cramped office and bluntly told him: "You won't be playing against Arsenal on Saturday. Your place is going to Laurie Brown."

"Laurie Brown?" Bobby said, his mouth agape. "But he's with the Arsenal."

"Not now," Bill replied, enjoying his moment of humiliating a man he had always considered lacking in morals. "I've just signed him and he is on his way here to meet the rest of the team."

Bobby could not believe what he was hearing. "But he's a bloody centre-half and a carthorse," he exploded. "He can't possibly play in my No.9 shirt."

"He can and he will," said Bill, as the two Yorkshiremen spat blood at each other.

Bobby got up and, as he stormed out of the office, shouted over his shoulder: "You've lost it, Bill. I always thought you were a good judge. But you've got this one so wrong." There were three 'f-bombs' included in the tirade.

At what was then a hefty £40,000, Brown became the first player to appear for both clubs in the North London Derby that Saturday, and

THE DARKEST DAYS

he played in Bobby Smith's No.9 shirt alongside Jimmy Greaves. Tottenham beat Arsenal 3-1, with two goals from Cliff Jones and a penalty from Greavsie, who told me:

"None of us could believe what was going on. Laurie was a lovely bloke but not fit to tie Bobby's bootlaces. He'd made his name as an amateur with the British Olympic team and, to be brutally honest, that was how he played the game, amateurishly. There was no way it was going to work out and after a handful of matches he was back at centre-half, where he played until – thank goodness – Mike England arrived from Blackburn. The atmosphere in the dressing room was terrible and Bobby Smith had suddenly become *persona non grata*. I still spoke to him but it was very strained. He had painted – or gambled – himself into a corner, and he went around openly criticising Bill Nick and the board. There was no way he was going to survive at Spurs after that."

On the Monday morning after a weekend of stewing, Bobby burst into Bill's office and told him: "After all we said to each other on Thursday, there's no way we can carry on. Put me on the transfer list."

Nicholson shot back: "The board have already made up their mind not to retain you next season. We're circulating to the rest of the clubs to say you are available."

Bill hated hostility, and refused to discuss the Bobby Smith incident for years afterwards until I once got him relaxed for an interview approaching one of his two long overdue testimonials granted by the club. At first when I brought up Bobby's name he went strangely quiet, as if having a silent debate with himself, and then he finally opened up:

> "Bobby was his own worst enemy. He got himself into a right old mess with his gambling and lost all his judgement. I will be very happy to talk about Bobby the player, but am not interested in talking about him as a person. We did not get on with each other, and that's all I want to say on the matter. But let me tell you that there has rarely been a braver footballer. He used to give every ounce of himself to a game in an era when you had to be ready to take a lot of knocks when leading the attack. It was not a game for faint hearts, and he was prepared to get hurt for the team.
>
> "Bob was unstoppable in our Double year. Managers used to try putting two defenders on him but he would bash them out

of the way as if swatting flies. But there was a lot more to him than strength. He had plenty of skill and could get instant control of a ball and then use it for the good of the team.

"His speciality was collecting the ball with his back to a wall of defenders and then cleverly holding and shielding it until laying it off. He was always getting bruised and battered, often illegally, but gave as good as he got, and I saw many defenders out-muscled by him. He was a goalkeeper's worst enemy. It was not foul play when he used to shoulder charge them as they took the ball, because it was within the rules of the time.

"Then there was his partnership with Jimmy Greaves. They complemented each other perfectly, Bobby with the muscle and Jimmy with his own special magic. What a wonderful sight they were when on song, which was often. It's fair to say they brought the best out of each other.

"They would have played together in the 1958 World Cup finals if I'd had my way, but our selectors knew best! Bobby spent the tournament on the bench and Jimmy wasn't even picked for the squad.

"It was my idea to bring Bob to Tottenham from Chelsea. At first he did not want to come, but both he and I are so pleased he changed his mind. It all went sour at the end but when you look back on his career he was a great, great signing for Spurs. I'm glad I nagged Jimmy Anderson into buying him. As we say in Yorkshire, 'He were a reet good 'un'."

Tottenham circulated to all clubs that Bobby was for sale, and everybody expected the fee to be around £15,000. He was 31 and still had petrol in the tank. Plenty of clubs considered signing him but were put off by the stories of his gambling. This was all at the time of the sensational football bribery scandal, when several players, including England internationals Peter Swan and Tony Kay, were jailed for match fixing.

Bobby revealed after his retirement that he had been approached by shadowy figures among the betting fraternity to organise the fixing of a North London Derby with Arsenal. "I refused them point blank," he said. "I was addicted to gambling but was never ever crooked on the football pitch."

THE DARKEST DAYS

Greavsie scored four goals and Smith one in an 8-3 rout of Northern Ireland in the first match under the Wembley floodlights on 20 November 1963. Difficult to believe, but it was the last time the Greaves/Smith partnership would operate at international level after they had scored 32 goals between them in 14 England matches (Greaves 19, Smith 13). It was a phenomenal goalscoring rate, yet within seven months Bobby Smith was playing down in the Fourth Division following that earthquaking row with the placid Bill Nicholson.

It was one of the quickest descents into relative obscurity in English football history, and right up until his passing, at the age of 77, Bobby considered he had been ill-treated by Tottenham.

The only club to publicly show interest in signing him when Spurs transfer-listed him were Fulham, where their former top goalscorer Bedford Jezzard was in charge. He discussed the idea of signing Smith with club legend Johnny Haynes, who had played with the Tottenham centre-forward for England, including in the unforgettable 9-3 dismantling of Scotland in 1961 when Bobby was among the players who chaired him off the pitch shoulder-high in triumph. Johnny's view was: "Bobby could not have become a bad player overnight, and he's hardly the first player to have trouble finding a winner at the races. Test them with a bid."

Bedford duly did what 'Mr Fulham' advised and rang Bill Nicholson and made a tentative offer of £12,000.

Bill said that he would put it to the board, while privately hoping they would turn it down. The last thing he wanted was Bobby becoming a hit alongside Johnny Haynes for a rival London club.

On 21 April 1964, Smith played his final match for Tottenham, a 7-2 defeat by Burnley at Turf Moor. Twenty-eight days later, having turned down the Fulham bid on the advice of Bill Nick, the Tottenham board were happy to send Bobby Smith down to the Fourth Division with Brighton & Hove Albion. The fee? £5,000. This for a player who had helped crush Northern Ireland 8-3 just six and a half months earlier. As a hush-hush part of the deal, his gambling debts were cleared by a wealthy Brighton fan who just so happened to be a bookmaker.

To help pay off another betting debt, Bobby sold a sizzling tell-all series to a Sunday paper in which he blasted Bill Nick's managing methods ("He's a dictator") and he revealed that he and the Tottenham boss hated each other. Spurs chairman Frederick Wale reacted by banning him from the club for life, announcing the draconian decision in the club programme. Bobby later made his peace with Bill and apologised profusely for his comments, confessing that he had done it purely for money. New chairman Irving Scholar rescinded the ban order and a contrite Bobby was allowed back into the Tottenham fold.

Clandestinely, Nicholson had tried to bring Edmonton-born England skipper Johnny Haynes to White Hart Lane to team up with his old England sidekick Jimmy Greaves. But the bold attempt fell through, and the Blanchflower-White roles went to Mullery and Venables; good as they were, they were never in the Blanchflower-White class.

Greavsie had become accustomed to the pace set by Danny and John, and he struggled to adapt to the new midfield's style of delivery. He expected the ball to his feet, but Venners and Mullers both continually pushed the ball ahead of him and expected him to chase after it. No chance! Both were given a tough time by the Spurs supporters, who had been spoiled over recent years. They unkindly but understandably compared the newcomers with their great idols.

It took months for the demanding Tottenham fans to accept the new players, and Mullers told me some time later:

"I hated my early days at Spurs. Danny was an impossible act to follow. The fans wanted me to play the Blanchflower way. No hope. He was an artist who liked to play with what was something of a luxury style. I was a much more physical player, and made my presence felt. Those early days at the Lane were a complete nightmare. I used to play my heart out and all I got was barracking by supporters who had been spoiled watching one of the great teams – the Double side – and an outstanding footballer and captain in Danny.

"The only thing that saved me from asking Bill Nick for a transfer was watching Dave Mackay battling every day for fitness, giving it 100 per cent when most players would have been ready to throw in the towel after he had broken his leg for a second time.

"It made me realise that I had nothing to complain about by comparison, and I put my head down and got on with it. After literally months of jeers from impatient fans I realised I was gradually being accepted when a supporter shouted from the terraces, 'Come on The

THE DARKEST DAYS

Tank!' At last I knew that somebody was starting to appreciate the effort I was putting in.

"I was a huge fan of Blanchflower. He was overflowing with skill and inventive ideas. But not everybody plays the game the same way. I brought my own game to White Hart Lane but it was a long while before I really felt at home. They were challenging times."

The mercurial Terry Venables was not always happy playing at White Hart Lane after his success as the midfield boss at Chelsea, and when he eventually moved on to Queens Park Rangers, who would have taken any bets that one day he would return and buy the club! Yes, as Greavsie says, it's a funny old game.

One of the new-look squad who did win the hearts of the fans was Alan Gilzean, who formed a wonderful partnership with Greavsie. Jimmy found Gilly a joy to play with, and often felt like applauding his delicate touch play and finishing finesse in the penalty area. He was a master of the flick header, and could bamboozle defences with deceptive changes of pace and clever ball control.

I wrote a book called *The G-Men* [still available from the website in the About the Authors section, with a share of profits going to the Tottenham Tribute Trust], and one of the features was how Gilzean gave Bill Nick no problems compared with the many that he had with the mean, moody and often magnificent Bobby Smith.

"I had not heard that story before – that Bobby Smith was banned from the club. I knew about his reputation as a gambler but did not realise that he and Bill disliked each other to that extent. Bill would have detested anybody who lived off gambling on the horses and dogs. That was a million miles from his lifestyle.

Several of my Tottenham club-mates liked a flutter on the gee-gees, but in my time nobody let it get out of control. But it was a problem in the game, as we all learned when Paul Merson and Stan Bowles made the headlines with their massive gambling problems.

When I got chatting to Bill once, long after he had retired from managing, he told me that he had tried to get Stan Bowles from QPR and had offered Martin Chivers in part-exchange. That would have been exciting because he was one of the most skilful and imaginative forwards in the game. But as Crewe Alexander manager Ernie Tagg once said about him: 'If only Stan could have passed a betting shop like he could a football.'"

Next up for our hero Bill was completing a hat-trick of FA Cup final victories in the 1960s. What would the modern Spurs fans give for that!

CHAPTER 14

COMPLETING THE FA CUP HAT-TRICK

Bill Nick's latest team saved their peak performances for the FA Cup in the 1966/67 season, culminating in a well-earned FA Cup final triumph over London neighbours Chelsea at Wembley. It was the first-ever all-London final and, for Bill, completed a remarkable 1960s hat-trick that put him on a pedestal as one of the all-time great managers.

Liverpool's larger-than-life Scottish boss Bill Shankly – a good friend as well as a fierce rival to Nick – summed it up in typical hyperbolic style: "To win the FA Cup once is a great achievement, to win twice is extraordinary... and a third time, bloody miraculous. Surely Bill Nicholson must get a knighthood!"

Of the side that won the trophy in 1962, only Dave Mackay and Greavsie had survived, along with Cliff Jones on the substitute's bench. Greavsie had recovered from the hepatitis that had robbed him of half a yard of pace during the build-up to the 1966 World Cup finals; few ever take that illness into account when discussing Jimmy's contribution to the World Cup triumph, halted by a shin injury received in a group game against France.

An interlude in our Bill Nicholson story here while I give an action replay of the match and a summary of the players that first appeared in the *Daily Express*, where I was informing (Steve says boring) readers as chief football writer:

The fact that Dave Mackay was there at the 1967 FA Cup final to lead out the Tottenham team as skipper was the sort of story that you would expect to come from the pages of *Roy of the Rovers*. 'Miracle Man' Mackay had made an astonishing recovery after breaking his leg a second time following his controversial collision with Noel Cantwell at Old Trafford in 1963.

Mackay motivated a team that had Pat Jennings building himself into a legend as the last line of defence. Baby-faced Irish international Joe Kinnear had come in as right-back in place of the energetic Phil Beal, who was unlucky to break an arm after playing an important part in getting Spurs to the final. Joe, a neat, controlled player, was partnered at full-back by Cyril Knowles, a former Yorkshire miner who took the eye with his sharp tackling and some polished, if at times eccentric, skills. He was to become a cult hero, with anything he attempted – good or bad – accompanied by chants of "Nice one, Cyril" from the White Hart Lane faithful.

Standing like a Welsh mountain in the middle of the defence was the majestic Mike England, one of the finest centre-halves ever produced in Britain. He was a class player from head to toe.

Dave Mackay was the immoveable link between defence and attack as he adapted his game from buccaneer to anchorman, helping to stoke the fires of the engine room where Alan Mullery and Terry Venables were forging a productive partnership. They never quite touched the peaks that Spurs fans had seen in the 'Glory Glory' days of Blanchflower-White-Mackay, but – let's be honest – few midfield combinations have ever reached that sky-scraping standard.

Jimmy Robertson was a flying Scot on the right wing, where his speed was a vital asset for the G-men – Gilzean and Greaves, who had a radar-like understanding for where to be to get the best out of each other. For the final, Bill Nick preferred Frank Saul to Cliff Jones for the No.11 shirt. Frank, who had been a fringe player in the Double-winning squad, was more of a central striker than a winger, but he was a direct player with a good nose for goal. Cliff, and Joe Kirkup for Chelsea, were the first players to wear No.12 shirts in an FA Cup final.

The Tottenham team, in 3-3-4 formation:

Jennings
Kinnear   England   Knowles
Mullery   Venables   Mackay
Robertson   Greaves   Gilzean   Saul
Sub: Jones

COMPLETING THE FA CUP HAT-TRICK

Facing Tottenham in the first all-London final were Tommy Docherty's elegant but unpredictable Chelsea team. They had gone through an even more drastic rebuilding programme than Spurs, with Terry Venables being part of the upheaval when he moved on to Tottenham to make room the previous year for the arrival of Scotland's 'Wizard of Dribble', Charlie Cooke.

Peter 'The Cat' Bonetti was their goalkeeper, as good a catcher of the ball as there was in world football. Allan Harris, preferred at right-back to usual choice Joe Kirkup, was a solid defender who balanced the marvellously skilled Eddie McCreadie, who had the ball control of a winger to go with his scything tackles.

Marvin 'Lou' Hinton was a sound centre-half with a good footballing brain, and making the earth tremble alongside him was poker-faced Ron 'Chopper' Harris, Allan's brother and one of the most feared ball-winners in the game. Young John Hollins was a bundle of atomic energy at right-half, and the aggressive Scot John Boyle played a utility role in midfield while wearing the No.11 shirt.

Filling the scheming role for Chelsea that had belonged to Venables was the dance master Charlie Cooke, a charismatic character known to his friends as 'Bonny Prince Charlie'. All the people who tried to compare Charlie with his predecessor Venables were wasting their breath. They were as alike as grass and granite. Charlie liked to hang on to the ball and run with it as if it was tied to his boot laces, while Terry let the ball do the work with precise passes that could have come out of the 'Push and Run' coaching manual.

Chelsea relied on three main marksmen to get the ball into the net. Bobby Tambling, a faithful Stamford Bridge servant who had recently overtaken Greavsie's club goal-scoring record, had a terrific turn of speed and was a deadly finisher. Tommy Baldwin, who had joined Chelsea in a part-exchange deal that took George 'Stroller' Graham to Arsenal eight months earlier, was nicknamed 'Sponge' because of the way he soaked up work – and, off the park, beer!

Then there was Tony Hateley, a master of the airways whom Tommy Docherty had bought from Aston Villa for £100,000 after his silkily skilled centre-forward Peter Osgood had broken a leg. While weak on the ground, Tony was a powerhouse header of the ball who learned a lot from the old head master Tommy Lawton while at Notts County – one day he would pass on all he knew to his son, Mark Hateley.

Masterminding the Chelsea team was manager Tommy Docherty, one of the game's great personalities. He had a razor-sharp Glaswegian wit and was in complete contrast to the dour and often tight-lipped Bill Nicholson.

On paper, it looked certain to be a cracker of a match. But on the pitch it turned out to be something of a damp squib. The whole day fell a bit flat, mainly due to the fact that both teams were from London. That robbed the match of much of its atmosphere, because the supporters were not in that bubbling 'Oop f'the Coop' day-out mood.

Spurs skipper Mackay had a personal mission to win after having been inactive for so long, and he drove the Tottenham team on like a man possessed. He had unnerved the Chelsea players as they waited in the tunnel before the kick-off by winding them up with verbal banter. Dave knew every way there was to get under the skin of the opposition.

He then put action where his mouth was, demanding that Spurs play the more positive and purposeful football. They deserved their lead just before half-time, Jimmy Robertson crashing a shot wide of Bonetti after Alan Mullery's long-range piledriver had been blocked.

Robertson, proving one of the most effective of all the forwards, set up a second goal in the 67th minute when he steered a typical long throw-in from Dave Mackay into the path of Frank Saul, who pivoted and hooked the ball high into the net.

Tottenham then slowed the game down to suit themselves, playing possession football so that Charlie Cooke could not get the ball to take command with his mesmerising control. Bobby Tambling was allowed in for a goal five minutes from the end, but Tottenham tightened up at the back to hold out for victory.

Three months after this triumph, Tottenham drew 3-3 in the Charity Shield against Manchester United at Old Trafford, a match that has gone down in footballing folklore because of a goal scored by Pat Jennings. The Irish international goalkeeper hammered a huge clearance from the Spurs penalty area that went – on the first bounce – over the head of Alex Stepney and into the back of the United net. The bewildered look on the faces of the players of both teams was hilarious to see. I was reporting on the match for the *Daily Express*, and afterwards Pat told me: "I decided to clear the ball up to Greavsie and Gilly, and a strong following wind grabbed it and took it all the way to the United net. Jimmy and Alan had their backs to me and could not believe it when they realised it was me who had scored. Greavsie said he told Alan: 'D'you realise this makes Pat our top scorer for the season? He'll never let us forget it.'"

Bill Nicholson counted the 1967 FA Cup final triumph as one of his more memorable achievements...

> "I was confident we would win from the moment Tommy Doc let slip a tactical decision when we were being interviewed together at a function at the Hilton hotel on the Monday before the final. He said he was dropping his sweeper system, and I was delighted to hear it because I knew Alan Gilzean hated playing against it.
>
> "It was one of those matches when I felt we were always in control. They concentrated so hard on stopping Jimmy Greaves and Gilly playing that it left time and space for Jimmy Robertson and Frank Saul to pick their spots.
>
> "It was far from a classic match, but particularly satisfying for Dave Mackay. When he broke his leg for a second time in a reserve match that he was using for match-fitness, nobody would have guessed that he would be back at Wembley to collect the FA Cup.
>
> "He was a remarkable competitor and after his career-threatening injuries adjusted his game so that he was more defensive but still looking for the chance to prompt the attack. Dave could get through a game on his reputation for being rugged and tough – opponents always treated him with great respect, even after his twice-broken leg.
>
> "There was that famous incident at the start of the 1966/67 season when he grabbed hold of Billy Bremner, providing one of the best-known photographs in football. Dave hated the picture, because it gave the impression he was a bully. He was hard but never dirty.
>
> "He showed his character when he led the Derby County team to promotion as a skipper while playing a purely defensive sweeper role. We had agreed to let him move back to Hearts as player-manager when Brian Clough intervened and persuaded Dave to join him at the Baseball Ground after locking him in my office and saying he would not let him out until he had

signed for Derby. All sorts of inducements were offered, including, I believe, Dave being paid more for his programme notes than I was receiving each week from Spurs.

"Cloughie was quite a character who I had known since his England Under-23 days, when I was the manager who dropped him! He told me privately many years later, 'You were so right, and as a manager I've insisted my players train as hard as they play. It's the only way.'

"In Dave Mackay, he had signed the most dedicated player I ever encountered, whether training or playing."

My co-author Steve Perryman was a spectator at the 1967 FA Cup final…

"The nearest Bill got to bribing a player to join Spurs was when he gave me and my Dad tickets to watch Spurs play in the 1967 FA Cup final against Chelsea. I'd also been offered tickets by Chelsea, plus a place on their team coach going to and from Wembley. Back then at 15, I was quite popular with scouts and managers! But it was meeting Bill that clinched it for me. Honesty and integrity shone out of his every pore, and he didn't try to offer me the Earth. He just promised the right football education, and that's what appealed to me. Just being in the great man's presence filled you with confidence and trust. You couldn't buy it.

"The final fell a bit flat, but to my schoolboy eyes it was a wonderful experience going to Wembley, back in the day when there were twin towers and those magical 39 steps to the Royal Box to collect the trophy. It was a great sadness to me that when redesigning the new Wembley they could not find room for the towers, and winning captains now have to take a meandering journey before reaching the Royal Box.

"As I watched Dave Mackay – the Miracle Man – climb those steps to collect the FA Cup, I dreamt of the day I would do it as captain of Tottenham, my chosen club. And I was joining them simply because I had total faith in Bill Nicholson…"

CHAPTER 15

A LEGEND DEPARTS

My writing partner Steve Perryman now enters our storyline with first-hand evidence of life under Bill Nicholson, and no player in the history of the club has given more sterling service to Tottenham Hotspur. After two educational, learning-curve years as an apprentice, he made his first-team debut in 1969 and went on to famously skipper the side through a glorious period on his way to a club record 854 appearances. His reign included back-to-back years collecting the FA Cup in 1981 and 1982, all post-Nicholson's management but certainly doing it the 'Sir Bill' way.

In my reporting role, I got a distinctly different perspective of Bill than Steve, who watched him through a player's eyes while in our many interviews he was often guarded and careful about what he said to me (Sir Matt Busby had once advised him to "treat the press like you do the police; tell them only what they need to know..."). Steve got a close-up view of Nicholson the manager at work and, later, Nicholson the relaxed friend as the Victorian-strict Bill mellowed following his retirement...

> *"I cannot beat the Cliff Jones description that Bill was in charge from the boot room to the boardroom. He ruled White Hart Lane like an emperor, often kindly but also with a rod of iron when he felt it necessary. Cliff tells a story that always amuses me. It was in the early '60s and everybody was describing him as one of the world's greatest wingers.*

"With the mischievous Greavsie gleefully egging me on, I plucked up the courage and decided to ask Bill for a raise," Jones recalled. "I knocked on the door of his cramped little office on the corner of the High Road and what was later renamed Bill Nicholson Way.

"'What d'you want?' Bill asked irritably. 'Well, Bill, people keep telling me I'm the world's greatest winger and I'd like that to show in my wage packet.'

"Bill considered this and said: "'Well I'm not one of those people. Please shut the door on the way out.'"

"Bill could be a hard, hard man but I really respected him. I just wish he'd sometimes been more generous with Tottenham's money.

"When I joined Spurs in 1967 as a 15-year-old kid he was recognised as a 'master manager' along with Matt Busby at Old Trafford, Bill Shankly at Anfield, Jock Stein up at Celtic and, of course, England boss Alf Ramsey. The man chiefly responsible for us apprentices was loyal trainer Johnny Wallis, but everything he taught us came from the fount of all knowledge, Bill Nick. There was nothing we learned about football that was not touched with Bill's trusty hand. The Nicholson mantra of 'Everything must be done properly' ran right the way through the club. His was a presence you could feel at all times. That habit of always trying to do your best has remained with me throughout my life, and for that I thank 'Sir Bill'.

"He was too busy with first-team business to give us youngsters his undivided attention, but he was often lurking around making quiet notes on our attitudes, our work rate and our discipline, on and off the pitch. He always had a biro pen in his top pocket and used to make his notes in careful copperplate handwriting, and that was something we had in common from our schooldays, always trying to write clearly and elegantly. A small point but it gives an indication of a person's approach to life. Excuse the arrogance, but we were both neat, well-organised people.

"Bill surrounded himself with a very small, trusted team, unlike today's vast, well-oiled machine. He used his

faithful secretary Barbara Wallace (Mrs W) as a shield, and she vetted everybody – particularly pressmen like Norm, the Pest – who tried to take up his precious time. He was tunnel visioned and did not want to waste any time with non-club matters.

"I don't think Bill ever got the Army organisational routine out of his system and was continually demanding strict adherence to a code of good behaviour and recognition that football should be played 'the Spurs way'. He was neat and thorough in everything he did. Above all, you had to want to win. People happy to come second had no place in his life or thoughts.

"Eddie Baily played bad cop to Bill's good cop, and used to drop in on our training sessions to crack the whip. He had one hell of a tongue on him and could have given courses on how to swear. It is the industrial language of the game – if you have sensitive ears I would suggest that football apprenticeship is not for you. Bill only used to swear to make a point, while Eddie did not feel as if he had completed a sentence if he had not used a cuss word or two. But what a football man. Old timers always told me that without Eddie there would not have been a 'Push and Run' team. His control of the ball was uncanny and he could hit it accurately with either foot over prodigious distances. He had thick-thighed bow legs and used to stand in front of the young players challenging us to try to take the ball off him.

"'Come on, Perryman' he used to say, 'let's see what you're made of. Your job is to sicken the opposition with your use of the ball as well as tackling firmly and making yourself a bloody nuisance until they are sick of you.' I have left out the 'f' words that accompanied his taunts.

"He 'only' got nine England caps because that was in the era of a golden generation of inside-forwards, players like Raich Carter, Len Shackleton, Ernie Taylor and Wilf Mannion. You had to be really special to get into the England team ahead of players of that quality, and by all accounts – particularly his own! – Eddie was very special. He could blow his own trumpet better than Louis Armstrong, but

much of his boasting was tongue in cheek. Eddie lived up to his image as 'the cheeky chappie' like his hero, the 1940s Cockney-style comedian Max Miller, who I'm told actually came from Brighton but had the swagger of a London barrow boy. Eddie could wind you up to the point where you hated him, and then suddenly he would do something magical with the ball and you'd realise you could learn a lot by listening to him. And when you got it right, he'd put an arm around you and say in heavy Cockney tones, 'Well done, my son.' He was a hard taskmaster but knew when to drop the pollen of praise.

"I always remember in particular the way he used to drive Martin Chivers to distraction with his constant nagging and demands for extra effort. Yes, he could be a pain in the arse, but he had been there, done that and you were wise to listen to the points he was making between the cuss words. But 'Big Chiv' often shut his ears to him, which used to infuriate the man paid to coach. 'If you'd do the courtesy of listening to me, Mart,' he'd say, 'you could learn something that would make you a more complete player. You think you're God's gift, but you could be so much better. You're built like a Greek statue... and too often move like one.' He would then laugh at his alleged joke while the big man seethed. Behind his back, Eddie used to call him 'Mart the Fart' and he used to try to belittle him because he felt he was too big for his boots. You would almost have paid to watch and listen to their verbal duels. Then it would dawn on you that this was for real and that it was not a comedy show but your bread and butter. I used to put my head down and get on with trying to improve my game, hoping to avoid the Baily sarcasm. He really was like a real-life Alf Garnett (who in the TV series Till Death Us Do Part was portrayed by Warren Mitchell as a West Ham fan while in truth the actor was a fanatical supporter of Spurs).

"Eddie had taken over as Tottenham coach in 1963 after rejoining the club from Leyton Orient following the sad death from cancer of Harry Evans, John White's father-in-law. What a tragic family. I, of course, didn't know John

A LEGEND DEPARTS

but everybody to a man told me he was a gifted footballer who had so much more to give when he was so tragically taken from us. It does not bear thinking about.

"I clearly remember the first time I was invited to join the senior team for an eye-opening trip to an away match at Newcastle, and I saw at first-hand the iron grip Bill had on everything. It was in the 1967/68 season and I was 16 and feeling full of myself because I had been selected for the honour of travelling with the first-team pros.

"Bill quickly put me in my place. 'The only reason you're coming with us,' he said in a matter-of-fact way, 'is because our trainer Cecil Poynton has gone down with a bug and we need your help with the skip.'

"'Slave labour,' Greavsie called it, joking of course as he puffed on his ever-present pipe. He was a compulsive pipe smoker and told me he'd taken it up to try to control his cigarette habit. Like Bill Nick, I never smoked and it's one of the main reasons I survived a torn aorta a few years ago when a heart problem almost finished me off. If I'd been a smoker, I would not have been here to help tell the story of one of the greatest men I ever came across. End of medical advice!

"Jimmy was great at putting me at my ease on the long train journey to Newcastle, as were all the first-team squad – who I noticed were each very respectful of Bill. Nobody back-chatted him and they all behaved in a gentlemanly manner on the train, with no hint of boisterousness. We were like a team of respectable travelling businessmen in our club blazers and ties, and the joke was that I was there as the choirboy. I was quite cherubic in those days, and some say I still have those little boy looks. I try not to see the craggy bits!

"I was privileged to room with the great Pat Jennings in the Gosforth Park hotel where the team stayed on the eve of the Newcastle match. He lived up to his image of being a thorough gentleman and treated me as if I were a younger brother. That evening at dinner a waitress asked Pat to sign her autograph book. As she prepared to go off to the next table to get another autograph of an established star,

'SIR BILL'

Pat said, 'Excuse me, miss. Make sure you get this young man's signature. He's going to be some player.' The 'choirboy' felt six inches taller! What a thoughtful gesture from a great man. Nobody ever has a bad word to say about 'Our Pat', a wonderful ambassador for football, our club and for Ireland. Oh yes, I'd better add also for the Arse! Thanks to the Tottenham board, he became just as big a hero at Highbury. Idolised right across North London and Northern Ireland, where they have raised a statue to him in his hometown of Newry. Legend!

"As he gave the pre-match instructions in the dressing room before the match at St James' Park, Bill said, 'Don't forget, you're on a £20-a-point bonus, so a victory would be nicely profitable.' It was rare for Bill to talk about money and as we left the dressing room he suddenly remembered I was there. 'Not a word of what I've just said to anybody, Stephen,' he warned. 'Remember, what is said in a dressing room stays in the dressing room.' Anther lesson from The Master.

"I sat alongside Bill Nick and Eddie Baily in the dugout, and that was an experience and an education that money could not buy. What contrasting characters. Bill studiously made notes and kept tutting and quietly grumbling at mistakes, while Eddie shouted himself hoarse calling our players every name under the sun, and then going into an explosion of excitement as we scored one, then two and then – the cherry on the cake – a third goal. Bill showed little emotion, but Eddie could not contain himself, just like a frenzied fan. The huge Geordie crowd was amazing and kept on roaring their appreciation of their team until the third goal went in, then they started hurling insults at players of both sides.

"Hundreds of them were at the station to jeer us off, and it turned nasty when somebody threw a mug of hot chocolate at Alan Mullery. He ducked out of the way and it hit Mike England, making a mess of his pristine club blazer. Not a good idea. Towering Mike, always very proud of his smart appearance, responded instinctively by punching

A LEGEND DEPARTS

the Geordie fan on the nose. Police were called but let Mike off with a finger-wagging warning after he explained what had happened. Can you imagine that going unreported today, with social media being what it is?

"Bill Nick, ever a calming voice, told Mike: 'Sorry about your blazer. We'll pick up the cleaning bill. Best that we forget it happened.'

"This then 16-year-old looked on with wide-eyed wonder. I could not wait to be a first-team player."

One of Steve's fellow apprentices was a raw young Scot from Edinburgh called Graeme Souness. I need to share an off-beat story involving a talented player that Bill always considered 'the one that got away'. It shows off a different, hidden side of our subject.

By accident, I got an astonishing insight into the real Bill Nicholson. This was when he was overwhelmed by a story that made its way on to the front as well as back pages, and which gave him more distress than almost any other event in his career.

It was during the 1970/71 season and Bill was losing a battle to hang on to Souness, considered by many to be one of the finest young prospects in British football at the time. Born in the tough Broomhouse district of Edinburgh on 6 May 1953, Souness went to the same Carrickvale school that Dave Mackay had attended a generation earlier. They must have been hewn out of the identical lump of granite, because Souness had all the Mackay motivating mannerisms and liked to boss the pitch in the same intimidating way as his schoolboy idol.

His encyclopaedic knowledge of all that Mackay achieved swayed him to join Tottenham at the age of 15 when any of the Scottish clubs would willingly have opened their doors to him.

I learned earlier than most that Souness was not only a star in the making but also a headstrong boy who knew his own mind. Jim Rodger, a sleuth of a reporter on the *Scottish Daily Express*, was so close to Bill Nicholson that he knew all the Spurs secrets and kept most of them tucked to his chest, never sharing them with readers or colleagues. He earned a mutual trust with chairmen, managers and players that got him an ear in boardrooms and dressing rooms throughout football.

'SIR BILL'

Jim, standing 5ft 6in and almost as wide as he was tall, bespectacled and at least three stone overweight, was a legend in Scotland, on nodding terms with prime ministers and princes as well as most of the people who mattered in football. He telephoned me in the Fleet Street office of the *Express* one day in 1970 and whispered in the conspiratorial tone that he always used: "Get over to the North London digs of Graeme Souness and talk him out of doing anything silly. Bill Nick thinks he's going to walk out on the club."

"Graeme who?" I said. "I wouldn't know what he looks like, let alone where he lives."

"He's the hottest young prospect in the country," Jim said in a scolding tone, and proceeded to give me Graeme's address. "You'll be doing Bill Nick a big favour if you can tell him to just be patient and wait for his chance. He couldnae be with a better club. If you get him, put him on to me. I'll talk some sense into him."

That was how 'Rodger the Dodger' operated, working almost as a secret agent on behalf of managers across Britain, and then being rewarded with some of the hottest exclusive stories in the game.

In those days I was more concerned with trying to dig out stories on first-team players at all the London clubs, and could not see the point of chasing after a youngster whose career had hardly started. But as I had so much respect for my Glasgow colleague, I drove to Graeme's North London digs only to be told by his landlady that he had gone home to Scotland an hour earlier.

What a waste of time, I thought. As if anybody apart from Jim Rodger is going to be the slightest bit interested in this story.

Wrong!

It got to the point over the next few days when questions were asked in the House of Commons, as the story crossed from the back to the front pages. Graeme, then 17, had spent two years at Spurs as an apprentice who considered himself more of a sorcerer. He had gone back to Edinburgh because – he said – he felt homesick.

Spurs reacted by suspending him without pay for two weeks. Graeme's outspoken local MP, Tam Dalyell, took up the case, and questioned in the House what right a club had to deal with a minor like this when his only crime was to suffer from homesickness. "Is homesickness something that should be punishable?" demanded Dalyell, managing to make Souness sound as hard done by as

A LEGEND DEPARTS

Oliver Twist, while Bill Nicholson was somehow being cast as the Fagin of football.

The story became the property of columnists with poison pens, and Bill Nick, a fatherly manager if ever there was one, was unfairly pilloried. Souness, without having kicked a ball in senior football, was suddenly the best-known young player in the land.

The suspicion at Spurs was that their hot young property had been got at and was being tempted away from Tottenham.

I went hunting Bill for quotes and found he had gone home from his Lane office. It was never my style to trouble managers by invading the privacy of their homes, but I was under pressure from my editor to get a Nicholson slant on the story. So I drove down the road to Bill's nearby home in Creighton Road.

There was no reply when I knocked on his door, and I was just about to return to my car when an elderly lady sweeping the pavement in front of her house next door asked: "You looking for Mr Nicholson?"

I nodded, and she pointed to a side drive. "You'll find him around the back," she said. "He's in his allotment."

Allotment? Bill Nicholson, manager of Spurs, in his allotment?

Sure enough, I found Bill, dressed in shorts and Tottenham tracksuit top, digging with a spade in an allotment around the corner from his home.

"What the bloody hell do you want?" he said, as astonished to see me as I was to find him up to his ankles in shovelled soil. Pearls of sweat bubbled on that granite forehead of his and he leant on his spade like a farmer in his field.

"You spend a lot of time here?" I asked, my reporter's antenna on red alert.

"I'd love to so that I could escape the likes of you," he replied, without a hint of humour. "One day I want to find more time to take it up as a proper hobby, and if you say one word about it in your paper I will hang you from the nearest lamp post."

Goalpost would have been a better threat, I thought, but I kept that to myself...

I swore to secrecy, and it was many years before I told this story – I hope Bill Up There forgives me re-telling it here. I just feel it captures his (literally) down to earth personality. One of the nicest, kindest and most modest men ever to cross my path, but he could be brutal when necessary.

I pressed him for his take on Souness.

"I have never known such an ambitious and impatient young man," an exasperated Nicholson told me, putting his spade aside. "He has a wonderful future in the game, but he wants to run before he can walk. He can't understand why I'm not already considering him for the first team. He wants to jump ahead of established professionals like Alan Mullery and Martin Peters, and the very promising Steve Perryman. His chance will come, but he must show patience. If he's ever picked for Scotland, I wonder if they'll find a cap big enough for his head."

A suitably repentant Souness returned to the Lane after Bill had travelled to Scotland to have quiet, fatherly words with him, but he later wore out the carpet to Bill's office to the point where the Spurs boss decided he had no option but to let him go.

He had made one brief first-team appearance in a UEFA Cup tie (coming on for Martin Peters in a match in Iceland) before being sold to Middlesbrough in December 1972 for £27,000, which was a hefty fee in those days for a virtually untried player. Souness went on to become one of the most formidable midfield forces in football, his peak coming when he joined Bob Paisley's Liverpool for a fee of £350,000 in January 1978 – at the time the highest fee Middlesbrough had ever received for a player. Cue Bill Nick quietly spitting blood.

Forever afterwards Bill 'Digger' Nicholson considered Souness the one that slipped through the net.

While Souness was causing a ruckus due to a lack of first-team action, Steve had quietly arrived in the Tottenham first team in 1969 and was getting to witness close-up the final throes of Jimmy Greaves' legendary Spurs career...

> *"Just as I was getting my first-team career off the launching pad, Jimmy was losing his appetite for the game he had played better than possibly anybody else when it came to the fairly important job of putting the ball into the net.*
>
> *"There was a lot of tension in the dressing room and at the training ground because it was obvious Jim was losing interest and commitment. I was just a baby, 17 years old and full of energy and ambition, and here was one of my*

A LEGEND DEPARTS

heroes showing more enthusiasm for rally driving and his business interests than playing for Tottenham.

"Eddie Baily in particular was on Jimmy's case and it became very clear to me that they just didn't like each other. They were both powerful Cockney personalities and some of their verbal exchanges were vicious and shocking to my young ears.

"It all came to a head the day we lost a fourth-round FA Cup replay at Crystal Palace. Jimmy was one of several players who had a shocker. Bill Nick was fuming and I was among those left out of the team, although Bill stressed to me that he wanted to give me a rest and not to consider I had been axed. That was the caring side of Bill. He wanted to let me down gently.

"No such soft, comforting words for Greavsie. He was dropped for the first time since joining Tottenham and in the full glare of publicity as Fleet Street and all the broadcasting outlets made a full meal of the news. I don't know if Jimmy was acting, but at the time he didn't seem to care a jot about all the fuss and hoo-hah.

"I was later – after growing up and proving I could play the game a bit – to get very close to Jim, and he admitted that he had lost the edge to his game and a vital half-yard of his speed following a debilitating hepatitis illness of 1965. But he still wanted to play for Spurs.

"He said he felt let down by Bill Nick in particular. I was too young to make my opinion known but if anybody had asked me, I would have said: 'Whatever you do, keep Jimmy at Tottenham.' I agreed with Alan Mullery, who said publicly: 'To let Greavsie go is madness.'"

It was painful to watch the demise of Jimmy as a Spurs player, probably the biggest people's hero in the history of the club. Yes, even bigger than Harry 'One of Our Own' Kane. I've seen grown men brought to tears by a Greavsie goal and be distraught when Spurs decided to let him go.

Bill Nick told me privately that he was concerned that the Artful Dodger of the penalty area seemed to be showing more enthusiasm in his preparations to drive to Mexico in a 1970 World Cup rally than for playing football. By this time Jimmy had built up a flourishing sports shop and travel business with his brother-in-law, Tom Barden, and football was no longer the be-all-and-end-all for him. Yet he was still by some distance the most dynamic finisher in the 'old' First Division.

To try to bring the best out of Greavsie, Nicholson went shopping and bought Martin Chivers as a new playmate from Southampton.

How times change. In my reporting role for the *Daily Express* I met 'Big Chiv' at Waterloo Station and travelled with him by tube to Liverpool Street and then on to Tottenham as he prepared to start his new life at the Lane. These days, reporters cannot get near the players, who invariably arrive at their new clubs in chauffeur-driven limos with dark-tinted windows and an agent handing out second-hand quotes. To be honest, this star treatment might have been very much to the Chivers taste!

Martin, a grammar school boy educated at the highly regarded Taunton's School in Hampshire, spent the train journey from Southampton to Waterloo tackling *The Times* crossword. He told me on the way to the Lane: "This is like a dream for me. I have always been an admirer of the way Spurs play, and it's going to be a thrill as well as a challenge to play alongside Jimmy Greaves."

Sadly, the Greaves-Chivers experiment did not get off the ground as Martin suffered an awful knee injury that sidelined him for nearly an entire season, and by the time he came back Jimmy had reluctantly and sensationally moved on to West Ham.

> *"I was busy digging the foundations to my career and concentrated on keeping my nose clean and out of what was Bill Nicholson's business. It was a brave (some would say crazy...) call to let Greavsie go, and to this day some Spurs diehards have not forgiven him. But in his old age, Bill used to say with misty eyes that Tottenham had got the best out of Jimmy, and that by the time he joined West Ham he was a shadow of the player we had all loved and admired.*
>
> *"I remember Jimmy coming back to play in Bill's testimonial and he still looked as if he could do the business. It was difficult to believe the horrendous stories he later told about almost being killed by his alcohol addiction.*

A LEGEND DEPARTS

"By the time I had established myself in the first team, booze did not have quite the grip on players as in Jimmy's day. Some of the stories of drunken antics were mind-blowing – in the '50s 'and '60s there was a drinking culture that today's health-conscious footballers would find hard to believe.

"Jimmy told me that he would often drink himself unconscious, and to see him in later years totally in control of himself during his television career was nothing short of miraculous. Bill Nicholson used to say he had no idea of the extent that the players were drinking because he was a strict couple of glasses man who would then slip away to be with his wife and daughters.

"I was always quite entrepreneurial and liked to keep a clear head for my sports shop businesses away from football. But this book is not about me. It's about 'Sir Bill' and I was honoured to be part of his next successful team..."

Greavsie, whose Spurs career started with a reserve game at Plymouth in 1961, coincidentally ended it in March 1970 with a reserve match against the same opponents – this time at White Hart Lane. His next match, astonishingly, was for West Ham.

"Ron Greenwood had quietly tipped me off that he was prepared to let Martin Peters go if he could get the right deal. He knew I strongly fancied him, and we agreed to meet in secret the day before the transfer deadline. Our meeting place was the deserted car park at Walthamstow greyhound track. Ron and I sat in my car and after a long to-and-fro conversation agreed on Martin joining Spurs.

"Ron, a thoroughly good man who always represented football with dignity and pride, told me that Martin was an exemplary professional who wanted to move simply because he hated always coming third in the Moore-Hurst-Peters debates. He wanted to become his own man without constant comparisons. Ron said I needed to give him something more than just cash to prove he had done a good deal for West Ham, both in terms of the club and the supporters.

'SIR BILL'

"'How about Jimmy Greaves?' he asked. It was well publicised that Jimmy was no longer first-choice for our league team and so I agreed that he could go to Upton Park as a £54,000 makeweight in the transfer that would bring Martin to us.

"I obviously didn't tell Ron that I thought Jimmy, certainly in his own mind, was fed up with football after playing it every season since he was seven or eight. I knew that West Ham were getting a shell of the old Jimmy Greaves. All those Spurs supporters who heavily criticised me for letting him go were unable to see this. Jimmy had no greater fan than me, but the Greavsie I bought from Milan was no more. And his deterioration in that following season, his last in the league, proved my judgement right.

"It was well known that Jimmy liked a drink, but I was as shocked as everybody else when it became public that he was a seriously ill alcoholic. The way he pulled himself together was an enormous credit to his strength of character and nobody was happier than me to see him become a very successful and popular television performer.

"I was and always will be very fond of him, and I repeat – there has been no better finisher in my lifetime. It was a pleasure and a privilege to enjoy him at his peak. Tottenham have not had a better goal-scoring player, and neither has England. We saw the best of Greavsie."

Now Bill turned his attention to the next team he was building, and there were more trophies on the horizon.

CHAPTER 16

A TALE OF TWO STRIKERS

We now reach the post-Jimmy Greaves period in our Bill Nicholson story, and there will be a generation out there who will remember it as the summertime of their supporting Spurs. After playing in the 'Push and Run' era, then managing the Double team, guiding the first British side to lift a major European trophy and completing a hat-trick of FA Cup final triumphs, Bill was ready to embark on yet another silverware adventure. And Steve Perryman was at the heart of it all...

"People questioned Bill Nicholson's judgement in putting me under the wing of the seasoned 'man about town' Alan Gilzean when I became a regular in the Tottenham team following Greavsie's shock departure. But it was a masterstroke as rooming with Gilly helped me learn so much about how to cope with being a footballer right at the top of the mountain. I was a boy when I first made it into the senior squad and – thanks largely to Gilly's influence – I became a man after Bill paired us as room-mates for all Tottenham away matches.

"Alan was a modest, reserved, quietly intelligent man, who never shouted from the rooftops about his exquisite footballing skills. He had a wicked sense of humour but few realised it because he did it all with a straight face, making clever quips that went over the heads of many people who could not understand his thick Scottish brogue.

"Like Bill Nick, he was a methodical man and it was no surprise to me when he took up a career in transport organisation after retiring from football. Getting lorries delivering at the right place and at the right time suited his slide-rule mind. How many footballers that you know could do Pitman's shorthand and touch type? He was a one-off, our Gilly.

"He had roomed with his countryman and close friend Dave Mackay before I arrived on the scene and used to describe him as 'a walking disaster area'. Dave was in the habit of dropping clothes where he stood and was apparently the most untidy of people, yet on the pitch the man who always cleaned up the opposition.

"When I took over from Dave as his room-mate, Gilly used to ask if I'd been a hotel maid in a previous life because I always believed in keeping everything clean and tidy. I used to jokingly wait on him hand and foot, making him tea in bed and polishing his shoes. It was all a bit of fun and helped us bond, 'old Al' – who looked 10 years older than his actual age – and me, young, baby-faced Steve. We were the odd couple but it worked, we were great pals and had each other's backs on and off the pitch.

"It was my co-writer Norman who once described him as a 'Nureyev on grass' and that's exactly what he was, dancing through defences with a balletic rhythm. I used to love watching him partnering Greavsie when I first broke into the first team, and then he had another winning alliance with big Martin Chivers.

"Take it from me – it was hardly a coincidence that Chiv had his greatest moments playing alongside Gilly, who made him a better player with his skilled support play. There were at least three seasons when Martin could be described as one of the world's exceptional centre-forwards, and a lot of his success was down to the way Alan used to create openings for him with creative play that came naturally to him.

"Gilly was Greaves-class in the penalty area. There can be no higher praise. His flick heading, particularly at the near post, was his trademark; whenever I took corners I always had his bald bonce to aim for, and regardless of my accuracy he usually managed to flick it on for a teammate. He was the most unselfish of players and always put the needs of the team first.

"Bill and Gilly had a quiet respect for each other, and always got along. That could not be said about the boss and Big Chiv. Alan used to say he gave Bill a bit of distance because he did not want to be a bother to him. 'Och, he's busy managing,' he used to say. 'I wouldnae do his job for all the Bacardi in Cuba.'

"One of the few times Bill had to call Alan into his office, he said gravely, 'I've had a telephone call from a supporter who said he saw you coming out of a nightclub at two o'clock in the morning.'

'Och,' said Alan with that famous poker face of his, 'the man's a liar. I was going into the club.'

Alan, of course, could shift alcohol in the old-school Greaves style, but to watch him train and eat up long distances in the cross-country runs you would never believe he was a drinker who specialised in putting away Bacardi and Coke at a rate of knots.

"I loved the man and was delighted to play a secret agent role in getting him and Greavsie reunited after not seeing each other for more than 30 years. Alan had disappeared off everybody's radar while concentrating on his role in transport and living down in Weston-super-Mare in Somerset. I talked him into flying on the quiet to Guernsey, where Jimmy was doing one of his after-dinner speeches. We flew in from Exeter and Jimmy from Southend. Purely by chance the cabs taking us from the airport arrived at that evening's venue at exactly the same time and, as if choreographed, Alan and Jim fell into each other's arms like long-lost brothers. 'Where've you been?' asked Greavsie. 'Avoiding people like you,' cracked Alan, and they were back bantering as if they'd never been apart. Both agreed that the best manager they'd ever played for was our hero, Bill Nicholson."

'SIR BILL'

The latest 'team that Bill built' had the safe shovel-hands of Pat Jennings, the resistance of Joe Kinnear, the polish of Mike England, the tenacity of Phil Beal, the eccentricity and class of Cyril Knowles, the grit of Alan Mullery, the elegance of Martin Peters, and the driving power and anticipation of Steve Perryman, all serving twin strikers Gilly and Chivers. The mathematicians among you will notice that there are only 10 players. Bill could never make up his mind which winger to play, and he toyed with Jimmy Pearce and Jimmy Neighbour before bringing in Ralph Coates and Roger Morgan.

Bill was not a fan of Alf Ramsey's 'Wingless Wonders' but struggled to find flank runners who fully satisfied him. He was always looking for the 'next' Cliff Jones.

His main concern, as I often used to report in my Fleet Street days, was getting the best out of the enigmatic Martin Chivers. There were always sniping comments being made about Martin's perceived lack of determination and commitment whenever the going got tough – the most scorching of the criticism usually coming from the unforgiving, hard-to-please coach Eddie Baily.

In his early days at Southampton, I had watched Chiv alongside the young Mike Channon and I knew his apparent casual approach was deceptive. He had the physique of a heavyweight boxer, but to many spectators he seemed too often to have a punchless penalty area presence.

I recall helping Martin move into a smart new home in Epping with his first wife, Carol (shifting some furniture and generally getting in the way) following his move to Spurs. Chiv could appear confident to the point of arrogance and seemed like a young man with the world at his feet. "I've made a slow start," he said, "but I know I'll give the fans the goals they want once I've settled into playing with Greavsie, who has a style of his own. It will take us time to get on each other's wavelength."

But all his plans and ambitions nose-dived during a home match against Nottingham Forest in September 1968 when he felt a shooting pain in his knee and sank to the ground with his leg locked. It was even painful to watch from the press box, and it signalled a nine-month lay-off that understandably made Martin a little morose and moody.

He was still not firing on all cylinders when he made his comeback in August 1969, and there was obvious tension in the Tottenham camp.

A TALE OF TWO STRIKERS

Bill Nick got so frustrated with him that he once gave him a ticket to go and watch Geoff Hurst play for West Ham. "I felt quite insulted," Martin said later. "But I did what I was told and later thanked Bill, because by watching Geoff's positional play I learned a lot."

Chiv was always having verbal battles with Bill Nick about his game, but even more so with Eddie Baily. They had a continual war of words, and I was witness to two classic cases of Martin making Eddie hold up his hands in surrender.

The first time was in Romania in 1971 when Tottenham were playing Rapid Bucharest in the UEFA Cup, a second-leg tie that has gone down in the Tottenham 'hall of shame' as the 'Battle of Bucharest'. I reported in the *Express* that "Spurs were hacked and kicked about like rag dolls." Bill Nick went on record with the view that Rapid were the dirtiest side he had seen in more than 30 years in football.

The dressing room at the end of the match – which Spurs won 2-0 – was like a casualty clearing station, with six Spurs players nursing injuries caused by tackles that belonged in the house of horrors rather than on a football pitch. My writing partner Steve was in the worse state, with a sling protecting a broken collarbone.

I noticed that throughout the game Baily had been bawling at Martin Chivers from the touchline, calling him every name to which he could put his merciless tongue. You could not help but hear the insults being aimed at the 'Ambling Alp' of Spurs because the huge stadium was barely a third full. Big Chiv finally silenced Baily by scoring a superb goal, and you did not have to be a lip reader to know that Martin responded by shouting obscenities back at his nemesis.

We flew straight back to London after the match, and I took careful note that Baily and Chivers completely ignored each other at the airport and on the flight to London. Later that week I saw Bill Nick privately and told him I was thinking of writing a story about the obvious enmity between his right-hand man and his most productive forward.

Bill looked as pained as if I was telling him I was putting down his pet dog. "I can't tell you what and what not to write," he said, "but let me just say that you'll not be doing me any favours. Off the record, we're having problems with Martin. He's a strong-minded young man who thinks he knows it all. His attitude drives Eddie bananas, but you know Eddie – he often shouts things in the heat of a match that he doesn't really mean. I'm trying to make the peace between them, and any story about them will only make matters worse."

At Bill's request, I refrained from writing about the feud, and it was forgotten as Chivers hit such a rich vein of goal-scoring form that I compiled a feature in the *Express* suggesting he had become as powerful an England centre-forward as legends of the game like Tommy Lawton, Ted Drake and Jackie Milburn.

A frothing-at-the-mouth Eddie Baily went out of his way to confront me about the story, saying: "You have insulted truly great players. Chivers is not fit to carry their jock straps."

That's how angry Martin used to make Eddie, but he was forced to bend the knee to him again after the first leg of the 1972 UEFA Cup final against Wolves at Molineux. Before the game both Bill and Eddie had nagged Martin so much about his expected contribution that he snapped and walked out onto the pitch to get away from them.

During the match, with Baily bellowing from the touchline, Chivers conjured two magical goals that virtually clinched victory, before skipper Alan Mullery – back after a loan spell with Fulham – made sure of the trophy with a crucial goal in the second leg at White Hart Lane. The chanting, dancing crowd invaded the pitch that night and Mullery memorably performed a one-man celebratory lap of the pitch, hugging the trophy as if it were a baby. It was chaotic.

After Martin's phenomenal first-leg performance, a contrite Baily came into the dressing room, bowed down in front of the giant centre-forward and mimed as if to kiss his feet. "Here you are, Mart," he said in his loud Alf Garnett-style voice, "walk all over me. You've won me outright."

In those early '70s, Chivers was as potent and productive as any centre-forward in the league. Powerfully built and as wide as a door, he had a deceptively lethargic-looking bearing, but if a possible goal beckoned he would suddenly fire on all cylinders and leave surprised defenders in his wake as he accelerated away. He preferred the ball on his right foot and had a rocketing shot that brought him many of his 118 league goals. He also netted 13 times in 24 England games, and might have plundered many more goals but for a recurring knee injury.

The 1970/71 season saw the launch of Martin's peak years for both club and country. He played in all of Spurs' 58 league and cup games and scored 34 times, including both goals in the League Cup final against Aston Villa and 21 goals in the First Division as Bill Nick's side finished the season in third place (the bad news, however, was that Arsenal finished top and completed the League and FA Cup Double on the tenth anniversary of Tottenham's historic achievement). Martin also notched his first goal for England in a 3-0 win over Greece at Wembley in April 1971 to give a further golden glow to his resurgence.

It was in the following season that Chivers went into overdrive, netting 44 times in 64 first-team appearances. His seven goals in as many League Cup ties lifted Spurs to the semi-finals, where they eventually lost to Chelsea. Free from the worries about his troublesome knee, the rampaging Hampshire giant saved his most impressive form for that season's UEFA Cup, scoring eight times in 11 matches, including a hat-trick in a 9-0 annihilation of Icelandic side Keflavik ÍF and that superb brace against Wolverhampton Wanderers that brought Eddie Baily to his knees. In the First Division, he found the net 25 times in 39 appearances. After all that, even the bullish Baily had to concede that perhaps my article putting Chivers up at the top of the mountain alongside the greats of Eddie's playing days was in no way an exaggeration – those players could carry their own jockstraps from now on...

Tottenham's victory over Wolves – 3-2 on aggregate – in the 1972 UEFA Cup final was a particular, personal triumph for Bill Nicholson. Since taking charge of the club in 1958 he had steered Spurs to three FA Cup finals, one League Cup final, one European Cup Winners' Cup final and the UEFA Cup final – and they had won the lot!

There was some fallout between Bill and his players after the UEFA Cup final when he spent ages in the Wolves dressing room commiserating with the losers rather than praising the Tottenham team's triumph. "The better team lost," he told the Wolves players. Bill later had a clear-the-air meeting with the Tottenham team and conceded that he should have first congratulated his own players, but he could not resist adding: "But you were bloody lucky..."

The following season Bill had Spurs back at Wembley, where it was a Chivers long throw that opened the way for Ralph Coates – substituting for the injured John Pratt – to score the only goal of the 1973 League Cup final against Norwich City.

Martin – with the middle name Harcourt, after his German mother – continued his career in Switzerland with Servette and then had brief appearances with Norwich, Brighton and non-league Dorchester and Barnet, while also enjoying minor spells in Norway and Australia with Vard Haugesund and Frankston City respectively. In his post-playing career, he has owned a hotel and restaurant in Hertfordshire, dabbled with club management, had a spell as the National Development Manager to the FA and serves as a popular matchday host at Tottenham home games.

By his own admission, Martin has mellowed now all the shooting and shouting is over, and states his career turned round when he started finding the net in 1970/71. "It was all about confidence," he said. "I honestly feared my career was over with that knee injury against Forest. But I began to believe in myself again when I started scoring."

Remarkably, after he had taken his final shots, Martin became best of friends with Bill Nicholson, the manager with whom he had a long-running battle over wages, tactics and attitudes. Darkie, Bill's long-suffering wife, used to fume over the sleepless nights he gave her husband, but once she got to know Martin during his visits to their home, she was moved to say: "How on earth could Bill have got so upset about a proper gentleman like Martin?" Bill looked to the ceiling.

Big Chiv accepts that he was at times awkward. He always thought Bill was too miserly with the club's money in an era when footballer's wages were just beginning to take off. "Everything Bill did was in the interests of the club," Martin said. "He always had my full respect. We got to like each other a lot. And Darkie was a wonderful lady."

Martin Chivers. Enigmatic, but on his day as explosive as they come. At his absolute peak, as good a centre-forward as ever bred on the playing fields of England… despite what Eddie Baily thought. Bill Nick himself knew that if the force was with him, Chivers was as good as they came…

> "We would not have been nearly so successful in the early 1970s without the goals of Martin Chivers. But I wish it could all have been achieved without the hassle and the arguments. Martin was such a stubborn so-and-so, and his attitude often dropped a cloud on the dressing room.

Young Billy Nicholson, a month after signing for Spurs as a professional in 1938
Mirrorpix via Getty Images

It's the first season after the Second World War and Billy tests his tackling against clubmate Freddie Cox at White Hart Lane *Mirrorpix via Getty Images*

Bill Nick (far left) with the Spurs side that sealed the title in 1951 after defeating Sheffield Wednesday at White Hart Lane. Wednesday were the same opposition when Spurs secured the title again in 1961, with Nicholson as manager *Unknown*

Buddies Ron Burgess and Bill in 1952/53. They joined Tottenham on the same day in 1936. "Ron was the greatest ever player for Spurs," claimed 'Sir Bill' *Colorsport*

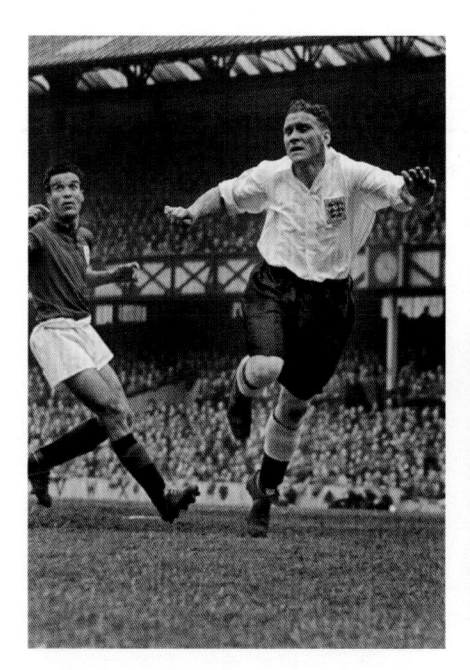

Bill's lone appearance for England against Portugal at Goodison Park in 1951. He scored with his first touch inside 30 seconds! *Colorsport*

Bill warms up for the home match against Huddersfield Town in 1952. He is using his left foot here, but was strongest on his right *Colorsport*

An early shot of Bill in his new role as Spurs coach on the eve of the 1956 FA Cup semi-final against Manchester City at Villa Park. That's his fellow Yorkshireman Bobby Smith with him *Mirrorpix via Getty Images*

Bill welcomes Forest captain and 'Cheeky Chappie' of the 'Push and Run' side Eddie Baily (second from right) back to the Lane. They chat with Welshmen Terry Medwin (left) and Mel Hopkins before a league match in October 1957. Eddie would become Bill's tough-talking assistant in 1963 *Mirrorpix via Getty Images*

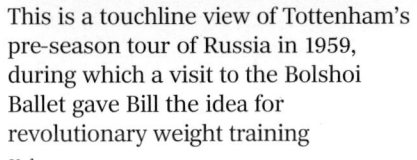

Bill on his memorable first day in charge as manager on 11 October 1958. The inset programme features the match in which Spurs marked his debut with an astonishing 10-4 victory over Everton *Colorsport*

This is a touchline view of Tottenham's pre-season tour of Russia in 1959, during which a visit to the Bolshoi Ballet gave Bill the idea for revolutionary weight training
Unknown

Bill and Falkirk manager Tommy Younger look on as John White signs as a Spurs player in 1959. The sublimely gifted forward, who completed the 'Double' jigsaw, died tragically in 1964, devastating the club *Getty Images*

Bill, in uncharacteristically jovial fashion, dons the club chairman's bowler hat during the celebrations after the 6-2 home win v Aston Villa. The victory, Spurs' 10th in succession from the start of the 1960/61 season, set a new record and they went on to win their first 11 games, a record that still stands *Popperfoto via Getty*

Typical Bill, insisting the Leicester City players share champagne from the FA Cup after Spurs completed the Double at Wembley in 1961. He often got criticised by his own players for spending too much time with beaten opponents *Getty Images*

It's May 1961 and skipper Danny Blanchflower holds the FA Cup aloft, while the League Championship trophy is in the safe hands of Ron Henry. The streets of Tottenham came to a halt during this Glory Glory parade. Never one to seek the limelight, Bill was not to be seen on the top deck *Getty Images*

Bill proudly shows off his star signing from Milan – the one and only Jimmy Greaves – in November 1961, while club captain Danny Blanchflower helps welcome the goal-scoring king to White Hart Lane *Getty Images*

Here we go again! Captain Danny Blanchflower and manager Bill Nicholson proudly hold the FA Cup trophy high on 5 May 1962 after the emphatic 3-1 victory over Burnley *Mirrorpix via Getty Images*

Another trophy for the Spurs shelf as Bill makes room for the European Cup Winners' Cup in 1963 after the 5-1 thrashing of Atletico Madrid *Getty Images*

Bill in his cubby hole of an office at White Hart Lane in 1963. He preferred being on the training ground at Cheshunt *Getty Images*

The 1967 FA Cup final against Chelsea is just days away and Bill reminds Frank Saul, Joe Kinnear, Terry Venables and Pat Jennings of their duties. Tottenham won 2-1 *PA Photos via Alamy*

It's the hat-trick of FA Cups, as 'Miracle Man' Dave Mackay shares exhibiting duties with 'Sir Bill' on the Tottenham Town Hall balcony of dreams in May 1967. You will notice our hero has the ever-present Biro pen in his top pocket. He was an inveterate note taker *Getty Images*

Spurs in Japan 1971 – this unusually relaxed picture of Bill Nick makes it rather endearing. Co-author Steve Perryman recalls that these summer tours were a chance for the Spurs squad to spend extended time together and to bond in a less formal environment *Unknown*

Aston Villa have been vanquished at Wembley, and Bill joins Martin Chivers and Alan Mullery in celebrating with the 1971 League Cup. The players got tankards instead of medals *Mirrorpix via Getty Images*

Spurs celebrate their 1972 UEFA Cup victory. Players from left to right: Ralph Coates, Alan Gilzean, Martin Peters, Mike England, skipper Alan Mullery, Pat Jennings, Joe Kinnear, Cyril Knowles, Martin Chivers and our joint author Steve Perryman. That's Philip Beal crouching in front *Mirrorpix via Getty Images*

Rival managers Bill Nicholson and Ron Saunders get the *Evening Standard* view on the eve of the 1973 Spurs-Norwich City League Cup final that was settled by a superb Ralph Coates goal. Bill was not naturally comfortable with any kind of PR shot but this one got through his defences *Getty Images*

Bill lifts silverware for the eighth and final time in his 16-year tenure at Spurs, making him unquestionably the greatest manager in the club's history *Colorsport*

The beginning of the end of Bill's managerial reign as he and his wife, Darkie, return to Heathrow after the nightmare UEFA Cup final defeat by Feyenoord in Rotterdam in 1974 *Popperfoto via Getty Images*

Bill gives a farewell wave to the Tottenham fans after his decision to resign in 1974. He is in his usual seat in front of the press box before the home match with Derby County. It was the last time he sat there *PA Images via Alamy*

Daughter Jean gets a shot for the family album as Bill, with Darkie at his side, shows off his OBE in the grounds of Buckingham Palace in 1975. All together now: "It should have been a knighthood…" *PA Images via Alamy*

New Spurs manager Keith Burkinshaw welcomes his fellow Yorkshireman back into the Tottenham fold following the latter's year like a fish out of water at West Ham *Getty Images*

'Sir Bill' – in charge from the boot room to the boardroom, and the keeper of the keys at White Hart Lane *PA Images via Alamy*

The ultimate tribute to Bill was when the road leading to White Hart Lane was re-named Bill Nicholson Way. Dave Mackay (far left, his first signing who always played the Nicholson way) was among those who joined Bill at the naming ceremony on 24 April 1999 *PA Images via Alamy*

To the astonishment of those who knew of the antagonism between them as player and manager, it was Martin Chivers who led Bill Nicholson out for his testimonial at White Hart Lane in 2001 *PA Images via Alamy*

White Hart Lane was like a second home to 'Sir Bill' and the fitting place for his memorial service on 7 November 2004 as well as for a huge display of flowers from Tottenham's adoring fans *Getty Images*

BILL NICHOLSON OBE
MEMORIAL SERVICE

WHITE HART LANE
SUNDAY, NOVEMBER 7, 2004

A TALE OF TWO STRIKERS

"I suppose I did go too far with my praise of Wolves after the second-leg in the UEFA Cup final, but I always had to call it as I saw it. That night they were the better team, but we virtually won the trophy at Molineux, where Martin was exceptional.

"He and Eddie were always at loggerheads and I had to try to keep the peace for the sake of the team. It was some time later when Martin finally climbed down off his high horse and accepted that everybody was doing their best for the club and the most important people of all – the supporters.

"If Martin and I learned anything from our tense stand-offs it was that the team must always come first. He was big enough in later years to concede that he had been out of order with some of his moods. Martin was frankly one of the most awkward people I ever had to manage, but on his day he could really play the game. Much to my wife's satisfaction, we got to quite like each other.

"The real highlight of that UEFA Cup triumph was our victory in the two-leg semi-final against Italian giants AC Milan. Stephen Perryman showed he had come of age when he scored two cracking goals to give us a 2-1 win at home in the first leg. We were so ravaged by injuries that I had to recall Alan Mullery from a loan spell at Fulham, where he had been playing to try to regain match fitness after an aggravating injury lay-off. He and Perryman were marvellous over the two legs.

"Most people did not think that – at 2-1 – we had enough of a lead going into the second leg at the San Siro, one of the hardest places in the world to be the visiting team. The crowd is so noisy and hostile that they're worth a one-goal start to Milan. However, thanks to a superbly struck goal by Mullery from a pass by Perryman we took a seventh-minute lead. Best Milan could do was make it 1-1 from a penalty and so we went through 3-2 on aggregate. Every one of us at the San Siro from Spurs that night – from players, staff, directors to travelling fans – were so proud of the performance. It was European football at its best and most dramatic. That was what I was in football for. It was terrific."

Steve has a special place in his memory box for the two matches with Milan:

"All these years later I still get a warm feeling thinking back on those battles with Milan. I'd been building a reputation as 'good old reliable Steve', winning the ball in midfield and then feeding it to a team-mate. Keep it simple, keep it flowing. The basics that Bill always demanded. But in that first leg against a Milan team dripping with star players like Gianni Rivera, Karl-Heinz Schnellinger and Romeo Benetti, I showed a side of me even I didn't know existed! I found the corner of the net with not one but two powerful long-range shots, and everybody hailed me as the man of the match.

"Did Bill come in to the dressing room to hug and congratulate me? Not a bit of it. That was never his style. All he did was warn us that it was only half-time and how much tougher it would be in the second leg in Milan.

"But I was feeling seven-foot tall at the Lane that evening and I knew I had pleased the Boss, who always kept on about wanting 20 goals a season from we midfielders. This is the motivational effect that Bill had on us. We never wanted to let him down. He gave the job 100 per cent at all times and he expected the same input from us. 'Do it for the supporters,' he'd constantly say. 'They pay your wages.'

"As he had warned us, it was much tougher in Milan, one of the most exciting and exacting matches of my life. The San Siro was a sea of noise, and all aimed in an anthem of hatred at us Spurs players. I'd never known an environment like it. Scary but exciting. This is the sort of night every footballer dreams about. It was a long way from my youth football in Uxbridge.

"We went out before the start of the match to inspect the pitch, but quickly retreated to the safety of the dressing-room when the fanatical Milan supporters started throwing firecrackers at us. None of us had experienced such a volatile pre-match atmosphere.

"Bill had cheekily accepted an invitation for us to train at the Inter Milan camp before the match and that was a red rag to a bull for their bitter rivals. It was the equivalent of AC Milan training at Highbury. This was Bill deliberately *winding up our hosts. He was always looking to be as competitive as possible.*

"It was bedlam as the first whistle blew and you could not hear yourself think. After just seven minutes I managed to squeeze a pass into the path of Alan Mullery and he hit it sweetly into the Milan net. How to silence 70,000 Italians! That gave us a commanding 3-1 lead on aggregate.

"We allowed them just one goal from the penalty spot in what the newspapers described as one of the great British performances in Europe. Somehow the referee managed to book me for a scuffle with their hatchet man Benetti, when it was actually my pal Phil Beal who had whacked the Italian. How on earth could the official have mixed up darkhaired me with blond Bealy? But I didn't say a dicky bird because Phil had already been booked once. Did we have a laugh over that one.

"As the final whistle blew, the crowd went potty and were throwing anything they could get their hands on. We players were instructed to stand in the centre-circle for 15 minutes while the fans ran out of missiles to hurl at us.

"Eventually we got back to the dressing room and Bill counted us back in like a mother hen. That was only half the battle. Next we had to negotiate getting back to our hotel. A brick was thrown that smashed our coach window, and Bill bravely got off and demanded that the police give us a motorbike escort through the streets packed with furious Italian fans.

"He was a happy man that night, and I felt as if I'd become a proper professional. The growing-up process was complete. Once you've survived a war of a match at the San Siro, you'll be a man my son!"

As we've seen, after Spurs' triumph in the San Siro Martin Chivers did the business at Molineux in the first leg of the final and his two goals virtually won the trophy for Spurs. An Alan Mullery-inspired 1-1 draw at White Hart Lane brought a 3-2 aggregate victory over Wolves and Tottenham Hotspur became the first name engraved on the new UEFA Cup.

'SIR BILL'

It should perhaps have read 'Bill Nicholson'. This latest triumph meant he had won more trophies than any other manager in the Football League. Statisticians almost trembled as they wrote down his record since taking over at Spurs: three FA Cup finals, one League Cup final and two European Cup finals. They'd won the lot and, oh yes, Nicholson's Spurs had also won the League Championship in the historic Double year. That made a remarkable seven trophies in 14 years. Add to that his back-to-back Second Division and League Championship medals as a player and he had a collection to truly envy.

But chaos and despair sadly waited around the corner.

CHAPTER 17

HAIR-RAISING FOR RALPH COATES

There was no indication of the misery waiting for Bill and his triumphant troops as they collected yet another League Cup trophy in 1973. The highlight for Tottenham on the way to Wembley was beating the season's form team, Liverpool, 3-1 in a quarter-final replay at White Hart Lane to put Bill's side in reach of their second final in three years. It was one of those special Lane evenings, the action and the atmosphere making the skin tingle just as it did back in the 'Glory Glory' days of the '60s.

Spurs subsequently saw off Wolves 4-3 on aggregate in the semi-final, which softened the blow of going out to Brian Clough's Derby County in the fourth round of the FA Cup and booked them a place in the final against Ron Saunders' Norwich. I dipped into my Tottenham archives for this summary of a mainly best-forgotten match:

Substitute Ralph Coates provided the only memorable moment in the final against a Norwich team bidding for a hat-trick against London glamour sides. They accounted for Arsenal in the quarter-final and Chelsea in the semi-final. Their second-leg tie against Chelsea had been abandoned because of fog, and some critics cruelly suggested that the Canaries were still in a fog when they got to Wembley to face Tottenham. Norwich played with a strangely negative attitude, and the game got bogged down in a midfield traffic jam.

Coates, a record £192,000 signing from Burnley in May 1971, had never quite lived up to his potential at White Hart Lane, and he was desperately unhappy to be relegated by Bill Nicholson to the substitutes' bench. But along with his much-mocked comb-over, Ralph gave his answer to the critics after being summoned into the goalless match midway through the first half following an injury to Tottenham loyalist John Pratt.

A long, powerful throw from Chivers was helped on by Jimmy Pearce and then Alan Gilzean before falling to the feet of Coates, who from just outside the 18-yard box cracked in a low right-foot shot that sizzled wide of goalkeeper Kevin Keelan's despairing dive. It was the only goal of a game that was described by one veteran reporter as "the dullest match ever witnessed at Wembley".

Match hero Coates, who settled down to score 23 goals in 229 league matches in a seven-year stay at Spurs, told me in his distinctive Co. Durham accent:

"I needed this goal as much for my own confidence as for the team. It was a bitter blow when I was told I'd be on the subs' bench. Norwich packed so many players into their own half that there didn't seem to be any room out there to breathe, let alone run. Happily, I got one sight of goal and let fly. It was one of the most satisfying goals I've ever scored. It was great to at last repay Bill Nicholson for having had the faith to buy me from Burnley. But I still think I should have started the game…"

The winning Spurs team:

Jennings
Kinnear England Beal Knowles
Pratt Perryman Peters Pearce
Gilzean Chivers

Sub: Coates

Bill Nicholson had mixed feelings about the victory:

"It was arguably the most disappointing performance we ever gave at Wembley, but I was so relieved and delighted for Ralph Coates. He'd been given a rough time by the spectators and even some of his own team-mates, having the mickey taken out of him because of his efforts to hide his increasing baldness. Ralph used to try to disguise it in the same way as Bobby Charlton, and it just became more pronounced. If you have

HAIR-RAISING FOR RALPH COATES

the sort of hairstyle he had, you'd better be able to play a bit because you couldn't miss him on the field. But the ball just wouldn't run for him and he was the target for a lot of cruel jeering and insults. I had been his manager for an England Under-23 match against Turkey in Ankara, and he scored a superb goal that made me think that one day I'd like to buy him. He was a lovely, unassuming boy who always gave 100 per cent, but after I'd paid a British record fee for him he found the weight of it like a sack of coal on his back. He really struggled to function, but he shut up a lot of his critics with that goal that won us the League Cup.

"A long throw from Chivers set up the Coates goal, an old tactic that we used in Dave Mackay's day because he could really hurl the ball prodigious distances. We would spend hours in training on the throw, and our two best headers – Mike England and Alan Gilzean – used to find positions in the penalty area to meet the ball. The idea was that if Martin held the ball in his left hand before throwing, it was going to be aimed at England, if in his right hand then Gilzean was going to receive it. Chiv, a very intelligent young man, kept forgetting which hand to signal his intent and – exasperated by the mix-ups – we told him to just concentrate on finding any team-mate. He certainly did that with the throw that eventually reached Coates!"

Steve recalls Ralph's anguish when he first joined Tottenham…

"From day one of Ralph arriving at White Hart Lane as the country's most expensive footballer you could almost see him questioning himself whether he had made a mistake joining us from Burnley, where he was the king of the castle and hugely respected. Now suddenly he was just one of a highly talented, tightly knit group of players and he struggled to settle into his new surroundings and find an identity. We were like a big family, and Ralph had to wait before he was accepted as one of us. He had the lovely, laid-back personality of a typical North-Eastener but had to run the gauntlet of the mickey-takers in our group, particularly John Pratt, Phil Beal, Terry Naylor and my best

buddy Phil Holder, a little man with a big personality who even Bill Nick called 'Chief'.

"Ralph was unfortunate to be losing his barnet at just the time he joined us and used to spend ages trying to comb over the growing bald spot. He had the same hairstyle as Bobby Charlton, who was getting loads of unwanted publicity because of his famous comb-over. Footballers are a cruel lot and we showed Ralph no mercy with our teasing and taunting; all in fun but it could cut deep with the man on the receiving end.

"Phil Beal was the most persistent prankster and nobody was safe when he was around (or when he was hiding after Ralph or anybody got caught out by his jokes). He used to make secret visits to party shops and buy the latest tricks to spring on unsuspecting victims, with Coates often in his firing line. While it was all good for team spirit, Bealy could often go a laugh too far.

"It did Ralph no favours that the supporters greeted him with loud choruses of: 'Ralph Coates, Ralph Coates, Ralphie Ralphie Coates; He's got no hair but we don't care, Ralphie Ralphie Coates...' Not the most flattering or motivational of chants.

"Bill called a meeting without Ralph and pleaded for us to go easy with the mickey-taking. He suspected with good reason that some of our squad slightly resented the money Ralph had cost and the handsome contract he was on. But that goal against Norwich helped give him new status and made him feel accepted, and Bill felt that he had not wasted that hundred and ninety grand after all."

Ralph ran leisure centres after his retirement from professional football but continued playing in Sunday teams until his late fifties. "I've always been happiest when playing the game," he told me during his period acting as a meeter-and-greeter with the Spurs legends. "I have to be honest and say my most satisfying time was when I was with Burnley. Everything came easily to me back then and I enjoyed being the leader of the pack at Turf Moor. There was too much pressure on me to live up to my fee when I arrived at Tottenham and suddenly it seemed more business than pleasure. But I eventually settled and always had huge respect for Bill Nicholson, who I know had to take a lot of stick because of all that money he spent on me.

"If I could go through it all again I would have more confidence in myself. I spent too much time worrying – about my form, my weight, my appearance, my hair, everything. I could play the game better than most, but never truly believed in myself until it was all over. Looking back, I was a much better player than I ever realised. Isn't that daft!"

Following a savage stroke, Ralph died in 2010 aged 64. He was much mourned by all those he had entertained with his skilled football. Ralph was a lovely bloke. If only he had believed in himself.

In the same month that he helped Spurs win the League Cup, the peerless Pat Jennings proved just why he was rated one of the world's greatest goalkeepers by making two penalty saves – from Kevin Keegan and Tommy Smith – in a First Division game against league leaders Liverpool at Anfield. No wonder he was elected Footballer of the Year that season. Bill Shankly, Liverpool's larger-than-life manager, one of Bill Nick's closest friends in football, said afterwards: "Jennings should be disqualified from playing with those hands, they're like bloody pink shovels." He was only half joking.

Spurs battled through to the semi-final in defence of the UEFA Cup. On the way they accounted for Lyn Oslo 12-3 on aggregate, Olympiakos Piraeus 4-1, Red Star Belgrade 2-1, and Vittoria Setubal 2-2 on the away goals rule as a Martin Chivers rocket in Portugal clinched a passport to the semi-finals. However, it was Spurs who would subsequently lose out on the contentious away goals rule after a titanic tussle with Shankly's Liverpool lions, despite two goals from Martin Peters in the second leg at White Hart Lane. The 2-2 aggregate scoreline signalled an end to Tottenham's momentous run. It was a cup campaign that stayed engraved on Steve Perryman's memory because, still short of his 21st birthday, he captained Spurs for the first time against Olympiakos in Greece.

"It was one of the proudest days of my young football life when Bill took me on one side as we prepared for the second leg of our tie with Olympiakos. 'Martin Peters has failed a fitness test,' he said, 'and I want you to take over as

skipper for this match. I'm also making you vice-captain so that in future you automatically take over if and when necessary.'

"Unusually for me, I was speechless. It seemed no time at all since I had been an apprentice at the club. Now I was going to lead the first team out in a vital European tie. I was enormously proud that Bill felt I was mature enough to skipper the side. He had never actually told me personally but said in several newspaper interviews how pleased he was with my progress. We go back to the very start of my league career when Bill told Norman Giller that I was 'a diamond of a prospect'. That was the only time he lavished me with praise. As I was to learn, it was not his style at all to compliment players, but he was very quick to give out bollockings to anybody giving less than their best.

"Bill just did not believe in praising players to their face because he wanted them always to keep their feet on the ground. I was content to accept that, although several of my team-mates thought he was mean not to pat them on their back occasionally. Some players need praise, like a comfort blanket. I was not one of them. I liked to be a self-motivator and I always played flat-out because I did not want to let Bill or the team down. I was my own biggest critic.

"The wonderful Cliffie Jones, who left Spurs for Fulham just as I was about to start my league career, still returns to the Tottenham ground at every opportunity as a distinguished club ambassador and loves tasting the atmosphere at the club. He told me that Bill had been just as miserly with his praise in the 'Glory Glory' days of the Double and the back-to-back FA Cup wins. 'I don't find it necessary to praise players for doing their job,' he used to say. 'Just remember that a pat on the back is only inches away from a kick up the arse.'

"I always played my heart out for Bill and the team. It reached the stage where my brother Ted, who had been a huge influence on my career, thought I overdid the running and hard work and he started to refuse to watch me play in a protest that really hurt me. Ted felt that I had *surrendered personal success for the sake of the team, covering for and encouraging my team-mates at the expense of my own game. He thought I had become such a committed team player that I had lost the individual flair that took the eye in my younger days. 'You've buried yourself so deep into the team ethic that you have lost the game that made you stand out,' he said, words that were possibly true but hurtful coming from my big brother. We had always been so close and he had supported and advised me every inch of the way in my career. Now he thought I had become the Invisible Man.*

"Maybe this is why I never got full England recognition apart from in the fairly meaningless match against Iceland, when I came on as sub. Didn't even start the game, so hardly the most auspicious international record, although I had 17 England Under-23 caps as consolation. But who was I to please – my brother Ted, or the master manager Bill Nicholson? I chose 'Sir Bill' and played the game the way he wanted me to. Team always first."

Sadly for those with Spurs in their blood, it was yet another final that was to spell the beginning of the end of the Bill Nicholson reign – and it was destined to end in tears.

Authors' warning: Tottenham fans of a nervous disposition might want to skip the next few pages. It does not make pretty reading.

CHAPTER 18

NIGHTMARE IN ROTTERDAM

Bill Nicholson called it "the saddest night of my life".

The night in question was 29 May 1974, which saw Tottenham take on Feyenoord in Rotterdam in the second leg of the UEFA Cup final. Unusually, Bill's misery was caused by what happened off rather than on the pitch, even though Spurs were soundly beaten 2-0 to give Feyenoord a 4-2 aggregate victory.

The UEFA Cup had been the exclusive property of Football League clubs for six successive years, but Feyenoord deservedly became the first Dutch winners of the trophy after a final that turned into the blackest event in Tottenham's proud history. And all this at the same ground where Bill's Spurs had experienced their greatest triumph, having become the first British team to win a major European trophy 11 years earlier.

Spurs had been flattered by a 2-2 draw in the first leg at White Hart Lane, a goal just before half-time from centre-half Mike England and an own goal by Joop van Daele cancelling out goals from the highly skilled midfield pairing of Willem Van Hanegem and Theo de Jong.

Feyenoord were comfortably the better team in the second leg, and a section of so-called Spurs fans could not stomach seeing their team being made to look strictly second best. Steve recalls:

"It was a match I've tried to erase from my memory. I had never known one like it. Usually you can blank out the crowd and get on with the game. But this night in Rotterdam was different. There was a sort of angry roar and we could see seats and bottles whizzing around as spectators fought

with each other and battled with the police. All the players had wives, girlfriends and relatives at the match and we could not help but worry whether they were all right.

"Gradually we pieced together what was happening and, sorry to say, it seemed as if our fans had started the trouble after we'd had a good-looking goal by Chris McGrath turned down. Then, when Feyenoord scored three minutes before the break, a mob of them invaded the pitch, clearly trying to get the game abandoned because we were losing. For the first time, I was ashamed of a minority of our supporters, who were rioting like a small army of Neanderthals. I wish I could claim it was the Dutch causing the mayhem, but it was the Brits. It was so-called Tottenham supporters blackening the club's good name.

"Bill Nick would normally have come into the dressing room at half-time and galvanised us with one of his rallying calls, but instead he had to arm himself with a megaphone and plead with the fans to behave themselves. I was in the dressing room getting ready for the second half so didn't see it, but I'm told he was crying as he called for an end to the violence. His words fell on deaf ears.

"The police were still battling for control as the second half started, and the Dutch spectators started to yell in English: 'Go home English thugs. We don't want you here.'

"It was sickening and our skipper Martin Peters was gesturing to the crowd to calm down. There was choking smoke drifting across the pitch from fires being lit in the stands, and it was the ugliest I have ever known it in a football stadium. I was amazed that the game was not called off, but the referee was determined not to let the hooligans succeed and he got the match finished, with Feyenoord deserving 4-2 aggregate winners.

"Bill was in a daze at the end, wandering around like a zombie. In the coach ride back to our hotel he kept repeating: 'What have they done to my game... what have they done to my game...?'

"It was an image that stuck with me for years and the lowest point in my career. Bill clearly felt the same."

NIGHTMARE IN ROTTERDAM

The Dutch masters made sure of their victory with their second goal – scored by Peter Ressel – minutes before the final whistle. This sparked another riot by Spurs followers that led to 70 arrests and 200 spectators being treated for injuries. It was like a scene from a Martin Scorsese film.

Bill Nicholson, choking back tears, had – as Steve confirms – appealed by megaphone and then over the public address system for sanity. "You hooligans are a disgrace to Tottenham Hotspur and a disgrace to England," he said. "This is a game of football – not a war."

That night Bill was close to walking out on the club that had been his life. He said in an emotional after-match statement:

"This is the saddest night of my life. It makes you wonder if it is all worth it when you see people behaving like animals. It is not just a football problem. It's a social problem, and hooliganism is eating into our great game. Questions should be asked as to whether there is enough discipline in schools. Feyenoord were worthy winners, and I am extremely embarrassed that a minority among our supporters – people we should disown – were unable to accept the fact that we were beaten by a better side."

Bill Nick festered and fretted throughout the summer, waiting for the new season for the first time in his career without enthusiasm. He felt his beloved Spurs had been badly wounded by the incident in Rotterdam, and he was disillusioned by the way widespread hooliganism was scarring the face of the once beautiful game. He had suddenly lost the ability to motivate his players, and he slipped into a deep depression as Spurs got off to their worst start ever with four successive defeats.

While his world was crashing around him, Bill got involved in a stand-off with his vice-captain Steve Perryman – my writing partner – and there was talk of literally sending him to Coventry... City that is, not to make him ostracised.

> *"Bill was a shell of the man he had been before that awful night in Rotterdam. I began to think that maybe I should have listened to my brother Ted rather than Bill. Selfish thoughts come to the surface at times of crisis like this. Had I given too much to the team and not done enough to promote my own skills? People thought of me as a 'fetcher*

and carrier' because that was the role I had settled for, putting team needs first at all times. It all came to a head when Charlie Faulkner, the scout who played a big part in me joining Spurs, telephoned to say he had got into a big row with Bill and his sidekick Eddie Baily, who both considered my legs had 'gone'. Not the sort of thing you want to hear at the age of 22!

"Bill contacted me to say that Coventry had asked for me as a part of a deal for two of their players coming to Spurs. Was I interested? The fact that he had even considered it showed that he would let me go. This was not the Bill Nicholson I had grown to admire and even love like a second father. This Bill Nicholson was shot to pieces. That bad, sad night in Rotterdam had sent him over the edge.

"I was in the process of discussing it with my family when news broke that Bill had resigned. I knew from our last conversation that Bill needed to make the break for the good of his health. The pressure of the job had broken Arthur Rowe and Jimmy Anderson before him. Now he had finally been beaten down after taking on far too much responsibility for too long. I had respected him for his decisiveness, and his constant encouragement for me to anticipate what was happening next on the pitch. It had become a trademark of my game, anticipation. Knowing what was about to happen and being there to take advantage of the moment. Anticipation, the word that Bill had kept drumming into me. Despite all that, I had not anticipated him wanting me to go to Coventry!

"It was a time of turmoil in both our careers, and suddenly the man I most admired in football had gone. And Coventry was never mentioned again."

It was not only hooliganism that had robbed Bill of his appetite, but also player power and greed, as he later revealed:

"Players have become impossible. They talk all the time about security, but they are not prepared to work for it. I am abused by players when they come to see me. There is no longer respect."

NIGHTMARE IN ROTTERDAM

He also dropped a bombshell at a press conference by divulging:

> "I have recently found it impossible to get the players I want because at Tottenham we pride ourselves in not making under-the-counter payments. It is expected in the London area for players to ask for £7,000 tax free. That's the minimum asking price by the agents of players. I want no part of that world."

Skipper Martin Peters and long-serving defender Phil Beal made a private visit to Nicholson on behalf of the players to ask him to change his mind and stay on, but he said there was no going back. Steve had been invited to attend the meeting but he politely declined. The other players did not know of his falling out with the manager and the suggestion that he should consider going to Coventry.

It was a confusing and contentious time – both for my co-author and for our hero, Bill. You couldn't make it up. The Tottenham directors wrung their hands and allowed the Master of White Hart Lane to leave, when an arm around the shoulders and warm words of encouragement could have made him change his mind.

There were strong rumours that Lane icon Danny Blanchflower would take over. Danny and I kept in close touch with each other after I had gone off into the freelancing world, when one of my roles was 'The Judge' at *The Sun*, answering readers' questions and settling pub arguments. One day I received a question on a postcard (those were the days, my friends) that read: "If the job offer came along, would Danny Blanchflower consider returning to football as manager of Spurs?"

I rang Danny boy at his regular hangout in the private members' lounge at Wentworth Golf Club, which he had made a second home. Danny, who could be witty, wise and weird in equal measure, and all within one thought process, prided himself on never ducking a question, but on this occasion he was unusually prickly.

"All right, what do you know?" he asked. "I'm sworn to secrecy."

Purely by coincidence I had stumbled on a developing story of major proportions.

"This is a genuine question from a reader," I told him. "What's going on?"

There was a long silence, which was a rare thing when talking to Danny, because he liked to fill every waking moment with original ideas and unique observations. To wind him up, I used to call him Danny Blarneyflower.

"I don't want to tell you on the telephone," he said, mysteriously. "Meet me at the Alex Forbes café tomorrow at noon." This was a coffee house near Blackfriars Station, a short walk from Fleet Street. It was years since it had been owned by former Arsenal star Alex Forbes, but it was still known to football journos by his name. It was the sort of nondescript place where you could melt into the background while meeting contacts.

There was a touch of the John Le Carré spy thriller about Danny's entrance into the coffee house. He was looking around furtively as if making sure he had not been followed.

"What's with all the cloak and dagger stuff?" I asked.

Danny was obviously agonising. "I'm going to have to ask you to give me your word that all I am about to tell you is confidential," he said. "You're going to be desperate to break the story, but because I cannot tell a lie, I'm going to take you into my confidence. If it leaks, it could stop me getting a job I have always dreamed about – manager of Spurs."

I spluttered into my coffee cup.

"You've known me long enough to realise you can trust me," I said. "Thank goodness I'm not a staff reporter anymore. My duty then would be to the newspaper."

"And then I wouldn't be telling you," replied Danny, with his usual distinctive logic. "The fact is that Bill Nick is on the point of resigning from Spurs, and he wants to put my name forward as his successor."

The newspaperman in me was aching to get that sensational story into print, but Danny had tied me into a straitjacket of secrecy.

"When you rang me and asked that question as 'The Judge', I thought it was your crafty way of saying you were on to the story," he explained. "Bill confided in me a week ago that he was going and that he wanted to recommend me as his successor. I've been trying to talk him out of it. But this is not the Bill Nicholson of old. I've never known him so low and so lacking in appetite for the game that has been his life. He is completely disillusioned with football, or the politics of it. Bill doesn't like what he sees with the galloping greed of the players, and the violence on the terraces has sickened him. I said that perhaps he was trying to pass me a poisoned chalice."

It was two weeks before Nicholson's stunning decision to quit became public, and the veteran manager made no secret of the fact that he wanted Tottenham icon Danny Blanchflower to take over from him. He had even teed-up ex-Leeds playmaker Johnny Giles as player-coach.

The board did not take kindly to Bill selecting his own successor and decided to show they were in charge. They instead chose to hand the reins to Danny's fellow Irishman Terry Neill, a man with Arsenal-red blood.

A desperately disappointed Danny told me:

"It can only end in tears. Terry is an intelligent man with lots of bright ideas, but he has as much chance of being accepted at Tottenham as the Archbishop of Canterbury has of being welcomed at the Vatican. He is Arsenal through and through. If I had got the job I would have kept Bill Nicholson on as a backroom consultant. It was madness that the board let him go with all his experience and knowledge. It was the one management job for which I would willingly have returned to the game. I guess the directors have got their own back on me because I always refused to bow the knee to them."

Bill Nicholson was devastated that the board had ignored his advice and told me:

"Danny was perfect for the job. He knew the traditions and the ways of Tottenham and would have slipped into my shoes comfortably and with style. The fans and the players would have welcomed him with open arms. He had Spurs in his soul. I have never been so embarrassed in all my life when the board totally ignored my advice and just refused to consider Danny.

"I thought that after all my service to the club I was entitled to think I could give guidance as to who would be right to take over. But they appointed Terry Neill without consulting me. I would have been happy to stay on and advise Danny, without interfering. He has always been his own man, but I know he

would have been willing to listen to me when there was any situation with which he needed my considerable experience.

"Everything I did was with the good of Tottenham in mind. I had given everything to the club and now they had turned their back on me."

CHAPTER 19

ON THE DOLE

On 29 August 1974, 'Mr Tottenham' handed in his resignation, bringing to a (temporary) end 39 years of service to the club, 16 of them as the most successful manager in Spurs' history. Meanwhile, instead of going to Coventry, Steve 'Skip' Perryman stayed on at White Hart Lane for another 13 years and 500-plus games.

Terry Neill started his brief reign by bringing in Scottish striker John Duncan, but it was an 'old hand' who saved Tottenham from what looked certain relegation. Martin Chivers, recalled after two months in the wilderness, scored one of the goals as Spurs just beat the drop with a 4-2 victory over Leeds in a nail-nibbling end-of-season game at White Hart Lane.

Bill Nick and Eddie Baily made quiet returns to football in the summer of 1975, both of them joining West Ham in scouting and consultant roles after the humiliation of signing on the dole.

Bill was restrained with his response to what virtually added up to a dismissal, even though he insisted he had resigned.

The man himself told me a little while after the dust had settled:

"The truth is I was burned out and could not have carried on in the state of mind I had got myself into. I needed a break and did not have the energy or appetite to fight my corner. Eddie was very, very angry and wanted me to jump up and down with him, but I just couldn't bring myself to battle on. My wife saw me in a dark place and was relieved that I was giving up the job. Something it had taught me is that nobody should manage a club for more than five years. It wears you out and you just cannot give the job the concentration it requires. There are so

many pressures. Just selecting the team is a bigger headache than most people face in their workplace. You immediately make yourself unpopular with the players you leave out and their relatives and fans. Everybody thinks they can pick a better team than you. Somebody once called it the 'Impossible Job'. There is no way you can keep everybody happy.

"Eddie didn't like it, but I told him we had become dinosaurs. The game has changed out of sight. Money is now the god, when in my professional footballer days playing the game was everything. Average footballers are asking for fortunes, and agents are playing clubs and managers off against each other.

"Worst thing of all, as was proved in Rotterdam, is that we have lost control of our younger supporters. They seem to think they are in charge, and if there's a decision they disagree with they want to referee the match. It's a sort of anarchy.

"What happened in Holland was the breaking point for me. Hooligans running riot. I want no part of that. One of my daughters travelled to the game by ferry and had to lock herself in her cabin because she was terrified of the many drunken fans on board. What sort of behaviour is that? It's a massive social problem and it's going to take strong discipline to sort it out.

"I've had some great times in the job and am proud of my record. Some of the football has been out of this world and I've been lucky to call on many of the greatest footballers of modern times. The likes of Greavsie, Dave Mackay, Danny Blanchflower, Pat Jennings and Jonesie have been world-class, and I was fortunate to play with wonderful footballers like Ronnie Burgess, the Duke and dear old Eddie Baily, whose bark is much worse than his bite. All he ever wanted was to get the best from our players. Sometimes he went too far with his demands, but that's Eddie.

"Signing on the dole was the most humiliating thing I've ever had to do. The West Ham pair of John Lyall and Ron Greenwood were among those who kindly came forward to help both Eddie and me in our hour of need and we are so grateful that they gave us employment in the game that we love. I always think of Eddie as your typical Cockney with a bit of the 'Spirit of the Blitz' about him. You can't knock him down for long and he has this bounce about him that is infectious."

ON THE DOLE

Meantime, Terry Neill was fighting an uphill battle to pump confidence and belief into his Tottenham players. He did not mince words after a goalless draw with Arsenal at White Hart Lane: "I apologise to everybody who paid good money to watch this rubbish. It made me feel ashamed. It was the kind of stuff that could kill football."

Ouch, that was tougher and more hard-hitting than anything 'Sir Bill' had needed to say in his 16 years in the hot seat.

Terry, whom I had known and liked since his days as a teenager under Billy Wright at Highbury, had a lot of big ideas but he never truly settled at White Hart Lane. Die-hard Tottenham fans could not accept him as 'one of us'. Most could not look at him without seeing red. They might have changed their mind if he had managed to pull off an audacious transfer deal in February 1976. He discovered that Johan Cruyff was unsettled at Barcelona and moved in with a bid that was ultimately turned down. Johan Cruyff in a Tottenham shirt. Now that would have been something special...

Three days after he had been rebuffed by the Dutchman, Neill gave a full league debut to a 17-year-old midfield player who would one day become Cruyff-class with his passing and ball control. Enter Glenn Hoddle, who marked his arrival on the senior stage by firing a spectacular shot past Stoke City and England goalkeeper Peter Shilton.

Glenn told me a lovely story about Bill, who was manager when he signed for Tottenham as an apprentice shortly before he quit his job:

"I was playing in a youth match for Tottenham and knew that the great man [Bill] was on the touchline watching as I scored a hat-trick. He came into the dressing room after the final whistle and I preened myself as I prepared to be praised.

"'Young man, you should have had only two goals,' he said. 'For that third goal you should have passed the ball to a team-mate who was better placed rather than taking a gamble on shooting.' That was it, and then he left me making goldfish movements with my mouth. And d'you know something, he was right! I should have passed the ball. He had made me think and analyse my play. It was a precious insight into why he was such a great manager."

Steve was now an 'old man' of 22 and has clear memories of that period in Tottenham history when 'Sir Bill' was no longer an influence on either him or the club he had served since the mid-1930s:

> *"They were strange times because few of us could remember a moment when Bill was not dictating things at Tottenham. I personally found Terry Neill and his assistant Wilf Dixon comfortable to work with, and I was encouraged by Terry's first words to me when he arrived at White Hart Lane: 'Steve, just so you know... you're not going anywhere.' That was all he said before walking away to drop pollen on somebody else, but it was reassuring to hear and proved that I was still wanted at Spurs.*
>
> *"You need to remember that Terry had not long retired and was still only 32. He was the same vintage as some of our senior players, who found it difficult to accept that he was giving them orders when just in the last few seasons he had been a rival – an Arsenal man – on the pitch. Within a year Mike England, Bealy (with his pranks) and Martin Peters had moved on, and Big Chiv and lovely Knowlesy were not far behind.*
>
> *"Our goalkeeper Pat Jennings was an old Northern Ireland team-mate of Terry's and he told me we could not be in better hands. 'Terry knows and loves his football,' Pat said to me. 'Give him your usual 100 per cent and he will respond in kind.' I had huge respect for Pat and took his word for it. Terry got my full concentration and effort. To be honest, I knew no other way.*
>
> *"It was a changing of the guard, and I was installed as club captain – an honour that I took very seriously. I was extremely conscious that I was walking in the footsteps of giants of the game... Ron Burgess, Blanchflower, Mackay, Mullery, Peters. All Tottenham gods. When Terry Neill told me I was confirmed as skipper, he said: 'Remember, you're MY captain.' I had the balls to reply, 'No, gaffer. I'm the Tottenham captain. I will be playing for the team.'*
>
> *"This proved that Bill Nicholson's 'team-first' approach had stuck with me, and I was delighted that Bill and I had mended our bridges and were back on good terms. I had*

bumped into him one day on my way to the ground when he was in his front garden, a few hundred yards from the Lane. We talked just as in old times as if the Coventry conversation had never happened. I would bet he did not remember it as he was in such a state at the time.

"I was moved later that day to telephone him. 'I just wanted to say that I'm sorry I did not do better for you last season,' I said, 'and I'm ringing to thank you for all you've done for me. You have made me what I am today.'

"Typical Bill, he was embarrassed to have somebody praising him. He thanked me and from that day on we talked at every opportunity like old friends. What a man."

Terry Neill was not at Spurs to see Glenn Hoddle grow into the footballing master he later became, nor Steve Perryman develop into a captain supreme. In July 1976 he followed his heart and went home to Highbury as Arsenal manager in succession to Bertie Mee.

Sometime later I caught up with Terry, who remained a close pal of mine, and he told me: "I was arrogant enough to think I could follow in Bill Nick's footsteps, but his boots were too big for anybody.

"I had always been fond of Bill, and I made a mistake not to appoint him as a consultant when I was first appointed. I took the old-fashioned view that I was a new broom who did not want the old broom getting in my way. He was and remains one of the all-time great managers, a thorough gentleman and an iconic coach. He deserves a statue at Tottenham. And please remind all those Spurs fans who hated me that I was the man who brought Keith Burkinshaw to Tottenham!"

The killer blow was that Terry later took the irreplaceable Pat Jennings to Arsenal with him after the board had refused to give the greatest of all goalkeepers a loan to help buy his house.

I contacted Bill Nick for his verdict on the transfer. He preferred not to be quoted. "It's none of my business," he said, adding under his breath, "The fools ... the bloody fools."

There was something to cheer up Bill and Darkie when he was invited to Buckingham Palace in 1975 to receive an OBE for his services to football. But we all know – we all know – it should have been a knighthood. Bill was now back in the game he loved as a scout with West Ham, but he was a fish out of water. Tottenham is where he belonged.

CHAPTER 20

BACK FROM THE WILDERNESS

When Terry Neill and his right-hand man Wilf Dixon departed for 'that other club' in North London, they left behind a little-known coach called Keith Burkinshaw. The Spurs directors promoted him to the Tottenham hot seat, and one of the first things he did – sensibly and obviously – was to invite Bill Nicholson back in a scouting and advisory role.

Everybody – fans, players, directors, the media circus – liked Keith, an ex-Barnsley miner who came up the hard way and had Nicholson-style principles and work ethic. He had been a peripheral defender at Liverpool before giving long service at the football outposts of Workington and Scunthorpe.

Keith learned his coaching trade in Zambia and then with Newcastle, joining Spurs in 1975 – one of Terry Neill's first signings for the backroom team. Terry had met him on coaching courses and was impressed by his ideas and initiative.

Like Bill Nick, Burkinshaw was a dour Yorkshireman who wore blinkers that meant he saw nothing but the world of football. He said after persuading Bill to leave his chief scout role at West Ham and return 'home' in July 1976: "Bringing Bill back into the Tottenham fold is a no-brainer. He's rich with experience and knows his football inside out. I have no thought or fear that he will interfere. His knowledge is there for me to call on if necessary and he's totally committed to the Tottenham cause. I cannot think of anybody more respected and admired throughout the game. It's a privilege to have him back at the club where he belongs."

Bill was like a boy who had got what he wanted for Christmas:

"It took me all of two seconds to make up my mind to accept Keith's kind offer to return to the club that had been my life, although I asked for time to think about it. I told Eddie Baily what I was going to do and he called me every name under the sun. I heard on the grapevine that the directors who were there at the end of my managing career were themselves being shunted out, so that removed the only barrier to my returning.

"Everybody seemed delighted with the move except Eddie. We fell out over my decision but made up later and got back on talking terms. It was such a relief to be back at the club I loved but without the strain and pressure of management.

"I was a huge admirer of Keith – I saw a lot of the younger me in him. He was conscientious, had an excellent grasp of football tactics, ruled the players with common-sense strictness but was flexible and approachable, and he delegated sensibly. His fine assistant, Pat Welton, shouldered a lot of the work and made Keith's life easier. I realised I had taken on too much in my time and it eventually caught up with me.

"Darkie was delighted that I returned because she knew how much I missed the club I'd been with since I was a 17-year-old boy, but she couldn't believe the time I spent travelling to midweek matches all over the country. I watched more games even than when I was managing, and poor Darkie just threw her arms up in the air in despair and told me that football was my mistress. She could be much funnier than me. I was very lucky to have her."

Bill was there to commiserate with and support Keith when his first season in full control climaxed in the ultimate humiliation: bottom of the pile and thus relegation to the second tier, ending a 27-year unbroken run for Spurs at the top table.

Today, Keith would have been hounded out by the keyboard warriors on social media, but the club's directors kept faith with him and he rewarded their confidence by leading Tottenham straight back up again – with Steve Perryman inevitably leading from the front...

"Relegation! I wouldn't wish it on my worst enemy. I don't think I'd ever been so miserable as the day we dropped into

the Second Division. I felt I'd let everybody down – the fans, the directors, my family. I quietly made a vow to myself that I'd lead the team right back up again. I didn't shout about it from the rooftops. The only person I told we'd come right back up again was Alfie Conn, a very clever – sometimes too clever for his own good – forward, who we had just sold to Celtic. He gave an interview to the Scottish papers in which he said 'the Cockney mafia' had driven him out of White Hart Lane, meaning, I guess, me, Bealy, John Pratt and Terry Naylor. I wasn't going to let him get away with that. I telephoned him and said I'd accept his apology when we were promoted. I thought it was an offer he couldn't refuse, but I'm still waiting for his call.

"By then 'Sir Bill' was back at the Lane in the capacity of chief scout. He kept his nose out of Keith's business but was there for us, encouraging and telling us to keep our heads up. One of his mantras was: 'You're too good for the Second Division. You have a target – promotion. Go for it.' He was a great shoulder for Keith."

With the season into its last embers, Tottenham, Bolton and Southampton were neck and neck at the top of the table, with Brighton just two points behind. Spurs clinched an instant return to the First Division with a tense, goalless draw against Southampton, pipping Brighton on goal difference for third place. This, of course, was before play-offs were introduced, and it was a finale that tested nerves like never before. Many Spurs fans talked of feeling physically sick during that last game against the Saints.

Few will forget the highlight of that promotion season, a 9-0 thrashing of Bristol Rovers at the Lane on 22 October 1977. Colin Lee – signed from Torquay just 48 hours earlier for £60,000 to partner the bullocking Ian Moores – found the passes from Hoddle and thrusting winger Peter Taylor like a silver-plate service after his days down the league, and he scored four goals in the humiliation of Rovers. Just a week earlier Spurs had gone down to a 4-1 defeat against Charlton Athletic. The ups and downs of football.

While Lee took all the headlines, the nearest rival to him as the man of the match was the unsung John Pratt, who continually won the ball in midfield and then fed it to Glenn Hoddle, who finished off the banquet with a stunning strike that put a golden seal on Tottenham's record league victory. It was just a glimpse of the Hoddle magic that was waiting to be unwrapped once the club returned to the First Division stage.

Bill watched it all from a distance...

"I deliberately stayed in the background, quietly letting Keith know I was there for him if he needed me. We had a lot of conversations, bouncing thoughts off each other, but I was careful not to interfere. I was a sounding board and tossed in the occasional thought based on all my years of experience. But I never volunteered an opinion unless I was invited to have a say. I'd done all the managing that I had wanted to, thank you very much. Keith kept his head and continued to concentrate on getting the basics right.

"I knew it would come right in the end because he was well-organised and had a strategy that called for the players to do the simple things well. He did not complicate matters with the sort of mumbo jumbo I hear from some coaches.

"The success I had with the 'Push and Run' team as a player and as manager of the Double side and all that we achieved in FA Cups and in Europe was because we kept everything simple – the Spurs way.

"The common denominator of all the great Tottenham sides in my time has been that they've had as their main asset outstanding teamwork. Of course there have been exceptional individuals, like Greaves and Gilzean, Blanchflower, White and Mackay, Burgess and Baily, and today Hoddle and Ardiles, but they have each followed the Tottenham tradition and put the team first. As I was told all those years ago in my young days with Gravesend & Northfleet – there is no 'I' in team. So, so true.

"It somehow got around that Tottenham's success under Keith was down to me. That was nonsense. Everything they achieved was because of what Keith and his coaching staff did. He deserves all the credit. I did nothing but give my best advice when asked."

BACK FROM THE WILDERNESS

Now comes one of our interludes here while I do some unashamed name dropping as I recall how I stumbled on the fact that Tottenham were involved in the most sensational transfer business the game had yet known – in an era when British football was played exclusively by British players.

The master of mirth Eric Morecambe – of all people – knew before most of us that Spurs were about to pull off the most sensational transfer coup in British football history in the summer of 1978, and it was Bill Nicholson, no less, who made it all happen.

Please be patient while I explain; or – as Eric would have said – while I try to get the words down, not necessarily in the right order.

For several years I had the privilege and pleasure of working with Eric on regular newspaper columns for the *Daily Express* and the magazine *Titbits*, which I assure you was a weekly, all-topics chat publication and nothing to do with a woman's anatomy. Eric's share of the fees used to be paid to Luton Town Football Club, where he was the jester director who got the Hatters more publicity than they'd had before or since.

The manager at Luton for much of Eric's time on the board was a charismatic character called Harry Haslam, who was rarely seen without a smile on his face as he lived up to his nickname 'Happy Harry'. Whenever I used to be in the company of Eric and Harry at Luton's Kenilworth Road ground, it was a toss-up who got more laughs. Yes, Harry was that funny.

Now to get to the point: in 1978 Haslam took over at Sheffield United but still kept in close contact with the Harpenden-based comedian. I was discussing our column with Eric when he said: "Shall we write about the two Argies who are going to play in England? You know, lines like it takes two to tango but it will be more of a knees-up when 'Bites Yer Legs' gets stuck into them?"

Eric often had me speechless with laughter, but this time I was lost for words because of the unusual facts he was offering.

"What two Argentines?" I asked. "Is this a joke?"

He then explained how Haslam had told him that his Argentine coach, Oscar Arce, had wanted him to buy two members of the squad who had just won the World Cup in Buenos Aires. Sheffield United could not afford them and so Harry had tipped off two of his closest friends in the game – Bill Nicholson at Tottenham and Terry Neill at Arsenal.

The names of the two players who were desperate to play in England: Osvaldo Ardiles and Ricardo Villa. I immediately telephoned Bill Nick and came straight to the point: "Bill, what d'you know of Osvaldo Ardiles and Ricardo Villa?"

There was a silence on the phone that could have been measured in fathoms.

"What do YOU know?" he finally asked.

I told him about my conversation with Eric.

"Well Eric is bang on the ball," he said. "Even as I speak Keith is in Argentina hopefully wrapping up the deal. I passed on Harry's tip to Keith and the directors, and they are as excited as me about the possibility of signing them. We know Arsenal are interested but thanks to Harry we've got a head start."

Driven by the hungry, freelance writer inside me, I contacted powerhouse *Sun* sports editor Frank Nicklin with the tip. "Too late, old son," he said. "It's just come over the wires from Buenos Aires. Burkinshaw has signed them both. We're leading the front and back pages on it in the morning. It's the soccer story of the century: Spurs Beat Arsenal In Argie Bargie." Yes, that was how Frank talked – in *Sun* headlines.

Sure enough, Ardiles and Villa arrived at the Lane at the start of what was a revolution in the British game. Both were wonderful ambassadors for football, for Tottenham and for their country, and Villa's magical solo goal in the 1981 FA Cup final replay against Manchester City has been cemented into Spurs folklore.

Spurs were boldly making the most of the Professional Football Association's decision to lift the ban on foreign players, and the newly introduced freedom of contract suddenly made the Football League an attractive proposition for overseas players.

It was a revolution started by Tottenham, and it quickly brought rewards.

Bill Nicholson, quietly looked on in the background with a satisfied smile knowing it was all being done the simple way. The Spurs way.

Meanwhile there was a boardroom revolution going on at the Lane while Burkinshaw was concentrating on the return to the top table. Property developers Irving Scholar and Paul Bobroff bought out the Wale family shares and floated the club on the Stock Exchange. It was a move that was to have massive consequences for the club.

After their 'lost' year in the Second Division, Tottenham took a season to find their feet back at the top table, and then came into the 1980s with something of a swagger, a lot of style and a hint of a smile as Bill Nicholson concentrated on his role as chief scout. He was proving he still had an eye for talent by organising the purchase of bargain buys such as Gary Mabbutt, Tony Galvin and Graham Roberts.

And, of course – almost as footballing folklore demanded – Spurs marked the first season of the decade, 1980/81, with a major trophy, and stamped for ever with that magical goal by Ricky Villa against Manchester City. Then, with a replay victory over Queens Park Rangers in 1982, they made it back-to-back FA Cup triumphs – and collecting the treasured trophy each time after the climb up the 39 steps was our very own Steve 'Skip' Perryman...

"What days they were! The excitement caused by the signing of Ossie and Ricky could be measured on the Richter scale. I became and remain very close friends with Osvaldo, a gifted footballer and a wonderful human being. I introduced them both to Bill, and explained how he was 'Mr Spurs' – each of them always showed him huge respect. They treated him like a favourite granddad.

"Bill, like me, was particularly taken with Ardiles. He was a very intelligent man who had studied for a law degree until football claimed all his attention. At every opportunity Bill and Ossie picked each other's brains about football tactics and discussed the differences between the game here and in South America. Two masters of the game finding common ground through the language of football that both spoke fluently.

"Ricardo was harder to converse with when he first arrived because his English was poor, but the man with a farming background was warm and friendly – like a big bear – and of course he will always be a cult figure because of that FA Cup final goal.

"I clearly remember Bill being concerned about controlling the number of foreign players allowed to play in the league. Sure enough, just as he constantly predicted, it is now difficult to find more than a handful of homegrown players in the top teams. And the Premier League clubs

continually prefer foreign managers and coaches to British ones. Bill was right to be worried. We now have a British game played at the top mainly by overseas footballers, coached and managed by foreigners and ownership of the major clubs is largely foreign.

"Bill warned of the dangers. He was always a visionary."

I interviewed Bill on the eve of him receiving an award from the FA Coaches Association for his lifetime service to the game. He told me:

"It is a great honour to be recognised by my peers. I have been dedicated to coaching ever since Walter Winterbottom introduced coaching courses immediately after the Second World War. With the right instruction and discipline, good footballers can become great and great footballers geniuses. There is not a player in the world who cannot be improved by the wisdom and vision of a good coach. I will also concede that bad, blinkered coaches can do great harm. Packing nine players in defence has never been my idea of how to play the game. My mantra has always been: 'Make it simple but make it positive.' We should always remember to try to entertain the spectators, not bore them.

"I care deeply about the future of our game, and we must be careful to protect it. We must control too much of a lurch towards commercialisation, and I have to say I am concerned about too great an influence by television. We must make sure the tail does not wag the dog. The day television is allowed to dictate where and when games should be played will be a defeat for the football spectators, who should always come first in our consideration.

"The powers-that-be must be careful not to let the game be run by outsiders. I am all in favour of allowing foreign footballers and coaches in but not to the detriment of encouraging home-grown talent.

"I have devoted my life to football and have been proud to have had such a long association with Tottenham Hotspur. This award from my fellow coaches fills me with great pride. It is the icing on the cake of my career."

Bill Nicholson, the coach's coach.

CHAPTER 21

AT HOME WITH THE MASTER

Another of our interludes, this time to visit 'Sir Bill' at home. This was an interview he gave me when I was sounding him out for a proposed appearance on a television programme I had devised in my previous life as a scriptwriter (14 years with the *This Is Your Life* team). Come with me back to the summer of 2001 and shortly before Bill was awarded the second of his long overdue testimonial matches, and please forgive some doubling up of quotes from earlier in the book. Bill the Sage was always worth repeating…

It was a double-decker red bus that had taken me to my first meeting with Bill Nicholson in 1958, and now here I was 43 years later in my Spurs-blue 4.2 Jaguar driving to see The Master for what was to prove our last face-to-face interview in which I was sounding him out for a proposed appearance on a television programme I had devised.

This was a series called *Who's the Greatest?*, and we were planning to feature Jimmy Greaves against Kenny Dalglish in a revival of my show that had run on ITV in the 1980s. I wanted to know whether Bill would be prepared to appear as a witness for Greavsie, while also craftily picking his brains for more treasured recollections about all things Spurs.

I prepared to park my flash car outside his modest but welcoming home, a small, unpretentious house once owned by Spurs and rented to him until he became sole owner in the 1960s for a couple of thousand pounds. It was close enough to the Lane that on match days you could hear the roar of the crowd.

Bill opened his front door as I pulled up, leaning heavily on a stick that was his one concession to galloping old age. "I remember you when you couldn't afford a bike," was his opening shot, immediately reviving memories of the banter we always used to share when I was doing my bread-and-butter job of football reporting. "You can't park there," he said. "You'll get a ticket. Drive round the back where you'll find our garage in a block. I won't charge you for taking our space. First right and then an immediate left."

Bill Nick, looking all of his 82 years, was still showing the way; still giving directions. Keep it simple. Give it and go. When not in possession, get in position.

The delightful Darkie demanded I have a cup of tea and then disappeared to the local shops – walking, I noticed, rather than cycling – leaving her beloved Bill and I to our rose-coloured recollections; or perhaps that should be blue and white.

The Nicholsons, approaching their diamond wedding anniversary, had one of those end-of-terrace houses that hugs you – nothing whatsoever ostentatious yet warm, welcoming and filled with friendliness. Their snug lounge led into an extension that was decorated with family photographs, mostly of daughters Linda and Jean and much-loved grandchildren. Just a framed photo of Bill with Darkie proudly showing off his OBE medallion in the Buckingham Palace forecourt gave any hint that this was the home of a hero. On the far wall hung the only sign that this was a football abode – a print of an oil painting depicting an FA Cup final at Wembley, sent out by the Football Association to mark their centenary. The match in question? The 1962 FA Cup final, which saw Spurs defeat Burnley 3-1 – one of Bill's most memorable triumphs.

This was the comfortable sanctuary to which Bill used to escape after all those matches in vast stadiums filled with cheering, chanting fans. What a contrast.

"Still tending your allotment?" I asked from my seat on the sofa, with him relaxed opposite me in his favourite, well-worn armchair, wearing a cardigan and Marks & Spencer slippers.

His hair was still military-short, but the once gingery, later steel grey mane had surrendered to a whiteness that would have matched a Spurs shirt.

"No, the old joints are not up to it now," he said. "But the neighbours keep it tidy and under control. The blackberry bush I planted is still there and giving us fruit."

Just a few months earlier, during the welter of litigation that surrounded the club that summer, there had been a tense exchange in the High Court. Former chairman Sir Alan Sugar, in his libel action against Associated Newspapers, denied vehemently the accusation by the newspaper's QC that, "On one occasion you were introduced to Bill Nicholson and were heard to say: 'Who is that old git?'"

When it was reported I remember all supporters with Spurs in their soul were outraged. This was like not knowing who lived at Buckingham Palace.

"What did you think of that?" I asked Bill, convinced he would give me one of his famous blanks.

"I thought it was hilarious," he said, unexpectedly. "I could have said exactly the same thing about Sugar, who looks nearly as old as me!"

When I tried to press Bill on the subject of boardroom battles and bungs, he waved a finger at me like an admonishing headmaster. "How long have we known each other?"

"More than 40 years," I said.

"And when have you ever known me get involved in politics? It is just not my scene. All I was ever interested in was the football. Keith Burkinshaw shared my views on that and it's why he quit the club. He was a first-class manager and I thought it was bonkers when the board let him go. The only time I got into politics was when I tried to get Danny Blanchflower appointed as my successor as manager, and all that got me was the embarrassment of having the board completely ignore my advice."

I could sense Bill was uncomfortable talking club matters, perhaps conscious that he was still Tottenham's Honorary President, so I changed the subject.

"We are reviving a TV series I dreamt up in the 1980s called *Who's the Greatest?*" I explained, "and one of our first shows will feature celebrities arguing the case for Jimmy Greaves against Kenny Dalglish."

"Hasn't that already been on?"

"No, that was Greaves against Ian Rush. We had a jury of 12 people and they voted eight-four in Jimmy's favour."

It set Bill off on the road down memory lane. "Should have been 12-0! Jimmy was the greatest scorer of them all. I've never seen a player touch him for putting the vital finishing touch. While others were still thinking about what to do, whoosh, he would just get on and do it. He would have the ball into the net in the blinking of an eye and then amble back to the centre-circle as casually as if he'd just swatted a fly. A genius."

Bill's mind was now filled with action replays of golden goals from the boots of our mutually favourite footballer, Greavsie. Not the rotund, funny one on the telly. Instead, the 10st 8lb, lightning-quick, darting, dribbling, twisting, turning and passing the ball into the net Jimmy Greaves, the Artful Dodger, the penalty area pickpocket who snaffled more memorable goals than many of us have had hot baths.

"He was never any trouble to manage, you know," Bill continued, now thinking aloud rather than talking direct to me. I need not have been there. He was wandering around a precious past and did not need any prompting or interruption. "Even when it came time for us to part company he knew in his heart he'd lost his appetite for the game. People who didn't know what they were talking about sometimes described him as a bit of a faint-heart, but in all the years I watched him I never ever saw him shirk a tackle. And I'll tell you what, there were at least 10 goals that should have been added to his career total. Time and again he would be flagged offside simply because his movement was too quick for the eye of the linesman.

"The hardest of all to take was in the 1962 European Cup semi-final against Benfica here [Bill waved a gnarled hand at the wall in the direction of nearby White Hart Lane] when he scored a perfectly good goal that was ruled out. That broke all our hearts. We might have beaten Jock [Stein] and his great Celtic to become the first British team to win the European Cup.

"Jimmy had two great partnerships for us, first with Bobby Smith who provided lots of muscle in making openings for Jimmy, and then with Alan Gilzean, one of the most elegant forwards I've ever clapped eyes on. Greavsie and Gilly together were like poetry in motion. I was hoping for a third one when I put Jim together with Martin Chivers, but by then he was only giving half his attention to the game. He was quite the businessman off the pitch, and that took the edge off his appetite for football.

"But even with half his concentration he was still twice as good as any other goal-scoring forward. It hurt like hell the day I decided to let him go in part-exchange for Martin Peters. But as a manager you often had to do things that hurt you inside but were necessary for the team and the club. Martin was another wonderfully gifted footballer, but completely different to Jim. Alf [Ramsey] described him as being 10 years ahead of his time, and I knew exactly what he meant. He was an exceptional reader of the game, a bit like Danny and dear John White, and knew where to be before anybody else had spotted the gap.

"Nothing's changed. The game is still all about positioning. If you're not in the right place, then you're not going to be able to do the right thing. Positioning, positioning, positioning. The three Ps. Now Jimmy always knew where to be to make the most of a goal-scoring opportunity. It came naturally to him. You couldn't teach it. Quite a few of his goals were tap-ins, and people said he was lucky. He made his own luck by being in the right place at the right time."

I reluctantly brought Bill out of his golden reminiscing. "Would you be prepared to come to the studio and say that on camera?" I asked.

Bill looked at me as if I had just awoken him from a wonderful dream.

"You know I hate appearing in front of TV cameras," he said. "Hated it when I was a manager, hate it now. I'm a football man, not a song and dance man. Mind you, I got a lot of pleasure watching Jimmy on the *Saint & Greavsie* show. Why did they take that off? I thought it was a good thing to show football could laugh at itself."

My eyebrows reached for the sky. "That's rich coming from you, Bill. You were Mr Serious throughout your managerial career."

"That's true," he admitted. "I found it difficult to unwind. I could never understand how the likes of Tommy Docherty and Malcolm Allison could sometimes act like clowns. I never had that sort of release. For me football was, still is, much more than just a game. It was my life."

"You and Tommy Doc were big rivals in the 1960s," I said, "but you got the better of him in the one that really mattered – the 1967 FA Cup final."

Suddenly the years fell away from the octogenarian as he dipped back into his peak seasons. "I was really worried about that one because Chelsea had stuffed us good and proper at the Bridge – 3-0 and it could have been five," he recalled. "They were playing a sweeper system, with Marvin Hinton very efficient in the role. Alan Gilzean detested the system and was much less effective against it. I was really concerned. Then, during the week of the final, talkative Tommy gave an interview in which he said he was dropping the sweeper formation and playing orthodox. I was delighted to hear it, and we were able to beat them 2-1. Dear old Tommy should have kept his trap shut."

"Which was the most satisfying of your FA Cup final victories?"

Bill gazed into space, like a man trying to choose between sparkling diamonds sitting in his memory bank. "Obviously from an achievement point of view it has to be the 1961 final because it completed what people described as the 'Impossible Double', but to be honest I felt flat at the end of it because we did not play anything like our best against a Leicester team playing above itself. They were down to 10 men because of injury, and it somehow made the game lopsided. There was no rhythm or pattern, while most of that season we'd played some of the finest football I've ever seen from a club side. You could have set it to music, it was so rhythmical. But the final turned out to be a big anti-climax. We got the Double, yes, but I wanted us to do it in real style, as much for our wonderful fans as for me.

"The following year Jimmy gave us a great start with a magnificent goal after just three minutes, rolling the ball into the net past half-a-dozen players as casually as if he was playing on his hall carpet. We went on to beat a very talented Burnley side 3-1. That was probably the most satisfying, because we played it the Spurs way. Quick, simple, beautiful football. Never complicate what is basically a simple game, and treat the ball with respect, not as if it's your worst enemy and needs a good, hard kicking. Caress it, play it with care, make every pass count, and when not in possession get into position."

I dragged Bill away from the mantra he had been preaching for more than 60 years. "If you had to pick one match from all those in which you were involved as manager, which gets your vote as the most satisfying?"

Back to the bank vault, and this time he had little hesitation in replying. "It has to be the 5-1 victory over Atletico Madrid in the 1963 European Cup Winners' Cup final," he said firmly. "This made us the first British team ever to win a major European trophy. That's in the history books forever. A bit special. That was little Terry Dyson's big night. He scored two storming goals. I remember that old rascal Bobby Smith saying to him in the dressing room afterwards that he should retire because he would never top that performance. Terry played on for another six years!"

Bill chuckled to himself over that suddenly uncorked memory, and I stupidly ruined the mood by introducing a sombre topic. "Eddie Baily told me he was disappointed with the pay-off he got from Spurs, and that you didn't get much more."

I had dropped winter's discontent into his glorious summer. Bill was clearly not keen to discuss the subject, particularly with his testimonial match just a few days away. "Let's just say it was more a paper tissue than golden handshake," he said. "Eddie was bitter for a long time, and we fell out over it. We've since patched it up and when we get together we talk about the many good times we enjoyed rather than the unhappy finish. I prefer to remember the positive things that came out of it. I got the break that I desperately needed and we found out who our true friends were. Ron Greenwood and John Lyall at West Ham came up trumps and were magnificent. Two of the most honest and caring people I have met in my long life. That year I went was a weird one. Bill Shankly, one of my best friends in football, resigned from his job at Anfield and things were never quite the same again. The football world was changing, and if I may say so, not for the better. As Shanks said to me once: 'The lunatics have taken over the asylum.'"

Ignorantly, I continued with the negativity: "Martin Chivers gave you a lot of headaches in your last couple of seasons as manager."

"Yes, he became a real handful," Bill admitted, shaking his head as if to get rid of bad thoughts. "As you know, he and Eddie really disliked each other, which led to a heavy atmosphere. There were a couple of seasons when Martin was comfortably the outstanding centre-forward in the country, and it seemed to go to his head. He more than anybody put me in the mood to resign with his continual beefing about his wages – that and the terrible hooliganism that started to ruin so many games. Since he retired, Martin has gone out of his way to make amends by visiting me a lot, and he has apologised for his behaviour. He has developed into a really nice person, and we get on just fine. When Darkie meets him he makes a fuss of her, and she says, 'How on earth did a nice young man like that manage to upset you so much? You were always moaning about him yet he strikes me as being a real charmer.' But Darkie did not have to put up with him constantly complaining about his wages and sulking when things didn't go his way."

I was kicking myself for bruising our conversation by bringing in bad vibes from the past, so looked to put us back on smiling ground. "Of all the managers of your era, Bill, who did you get on with best of all?"

This was much more acceptable ground. "No question, it had to be Bill Shankly," he replied, his eyes twinkling at the thought of his old friend. "We used to talk regularly on the phone at least once a week. Bill was a very funny man, but deadly serious about football in something of a fanatical way. We both agreed that the hardest thing about managing a football club was being judged by people who could not trap a bag of wet cement."

Bill let that thought sink in, and then added: "Once after Jimmy had scored one of his magical winning goals against Liverpool, Shanks phoned me on the Monday and said, 'Billy, there's one thing wrong with that wee Greaves feller of yours. He wears the wrong colour shirt. He deserves to be in Liverpool red, playing for a proper team.' Shanks continually asked me to name a price for Jim, reminding me that I had once, when he was Huddersfield manager, tried to buy Denis Law from him. Shows what a good judge I was. Few people had even heard of Denis then. Bill and I would discuss all the football gossip and put the world to rights. Darkie used to tease that we were like a couple of old women. Both Bill and I agreed that Brian Clough needed reining in. Shanks used to say to me, "When I talk to that man on the phone, I'm never sure if he's drunk with arrogance or alcohol."'

Bill peered into his teacup as if searching for a lost memory.

"I don't think Brian ever forgave me for dropping him when I was manager of the England Under-23s," he confided. "It probably held back his promotion to the senior team, because I told England manager Walter Winterbottom that I considered him a bit of a lazy so-and-so who played more for himself than the team. I had to call it as I saw it."

And there it was. Bill Nicholson, in a sentence, "I had to call it as I saw it."

As honest as the day is long, he was the most refreshingly candid and trustworthy man I ever met in football.

Bill tossed in one surprise that took my breath away as I was preparing to leave. "I wonder how different my life would have been," he said, "if I'd taken the offer to manage Sheffield Wednesday?"

"When was that?" I asked, wondering if he was pulling my leg.

"After the World Cup in 1958," he said. "Wednesday general manager Eric Taylor sounded me out. He said he'd been impressed by my coaching work with England during the World Cup finals in Sweden and wanted to know if I would be interested in taking over as team manager at Hillsborough. 'Come home to Yorkshire,' was his selling line. But I was happy coaching at Tottenham, and living here with our young family. Within a few weeks of being offered the Wednesday job I was promoted to manager at Spurs. Wednesday appointed Harry Catterick, and he turned them into our biggest rivals in that Double season. As your mate Greavsie would say, it's a funny old game."

I could not get my head round what Bill had told me. Manager of Sheffield Wednesday rather than Spurs? No, that was too much for my poor old brain to handle.

Incidentally, I never did get him to appear in front of the cameras, but he will always remain on my memory screen.

My last view of Bill that memorable day that I visited his home was him leaning on his stick, waving me goodbye with a wide smile on a friendly face far removed from the dour Yorkshireman description that accompanied so many of his interviews in his managing days. He was enjoying the last of the summer wine, and it was vintage Tottenham. Just for the record, my *Who's the Greatest?* idea morphed into *Petrolheads*, a series I devised for BBC2. I could not see Bill appearing in that. The panel, headed by *Top Gear's* Richard Hammond, would have mocked him unmercifully for driving an unfashionable Vauxhall Cavalier.

Bill would not have cared less. After all, he had driven the best: a Rolls-Royce of a football team called Tottenham Hotspur.

As I drove away from Creighton Road, the thought sat in my mind: shouldn't the people of Tottenham have been campaigning to put up a Spurs-blue plaque outside No.71? Bill Nicholson, Mr Spurs, lived here.

A week after my visit to see Bill at his home, the old master came out on to the pitch before his testimonial match to acknowledge an explosion of cheers from a ground full of worshippers, and we were astonished to see he was balanced on the supporting arm of his old nemesis, Martin Chivers. For those of us who were close to Bill and all things Spurs in the 1970s, this was the last pairing we ever expected to see. It just shows how time really can be a great healer. Big Chiv – now big, affable Chiv – was looking after Bill like a caring son.

It was Martin who told Bill to leave his walking stick in the dressing room. "You don't want your fans to see you needing that," he told him, and used his considerable strength to help him walk out on to his beloved White Hart Lane pitch to the sort of reception reserved for gods.

There was a near capacity crowd of 35,877 to see Spurs play Fiorentina in a pre-season friendly, but much more than that, they were there to pay homage to the man who for so many years represented the soul and the spirit of Spurs.

Bill was visibly moved by the warmth and the love that showered down on him. He had never been demonstrative, an exhibitionist or a braggart; had never chased the cheers. Yet here was proof positive that the quiet man from Scarborough had won the hearts of an army of fans who appreciated and respected his lifetime's service to Tottenham and to football.

"This is one of the proudest nights of my life," Bill said through a boulder in his throat as the roar of the crowd almost deafened him. "I always told my players that the most important people were the supporters who paid their wages. Here they are proving it. I am overwhelmed."

Chivers, holding the elderly and now frail Nicholson steady, told him: "You can feel the love, Bill. You've earned every one of these cheers."

The cynics among us could not believe that this was the same Martin Chivers who had battled with Bill on every front, from contracts to tactics, and had shown him scant respect. Big Chiv would later explain: "My differences with Bill and Eddie were greatly exaggerated and a lot of things were said in the heat of the moment. Bill knows how I feel about him, and how much I respect all he has done for this great club. He should be knighted for his services to football. Nobody has put more into the game than him. It's a pleasure for me to have him and Darkie as good friends."

Many eyes, including Bill's, were filled with tears as a parade of his old players lined up to pay tribute to him, including Mel Hopkins, Cliff Jones, Bobby Smith, Dave Mackay, Ron Henry, Tony Marchi, Les Allen, Pat Jennings, Martin Peters, Ralph Coates, John Pratt, Terry Naylor, the contrite Chivers and one of his last signings, Gary Mabbutt.

"The clock has turned back for me tonight," Bill said. "To see all my old players here is just wonderful. We had so many good times together, and throughout my managing career I tried to make it a family club... and all the supporters were part of that family. I want to thank everybody a million times over for coming out for my special night. They have, as they say, made an old man very happy."

Once the shooting and the shouting was over (Spurs beat Fiorentina 3-0) I was delighted to be reunited with one of the great characters from Bill's Double-winning team, the one and only Bobby Smith. He was not in the greatest shape following a series of operations as his past caught up with him. During his career he continually played through the pain threshold with the help of cortisone injections, and he was hobbling more heavily than Bill. The price our heroes pay for their fame.

"One of the bravest footballers I ever knew," was Bill's sincere tribute.

"I had my ups and downs with Bill," said Bobby, "but I was never anything less than in awe of his knowledge of the game, and he was the master of tactics. He always got me playing to the best of my ability. He was a born coach."

Bobby and I got on famously, just as back in the old days, and we agreed to work together on his autobiography. Sadly Bobby died before I could bring out the book and I had to write it solo. A share of the profits from sales of the book go to the Tottenham Tribute Trust and it is available from the website mentioned in the About the Authors section of this book.

My co-author Steve Perryman was spreading the football gospel in Japan when the tribute match was staged, but he was with Bill in spirit on his special night...

"I played in Bill's first, long-overdue testimonial match against West Ham at White Hart Lane just before the start of the 1983/84 season. I remember Alan Brazil scored our

goal in a 1-1 draw with the Hammers, a match both sides took seriously. The fun came in the warm-up match featuring such club legends as Greavsie and Gilly, Pat Jennings, Cliffie Jones, Cyril Knowles and Martin Peters. Who would have thought it would be the last time not only that the 'G-Men' played together but that it would be many years before they saw each other again?

"Nobody was more worthy of two testimonial matches than Bill, who had given most of his life to the club. In the old days they were called benefit matches and it was a way for clubs to show their gratitude outside the straitjacket of the maximum wage. There was just a meagre £25,000 raised in the first match, but there was nearer £40,000 in the second testimonial.

"In fairness to Big Martin, his beef about poor wages was shared by most of us players, and I also used to often knock at Bill's door and ask for a raise. He would suddenly go deaf! Bill used to treat Spurs money as if it was his own, and he was as tight as a drum. But we still loved him! He hated it when agents started negotiating on behalf of their players. Goodness knows how he would cope today when managers are confronted not only by agents but their lawyers, too! Bill would have been much happier if everybody had played for nothing!

"I was proud to play a small part in the tributes to Bill when he was first to be inducted into the newly established Spurs Hall of Fame. It was in a memorable ceremony at Whites in Paxton Road adjoining the White Hart Lane stadium in the spring of 2004. Bill was very frail, I recall, and it was Big Chiv who collected him from his home and brought him to the venue.

"The place was packed with old Tottenham players wanting to pay homage to 'Sir Bill', and joining me in saying a few words were the likes of Dave Mackay, Cliff Jones, Pat Jennings and 1980s manager David Pleat.

"We were unanimously agreed he should have been 'Sir Bill'."

AT HOME WITH THE MASTER

BBC commentator John Motson was Master of Ceremonies for the event, and introduced among others John Ryden, Tommy Harmer, Tony Marchi, Mel Hopkins, Peter Baker, Ron Henry, Maurice Norman, Dave Mackay, Cliff Jones, Bobby Smith, Les Allen, Terry Dyson, Terry Medwin, Eddie Clayton, Pat Jennings, our Steve Perryman, Phil Beal, John Pratt, Peter Collins, Terry Naylor, Jimmy Neighbour and, of course, Martin Chivers, on whose arm Bill was leaning as he arrived to a standing ovation. Peter Baker had flown in from his home in South Africa, and the only other surviving member of the Double team – goalkeeper Bill Brown – sent apologies for absence from his home in Canada.

As everybody joined in a chorus of 'He's a jolly good fellow' there was not a dry eye in the house.

One man knew Bill better than anybody: Eddie Baily, his right-hand man from 1963 until they departed together in 1974. The swaggering Cockney – known as the 'Cheeky Chappie' in his playing days – kept up a non-stop verbal barrage against the Tottenham directors, whom he accused of treating Bill with cruel contempt.

Eddie fell out with his old team-mate when Bill accepted the offer to return to White Hart Lane, and he swore he would never again walk into the ground where he had been the chief engineer in the 'Push and Run' team. But he and Bill ended their feud after seven years and he played a walk-on part in the veterans' exhibition game before Bill's main testimonial match at the Lane in 1983.

Ten years earlier Eddie had been allowed a testimonial, but no such thing as the luxury of the stage at White Hart Lane. He had to make do with playing the game at Enfield rather than Tottenham. It was feared it would flop until Alan Sugar sacked Terry Venables on the eve of the match and thousands of Spurs supporters descended on the ground to protest. 'I had an extra sugar in my cuppa,' cracked Eddie.

Still the Cheeky Chappie gave me his take on Bill while I was helping him publicise his testimonial game at Enfield:

"Bill Nick is the straightest, most honest man I've ever known... often too straight for his own good. Sometimes in this life you have to duck and dive and tell a few porkies to get the best out of a situation. But Bill will never go down that road, and his honesty has cost him quite a few major transfer deals. There's always somebody looking for a backhander, but that's foreign language to Bill.

"I really admire the man, and there's no better coach in the game. He's got vision and he has a will to win that he passes on to his players like a hypnotist. He can make ordinary players seem great by the instructions he gives them.

"Okay, I admit to being a bit of a mouth and trousers and like to gee-up players with my tongue. Bill does it quietly and with an authority that I envy. I lose my temper with players who don't reach their potential, but Bill has more patience and gets the best out of them with sound advice. He also stresses to keep it simple, which was the way we were brought up with that magnificent 'Push and Run' team.

"The only time we fell out as players was when I was advertising cigarette smoking in the 1950s. He thought I was being a hypocrite and, being honest Bill, he told me to my face. But in my defence, don't forget there had been no link with cancer back then and I needed the extra dough in the days when footballers were treated like slaves. I quit smoking soon after because I realised it was a mug's game. That pleased Bill.

"He was one of the greatest managers there has ever been. Matt Busby, Bill Shankly, Arthur Rowe, Stan Cullis, Alf and Bill, they were the best of my time. The only thing he was not good at was delegation. He tried to do everything and worked himself into the ground, making himself ill.

"It really disappointed me when he went back and I told Bill exactly what I thought of him, because that's the way I am. I always shoot from the lip.

"We've patched up our differences because, as I said to him, you're a long time dead. We talk about the great times we had together at Spurs, both as players and working as a tandem team to coach and train the lads to produce their best.

"All my shouting and cussing is aimed at making players better. I get under their skin and don't mind them hating me, provided they're giving it everything. Like Bill, I think not trying to do your best at all times is criminal.

"Both of us have had memorable careers, particularly Bill, who in my book is the king of managers. We're opposites in personality and I think that worked because we balanced each other. That good cop/bad cop description fits us perfectly.

"Bill has never been motivated by money, but by the satisfaction of a team playing to its peak. He is a one-off."

The most amazing thing of all about Eddie is that he even made his peace with old nemesis Martin Chivers. They found themselves as near neighbours in Brookmans Park in Hertfordshire and had a clear-the-air chat, and through a mutual love of golf became firm friends. You couldn't make it up.

CHAPTER 22

A FOND FINAL FAREWELL

It was a sad, sad day for football, Spurs in particular, when 'Sir Bill' passed away at the age of 85. He died on the morning of Saturday, 23 October 2004, within seven months of his induction into the Tottenham Hall of Fame and after moving with Darkie to a warden-assisted flat in Potters Bar, Hertfordshire. His final days were spent six miles from the old Cheshunt training camp where he had spent so many hours preparing his teams. That same afternoon Tottenham were beaten 2-1 at home by Bolton Wanderers. Many grown men and women cried when his death was announced. The Lane was awash with tears.

The tributes to a simple yet great man came tumbling in by the bucketload, and they feature later in this chapter. I gathered many of them in my freelancing role for several media outlets and added more following the moving memorial service staged at White Hart Lane on Sunday, 7 September 2004, where the loyal, loving Darkie and daughters, Linda and Jean, led what was in essence a huge family gathering. We were all there to say a fond final farewell to 'The Master'.

For me personally it was a hugely emotional time. My darling wife of 45 years, Eileen, was losing a fight with a terminal illness, and when the news broke that Bill had gone I don't mind admitting that I, too, joined in the crying game. I was distraught over the loss of one of the people I respected most in the world in which I have always cleaved a living by writing about the greats of sport. They did not come much greater than Bill, who represented the very best of men.

I thought back to when we had first met, and I include the memory here because it warms me to this day and justifies me combining with Steve 'Skip' Perryman in writing this tribute book as I approach the age Bill was when he sadly left us.

A ninepenny bus ride around the North Circular Road took me to my first ever meeting with 'Mr Nicholson'. It was just before Christmas 1958 and he had been in charge at White Hart Lane for a little over eight weeks. It is part of footballing folklore how in his first game as manager Spurs had beaten Everton 10-4 in a remarkable match. Now here I was on my way to interview him in my esteemed role as assistant sports editor of the *Stratford Express* (I had better own up here that there were only two of us on the sports staff – me and sports editor Harry Miller).

My meeting with the Spurs manager had been set up for me by Vic Railton, the best-connected football reporter in Fleet Street, and for whom I had been a dogsbody copyboy and unpaid statistician for the previous two years on the *London Evening News*.

At 18 and with the world at my feet, I was on the first rungs of the journalistic ladder. The local football club on my reporting beat was West Ham United. They were due to play Tottenham at Upton Park on Christmas Day 1958, with the return First Division match 24 hours later on Boxing Day at White Hart Lane.

Mr Nicholson had reluctantly agreed to talk to me at his cramped office at 748 Tottenham High Road, situated on the corner of an approach road to White Hart Lane that would eventually be renamed Bill Nicholson Way. It was just after lunch on the Thursday, a week before the Christmas Day match. First of all I had the challenge of trying to get past the formidable figure of Mrs Wallace, who sat in the outer office like a watchdog guarding her boss against all-comers.

She was receptionist, telephonist, ticket administrator and Mr Nicholson's personal secretary, who protected him from the many nuisances who were a drain on his precious time. To Mrs Wallace, that was anybody who tried to talk to him without an appointment noted down in her diary.

My name was not there and she was just about to get rid of me like a bad smell when Mr Nicholson appeared, fresh from a training session at the club playing fields at Cheshunt.

"It's all right, Mrs W," he said. "Vic Railton set this up. You can let him in."

Mrs W reluctantly waved me through to the inner sanctum where Mr Nicholson greeted me in a well-worn grey woollen tracksuit that had no name or logo on it, unlike today's sponsored club kit in which managers are like walking advertising boards.

He was in grumpy mood. "I hate being in the office," he said. "It's so claustrophobic. My real office is the training ground."

No wonder. There was not room to swing a cat, a dog or a cockerel in his tiny cubicle that was located at the back of the main ticket office, with the busy road sending in the uninvited noise and fumes of heavy traffic. Even Mrs W couldn't stop *them*.

He held up a fistful of letters. "Look at all these. I've got to find the time to answer them all."

I sat uncomfortably on a hardback chair facing him, tongue-tied and nervous at meeting a man who had been one of my heroes during his playing days that seemed just a blink of an eye ago.

He broke off from his grumbles as if suddenly realising he was being rude, reached across his desk, gripped my hand warmly and looked me straight in the eye. "You've got five minutes," he said, his Yorkshire accent watered down by nearly 25 years living in the south. "I'm chasing my backside. I'm only seeing you because that bloody nuisance Vic Railton nagged me into it."

An hour later we were still chatting and finally got round to talking about the West Ham games after I had pumped him for all I was worth on his days playing with the 'Push and Run' Spurs – the side that had won my heart eight years earlier. By the end of the interview we were on 'Norman-Bill' terms and bonded so well that from then on he always took my calls and granted interviews without the need for dear old Vic Railton's matchmaking or the ankle-snapping protection of faithful Mrs Barbara Wallace.

Our conversations were to bridge more than 40 years.

During this first meeting with Bill I found that he lived and breathed the game. It was a first impression that never changed through the next two decades, during which I got a close-up view of the Master at work – but rarely at play because he just never allowed himself leisure time. His life was football and Spurs. He, of course, found time for his charming wife, Darkie, and their two lovely daughters, Linda and Jean, but even they came second to his football calling. Bill famously cried when Linda got married because he suddenly realised he had not seen her grow up.

The reason I am focusing on my first interview with Bill is that it captures the man. Most other managers would have found an excuse to avoid having their time taken up by a young, nobody reporter. But he, beneath the gruff exterior, was warm and kind-hearted and could not bring himself to tell me to get lost. I never ever knew Bill be anything but a thorough gentleman – often a moaner and a groaner but never less than polite. Even when his world was crumbling in the mid-1970s, he still acted with dignity and took the sudden change of circumstances with a stoicism that epitomised the Victorian standards of discipline that he set throughout his life.

At this first meeting, I think he was surprised by my knowledge of Spurs. More like a starry-eyed fan than a professional reporter, I drew from him this assessment of that wonderful 'Push and Run' Spurs side in which Bill played a key role as a functional and thoughtful right-half, aware that I had been so lucky to have seen the team in action through schoolboy eyes...

> *"The beauty of that 'Push and Run' side is that we did everything simply, and yet to the naked eye it came across as artistry. We never tried to complicate things. Eddie Baily was one of the few players who used to dwell on the ball while looking for an opening. That's because he had such wonderful ball control. The rest of us moved it along swiftly and accurately. If we had a secret then that was it – accuracy plus anticipation. We were always thinking of the next ball. Where we should put it and looking for a free man who had found space. A bit like snooker or chess players, thinking ahead to the next move.*
>
> *"Football, good flowing football, is about utilising space. It's a big pitch that we play on. The opposition cannot cover it all, and the good players know how to find unoccupied space. It all comes together with teamwork. Each of us playing for the team and not being selfish. You have to remember that we had all come through a war; every one of us served King and Country (apart from Guernseyman Len Duquemin, who had his own peculiar war dodging the occupying Nazi forces). Playing football gave us*

freedom after years of tough discipline. Now, in the modern game, we are having to bring back discipline because there are too many players who want to be selfish and hog the ball. Here at Spurs we will be looking to use the ball, use the space, use our heads to think about the game. I was in Sweden for the World Cup and it opened my eyes to how we can play the game with more thought. We can't all be Peles or Garrinchas. We have to do it with teamwork."

Our chat was interrupted by veteran trainer Cecil Poynton popping his head around the door of Bill's office, not seeing me and saying in his West Midlands accent: "Alfie's playing up again, Bill. If he gave as much attention to his training as he does to following the dogs he'd be a much better and fitter player. He lost a packet again last night and is on the scrounge."

Bill pointed to me. "Got company at the moment, Cec," he said, giving me a quick introduction.

He then stared hard at me. "This is your test young man," he said in a warning tone. "If I read one word of what Cecil has just said about Alfie Stokes, you'll never again get an interview with me or any of my staff."

I would never have dreamed of reporting what I'd accidentally overheard. Alfie was notorious in the game for his gambling, and as far as I was concerned it was a private matter between him and the club.

For some reason Cecil felt he should add to my education. "Young fella," he said, "you'll find many of today's footballers are more interested in talking about shagging than football. You press people have a duty to make them take the game more seriously. I can't understand them. I'm at the age when I'd much rather have a good shit than a shag." (It took me another 50-plus years to understand what he meant...)

With that profound parting shot, Cecil left us to our chat, with Bill shaking his head as he watched the departing figure of Poynton, who had played for Spurs in the 1920s as a hard-tackling left-back. "Dear old Cecil," he said. "He's been here so long he's part of the furniture. We always encourage loyalty and long service at Spurs. We're like one big, happy family. As I said before we were so rudely interrupted, it's all about teamwork."

'SIR BILL'

Before Bill finally got rid of me, he said how much he was looking forward to the back-to-back matches against West Ham the following week. The Hammers were back at the top table after gaining promotion the previous season under the management of Ted Fenton, but with the club virtually run by the player power of skipper Noel Cantwell and senior professionals John Bond, Malcolm Musgrove and Malcolm Allison. In the wings were the young trio of Bobby Moore, Geoff Hurst and Martin Peters.

"West Ham have good footballing traditions," Bill said knowingly. "I think they'll be attractive games to watch, and we're confident of getting more than a share of the points."

In fact Hammers had the happier Christmas, winning 2-1 at Upton Park and by a thumping four goals to one at the Lane. Alfie Stokes played in both games but before the season was much older he found himself sold to Fulham.

Tottenham finished an uncomfortable 18th in the First Division table, but Bill Nick was rebuilding, dare I say, at the double! Today's keyboard warriors would have hounded him out, but the board fully supported their new manager.

All these memories came flooding back the day of Bill's memorial service, and 'Skip' Perryman was among those who played a prominent part...

> *"I had the honour of being one of the players called on to make a tribute on the special stage set up on the pitch at the Paxton Road End, facing the packed North Stand. It was one of the most moving moments of my life. The love for Bill was palpable, and you couldn't move without seeing a Tottenham legend, from veterans like Cliffie Jones, Bobby Smith, Alan Mullery and Greavsie, to the likes of Glenn Hoddle, Martin Chivers and the entire current first-team squad. They all did Bill proud. He was a stickler for decorum and ceremony, and everybody was at their most respectful. This was all for 'Sir Bill' – no slouching, hands out of your pockets...*
>
> *"It was a sad, sombre atmosphere, yet mixed with the pride we all had of having been part of Bill's life. He was a unique man and some of his gold dust had rubbed off on those of us lucky to have been close to him. To have known*

and worked with Bill gave you a special standing in the football world. We had been blessed to have been part of his universe. There will never be another like him.

"The Nicholsons were there in force, of course, with Darkie supported by Jean and Linda as well as grandchildren and nephews and nieces from Yorkshire, all underlining that he was very much a family man. I will get to say my piece on Bill in the final chapter of this journey through his life and times, but let me just say here how privileged I was to be there at White Hart Lane for this final, fond farewell to one of the greatest men I ever met in football. Thanks, Sir Bill."

Spurs chairman Daniel Levy, a life-long Spurs supporter, understood what Bill Nicholson meant to Tottenham Hotspur. He reflected the mood of the 8,000 people respectfully congregated at the Lane as he kicked off the tributes:

"Bill's passing is a tragedy for the whole of football but particularly so for his family and all of us at Spurs. He was loved by everyone at White Hart Lane, and there is no doubt that he in turn loved this club. Bill devoted his whole life to Tottenham Hotspur and to our fans, and he will never be surpassed as the greatest individual in our history. He lifted Spurs from mediocrity to the sublime as we became the first British club to win a European trophy and to so many wonderful achievements such as that special Double of 1960/61. He will never be forgotten."

The proceedings were performed with the dignity and precision – perfectionism even – that had marked Bill's life. Matchday announcer and BBC radio presenter Brian Alexander and the Reverend Toni Smith, a pioneering woman priest, were quietly in control of the low-key religious service that was punctuated with film highlights on the large screens of Bill's life in and out of football. His daughter Linda was spokesperson for her proud family, confirming that she, her mother and sister Jean had got accustomed to sharing Bill with Tottenham:

"The club was our second family and we were happy to accept that, because the club meant so much to our dear Dad. There are so many great memories we have and this ground at White

Hart Lane was at the centre of most of them. Dad always said that the most important thing were the fans. Without them, he used to say, there would be no game... There would be no chance for the players to play the game they love... There would be no spectacle. As a family, we have lots of fabulous memories of Dad, and all brought home by the book of condolences and the many tributes to him. On behalf of our Mum and our entire family, thank you to the club and you supporters for everything you have done for staging this fitting memorial. Dad would have been very proud of you all. Thank you."

There was a huge turnout of Bill's former players and personal tributes were delivered on stage by Cliff Jones, Jimmy Greaves, Martin Chivers, our Steve Perryman, Glenn Hoddle and Gary Mabbutt, before 85 white doves were released, representing each of his years on this mortal coil. Bill would have wanted them flying in 4-2-4 formation but at least they went off suitably in style – the Spurs way.

The singing of *Glory Glory Hallelujah* had never been so poignant, and the Nicholson family were rightly proud of the send-off given to Mr Spurs. Son-in-law Steve Bell had earlier been their eloquent spokesman at Bill's private funeral, and he told how the entire family had added notes to a kitchen wall list of just what Bill meant to them. In the end the lists were so long and so many that Steve had to take over the ruthless editing duties "otherwise I would have been all day telling the many reasons why he meant so much to us; he really was very, very special".

Bottom line, the family agreed that Bill was a model husband, much-loved dad, father-in-law and granddad, and fondly remembered as a loyal son, brother and favourite uncle; a man who was proud of his working-class roots and of always trying to do his best. He was never interested in fame and fortune, just in doing everything properly. And above all, he truly loved Tottenham Hotspur.

Bill did not have an arrogant bone in his body and never realised how popular he was with his fellow managers and coaches, internationally as well as domestically. Hardly a week went by at the Tottenham training ground at Cheshunt without overseas coaches dropping in to watch and monitor 'the Master' at work. He willingly shared his ideas and theories, so the Spurs way was spread far and wide.

A FOND FINAL FAREWELL

I got a close-up view of just what he meant within the game back in the 1960s when I went to a coaching conference at the Football Association training centre on the lush playing fields of Lilleshall in Shropshire (now moved to St George's Park in Staffordshire). I drove up from London with my close friend Dave Sexton, who was just starting his managing career with Leyton Orient. We had our mutual love of boxing and jazz as common ground, but it was football that ate up most of Dave's sleeping and waking time. He was a fanatic. Dave admired Bill to the point of hero worship, and wanted his Orient team to play the Spurs way. He told me:

"Bill represents football with dignity and style. His teams are always positive and a joy to watch. He is proving himself one of the finest managers the game has ever seen, but more than that he is an exceptional coach and fine person. I would travel to the ends of the Earth to hear him talking about his theories and tactics. He is the coach of coaches. Bill's strength is in the simplicity of his message. Everything is boiled down to simple instructions that the players can take on board, and he stresses the importance of teamwork. He encourages everybody to sing from the same song sheet; in that way lies harmony and a togetherness that is essential if a team is to have success."

Yes, Dave Sexton spoke like a true disciple.

Bill was the keynote speaker at the Lilleshall conference and got such a warm reception that for a moment he was almost lost for words. He had recently followed the Double by capturing the FA Cup again and then the European Cup Winners' Cup, but he was such a modest man that he had no idea how highly he was regarded by his peers.

This was underlined by everyone I spoke to in the weeks after his departure from this mortal coil, and it was a labour of love as I collected and collated these tributes to Bill following his passing. Many have come from legends no longer with us. Let's remember them all warmly and fondly as we recall their memories of 'Sir Bill'...

TERRY VENABLES
"Bill represented everything that was the best about our game. He was a man of dignity and dedication, and always wanted his team to win in the right style and the right spirit. I was privileged to play for him and against his teams. The biggest compliment I can pay him is that managers always talked about the 'Nicholson effect' in

their pre-match talks. They knew that his brain was behind the opposition, which meant we were pitched against one of the most innovative thinkers in football. He played in the Thirties, Forties and Fifties, and then poured all he had learned into the teams of the Sixties and Seventies. There was nobody better equipped to manage a side. Never once did I know of him boast or brag. He did everything with meticulous attention to detail and always insisted that his players represent Tottenham with a sporting attitude and with total effort. Bill could forgive anything but lack of commitment. He demanded and got 100 per cent input from all his players. If not, they were out. We have lost one of the great managers and coaches. It was an honour to have played for and against him."

DAVID PLEAT
"I don't mind admitting I cried when I heard that Bill had died. I idolised him as a man as well as a manager. His record at Spurs was second to none, and he achieved it all without blowing his trumpet. When I was fortunate to manage Spurs I had no hesitation in turning to Bill for advice and guidance. He never forced his opinions on me but was very happy and eager to share his great knowledge on all aspects of the game. He epitomised honesty and integrity throughout football, from the pitch to the boardroom, and he let his teams do his talking for him. I learnt so much from him and he was always happy to share his thoughts about coaching. He was admired and respected throughout the game by all his peers. We will not see his like again."

TOMMY DOCHERTY
"I played against Bill in his 'Push and Run' days and against his Double team, then took him on as a manager and usually finished second best. He was one of the most innovative of all coaches, and his next boast would have been his first. A thorough gentleman and sporting in defeat or victory. Alf Ramsey should have given him half his England caps, because Bill was always covering for him. It was my pleasure to have known him well. Socially he could be quite dull because all he wanted to talk about was football, but if you were sensible you listened because he always spoke such great sense. I had a quicker tongue than him but his football brain usually got the better of me. Football will miss him, and my deepest sympathy goes to Darkie and the girls."

A FOND FINAL FAREWELL

GEORGE GRAHAM
"I thought the world of Bill, and it's scandalous that he was not knighted. I attended many coaching courses when he was the main speaker, and he always came across as a man in love with his subject. I counted Bill as a friend, somebody I looked up to throughout my playing and managerial career, and he was never less than generous with his advice and encouragement. He was the guru of coaches, and it was Dave Sexton who introduced me to his style of preparing a team. Dave was my coach at Arsenal who was most responsible for me going to Highbury from Stamford Bridge. He told me how he had been inspired by Bill, and you only have to look at his record at Spurs to appreciate that the man was a genius."

SIR ALEX FERGUSON
"Football has lost one of its greatest servants. He and Scots Matt Busby, Bill Shankly and Jock Stein were the No.1 managers when I first came into the game with Dunfermline. He loved a Scottish player – Dave Mackay, John White, Bill Brown and Alan Gilzean as prime examples. In the game he was most respected as a coach and he allowed me to freely pick his brains when I was just starting out as a manager. He was always generous with his advice and had enormous knowledge of what makes players tick. Bill and Sir Matt were great friends, and the fact that Matt thought the world of him proved just how special he was. I mourn his passing and can safely say the game is poorer without him."

RON GREENWOOD
"There has been no better servant of football than Bill. He knew the game inside out and was always willing to share his knowledge. I went on many coaching courses with him and he was light years ahead of most people with his vision and understanding of tactics, which he always insisted should be simple. He did not like the game being complicated. I was delighted, along with John Lyall, to have him join us in the West Ham backroom team when he briefly left Spurs. We learned so much from him. When he told me he'd had an offer to return to Tottenham, I replied: 'That's where you belong.'"

'SIR BILL'

MALCOLM ALLISON
"Bill built one of the greatest of all British teams with that Double side of the early '60s and I used to go out of my way to watch them play because there was so much to learn. Bill was very generous with his time and advice when I started out on my coaching career, and there was nobody who had greater respect from his peers. Joe Mercer and I always looked forward to our jousts with Bill because we knew that in a Bill Nicholson team we were meeting the best-prepared side in the game."

DON HOWE
"I first met Bill when I was selected for England Under-23s and he was our manager, and from day one he put himself out to encourage my interest in coaching and getting a better understanding of the finer points of football. He was like a professor of the game and I learned so much from him, and when I was coach at Arsenal it was always a challenge to take him on. Never once did he get involved in the nonsense of allowing rivalry to spill over into hatred. For all his success, he managed to keep a perspective on things. A Bill Nicholson team was always worth watching because they were simply the best coached in the game."

BILL McGARRY
"I always looked forward to picking Bill's brains on coaching courses, and he was happy to share his thoughts and theories. People think of him as a great manager, which he was. He was an even greater coach, and we inside the game considered him the No.1 for many years. His silverware collection says it all."

ALLAN 'SNIFFER' CLARKE
"I was honoured to play for England Under-23s in Turkey in 1967 when Bill was manager, and I was impressed at how simple yet thorough were his pre-match instructions. He got the best out of our squad by his motivational words and was a manager in every sense of the word. We beat the Turks 3-0 and I got one of the goals. From then on I was a Bill Nicholson fan. He always behaved with great dignity and expected the same from his players. His death is a sad loss to football."

A FOND FINAL FAREWELL

RON BURGESS
"I have lost a dear friend and football has lost one of its greatest-ever managers. Bill and I joined Spurs on the same day in 1936 and we grew up together. He was always a great thinker about the game and had Tottenham Hotspur engraved on his heart. Bill always used to give me the credit for being first to mention a young lad called Pat Jennings to him. He kept a close eye on him from when I first signed him for Watford. I valued his life-long friendship. I never ever heard him boast, yet he had so much to boast about. Yes, the Master."

KEVIN KEEGAN
"Bill Shankly and Bill Nicholson, two legends of football. When I was at Anfield, Shanks used to talk of Bill Nick in hushed, reverential tones. They were very close friends, yet deadly rivals. When we were playing Spurs, Shanks always wanted us to pull out that little bit extra to win. 'This is a Bill Nicholson side,' he would say, 'There are none better prepared on this Earth.' Bill Nick has now joined Shanks Up There and they will be selecting the greatest team in heaven."

HOWARD KENDALL
"Bill Nicholson was one of those who was a massive influence on me becoming a manager after my playing career. He was in charge of the England Under-23s when I was establishing myself and I was impressed by the way he inspired and instructed the team before the kick-off. I used to sit at his feet listening because our manager at Goodison, Harry Catterick, said that he was the bee's knees. I learned so much by just listening, respecting Bill because he had been there, done that. The football world is a lot poorer without him."

RON 'CHOPPER' HARRIS
"I was Chelsea captain against Bill Nick's Tottenham in the 1967 FA Cup final, and I was struck at how he went out of his way to congratulate each Chelsea player after we had been beaten 2-1. It was a great example of how to react in victory. No showing off or gloating. He was genuinely sporting and made defeat easier to accept. He was a great ambassador for our game."

'SIR BILL'

SVEN-GORAN ERIKSSON
"Bill's fame as a coach transcended Tottenham and became synonymous with all that was best about football worldwide. I was one of many who attended Tottenham training sessions as a young coach to tap into the great man's secrets. He was always happy to share his immense knowledge, and we all felt privileged to listen and learn from one of the greatest of all coaches. Bill represented football with dignity and style, and I considered it an honour to have known him."

MARTIN JOL
"Everybody across the world of football knows the name Bill Nicholson. His deeds as a manager and coach are legendary. I felt so honoured to follow in his footsteps as manager of Tottenham. They are the footsteps of a giant. He set standards that were impossible to follow and gave Tottenham a worldwide reputation for producing football that was not only successful but also good to watch. When I took over as Spurs manager, there was a story published in several newspapers that I wanted to be the next Bill Nicholson. That was a misinterpretation of what I had said. There could only be one Bill Nicholson and it was a privilege to have walked in his shadow. The memorial service at White Hart Lane showed exactly why he was so revered. I bow my knee to his memory."

JIMMY HILL
"In many ways, losing dear Bill Nicholson is the end of an era. He played in the bad old days when footballers were treated like slaves, but Bill was never interested in money. His one aim in life was to manage a team that represented football as the Beautiful Game that it is. He and I were sad to see the freedom that we fought for become abused by the greed of some players. I would suggest that all players should take a leaf from Bill's book and play for pride. He was a great manager, a great coach and a great man. He was a wonderful ambassador for our sport."

SIR GEOFF HURST
"Bill's passing is a huge loss to football. He went out of his way to make it the Beautiful Game, and I remember nothing gave Ron Greenwood greater pleasure than when West Ham got the better of

Spurs because, to Ron, it meant beating the Master. I had many conversations with Bill and always found him not only knowledgeable but eager to share his beliefs that football was a game that should be kept simple and with the emphasis on attack. He and Ron were out of the same pod and always preached that the game was about being positive but all within the rules. Neither of them ever cheated. It was a pleasure listening to them both. My sympathy to Darkie and the Nicholson family. We have lost a great man."

Bill's former players lined up to pay tribute to the manager of managers:

ALAN MULLERY
"One word sums up Bill as a football manager: genius. Nobody read a game better than Bill, and he had a photographic memory of just about every opponent we faced. He could tell you the strengths and weaknesses of all the players. A test of a manager is what long-serving players think of him. I arrived at White Hart Lane when most of the Double-winning team were still playing, and the esteem in which he was held by them was unbelievable. Bill always gave it to you straight. He did not give false praise, and was quick to tell you when you did something wrong. Even in victory he would keep his feet on the ground and look for the things that needed tightening and improving. I remember a game when we beat Burnley 4-0 and he gave us a tongue-lashing because some of our play was loose and undisciplined. Bill didn't suffer fools, and gave all his concentration and time to the team and the club. He was always described as being dour, but he often had a twinkle in his eye and could be humorous in his own way. Bill will be remembered as one of the greatest managers of all time, and I considered myself very lucky to have played under him. If you ever got a pat on the back from Bill then you knew you had done something special. He will always be a legend at Tottenham."

PAT JENNINGS
"When you think of Tottenham you automatically think of Bill Nicholson – one of the legendary figures in football. He was like a father figure to me, and probably the biggest influence on my life. When I

first arrived from Watford I was young and inexperienced and had a bit of a wobbly time. But Bill stood by me and gave me the confidence I needed with his quiet words of encouragement and advice. His knowledge of football was second to none, and when he spoke about the game it came right from the heart. He'd been there, done that and so you listened with respect. He expected everybody to share his total commitment to Spurs and anybody who gave less than his best in the Tottenham jersey was going to get an earful. He could make players shake with his criticism, which was always constructive. Bill set the highest principles and expected his players to perform in a sporting yet competitive way. At all times he preached that the game should be kept simple and direct. He despised cheating in any form and never looked to take shortcuts to success. I remember he hated the way the game went very defensive in the 1970s. He thought football should be attractive and entertaining to watch, and he was always telling us to 'play for the fans'. Tottenham were so lucky to have him at the helm, and he was without doubt one of the greatest managers the game has ever seen."

JIMMY GREAVES

"You always knew where you stood with Bill, and I would rate him the greatest bloke I ever worked for. He knew which players needed a kick up the arse and which needed an arm around the shoulder. So many people in football say one thing and mean another. Bill was always straight and he said what he meant, and would shoot straight between the eyes to make his point, even if it upset you. He was very blunt and brutal when necessary, which is all part and parcel of being a good manager. Bill could be a miserable sod at times, but that's what the pressure of management does to you. When he let me go to West Ham in 1970 it broke my heart, but looking back it's easy to see why he thought I was a busted flush. I'd had my fill of football and Bill knew it before anybody else, apart from me. Once you got to know the real Bill Nick you found a warm, generous and totally trustworthy man. I used to watch him play when I was a kid and he was a true 100 per center who never gave anything less than his best on the pitch. And that was how he was as a manager, always pouring himself into his job. He expected the same attitude and effort from his players. It's well known that I was never a fan of coaches, but Bill kept it simple and you knew what he wanted from you. No mumbo jumbo. Spurs did not give him the sort of rewards he deserved for making them one of the most attractive teams in Europe. I couldn't believe it when they let him go, but Keith Burkinshaw had the sense to bring him back in a scouting and consultancy role. He had one of the best brains in football, and he was totally committed to Tottenham. Bill had blue and white blood and always put the club at the top of his agenda. My deepest sympathy goes to Darkie and the girls. He got away with being married to Darkie and Spurs... both Darkie and Spurs were the winners."

CLIFF JONES

"Bill would rarely praise a player because he thought that bred complacency. He always wanted us on our toes and not thinking we were the finished product. I remember feeling really pleased with myself after playing what I thought was a good game. As I waited for Bill's praise he said, 'Don't forget, son, that a pat on the back is only a couple of feet away from a kick up the backside.' He rarely swore. He left that to Eddie Baily, who could swear for Britain. How can I forget when I signed for Spurs? Bill was then coach, with Jimmy Anderson in charge. They tracked me down at my London barracks where I was completing my national service. The day before I had played for Wales against Israel. The date: 6 February 1958. That was the day of the Munich air crash and among those who perished was my regiment team-mate Duncan Edwards. What a player. So I was in tears when I signed for Tottenham, where Bill was already virtually in charge because Jimmy Anderson was unwell. There has never been a manager who paid such attention to detail as Bill. At our team talks he would go through the opposition with a fine toothcomb. His knowledge of every player was amazing, and he used to tell us how to play to make the most of the opposition weaknesses and would warn about their strengths. He managed the club from the boot room to the boardroom, and would never take any interference from the directors. They had such confidence in him that they left him to get on with it. He always insisted that the most important people at the club were the supporters and that we should feel privileged to play for them. I have never known a manager have as much time for the fans, and he always made a point of talking and, more importantly, listening to them. Time and again he would tell us to play for the supporters because they paid our wages. He will be desperately missed by everybody connected with the club, by everybody connected with football."

GLENN HODDLE

"I was lucky to play under Bill as a youngster but he had resigned by the time I made my league debut. I was in awe of him, and when I was a boy learning the game I considered him one of the greatest of all the managers. Nothing ever changed my mind. He was Mr Tottenham Hotspur and everything the club stands for emanated from Bill, who laid the foundations and gave the club pride and belief in itself. He always remained totally dedicated to Spurs. He had real, almost royal presence, knew what he wanted, knew how his team should and would function. Bill was a manager who truly managed. It was Bill more than anybody who established the traditions of Tottenham Hotspur Football Club. He never tried to complicate the game, and always sent his teams out to be positive. He preached that you must play for the team, not for yourself. Bill did not want flashy, show-off individualists. He wanted a team working together. That's how he built his great Double side, with the emphasis on teamwork. Bill was the Master and all of us in football must bow the knee to him. As long as footballs are kicked, Bill will never be forgotten."

MARTIN CHIVERS

"Bill and I had several ups and downs because I believed in speaking my mind, but we finished up the best of friends. My biggest beef was that he could never find it within himself to give us praise when we deserved it. He seemed to find it really hard to bring himself to say, 'Well done, lads.' Typical of him was that after our aggregate victory over Wolves in the UEFA Cup final he went into their dressing room and commiserated with them and then came into our dressing room where we were celebrating our win and gave us a going-over for our performance. I cannot think of any other manager who would have done that, perhaps with the exception of Brian Clough. Bill was brutally honest when sometimes it would have been better not to say anything. His record speaks for itself. He was one of the finest managers ever, as I often told him after he and I had retired. He was never driven by profit. He just wanted a perfect team and was always looking to build another Double side. Neither of us enjoyed our last season together, but these things happen and if I could turn the clock back I would probably have been less argumentative. I am just happy we made up. He was a good man, for whom I had the greatest respect, and I got on famously with his lovely wife, Darkie."

TERRY MEDWIN
"Bill was way ahead of his time in terms of coaching. When I arrived from Wales, I was used to doing training which was dominated by running and continual laps of the pitch, but he was doing things which most clubs hadn't even thought of. He insisted on a lot of ball work to go with our fitness training, and he made every player really think about his game and personal contribution to each match. He also had a lovely manner with the players and treated us as individuals, and that helped us to blend as a team. There was mutual respect. Bill lived a life that revolved around Tottenham Hotspur, the club coming first at all times. Nobody had a bad word to say about him because he was a gentleman. He was always asking after my kids, and was a really caring, warm man under that dour Yorkshire exterior. I can never recall him trying to claim the spotlight at the expense of his players, and he would always treat everybody with respect. Even when he was giving you a telling off you could not take offence because you knew he was doing it for all the right reasons. When I went into coaching, I took a lot of Bill with me. He showed that coaching should be inspirational and not boring or bewildering. I can hear him saying, 'Keep it simple!' Tottenham will never have a more loyal and conscientious servant."

GARY MABBUTT
"Bill had a special aura about him, and I was thankful to have him giving me fatherly advice when I was transferred from Bristol Rovers to Tottenham on his recommendation. He was up there with Bill Shankly, Sir Matt Busby and Sir Alf Ramsey for being respected throughout the game. Why he was not also a 'Sir' is one of the great mysteries. He had forgotten more than I knew about the game, and I was privileged to listen to him talking about football and the way Spurs liked to do things. I remember shaking with excitement when

he invited me to meet him for transfer talks. When we came face to face for the first time, I said nervously: 'Hello, Mr Nicholson, I'm Gary Mabbutt.' He shook my hand and said: 'Call me Bill.' He immediately put me at my ease and did not come the 'big I am'. He won me over easily and I had no hesitation in signing for the club. I never regretted it and was so grateful that Bill talked me into it. One of the main thrusts of his talk to me was that players should live the right kind of life and respect their bodies. I felt fortunate to have such a great man giving me sound advice that I always tried to follow. When I won a lifetime achievement award from the Professional Footballers' Association, I was extremely honoured to have it presented to me by Bill, who deservedly got the biggest ovation of the night. Everybody in the game thought the world of him. He was quite simply a legend."

JOE KINNEAR
"I had more than 10 years as a Tottenham player under Bill and could not have wished to play for a better manager. Every day working with him was like an education. He was a great manager, and an even greater coach. I can still hear his wise words in my head when I am out on the training ground today. I was brought up at Tottenham to train with the ball on the ground and I continue to use many of Bill's methods and sayings. 'Be first, be accurate, play the way you're facing, get into position when you're not in possession, when the ball is dead come alive.' All these simple instructions are going through my head as I think of Bill and the training sessions we used to have at Cheshunt. Today's players won't go far wrong if they do things Bill's way because it's the right way. Tottenham was his life and it was cruel for him when he was virtually forced away from the club, and I'm so glad they eventually took him back. Ask anybody who played under him and they'll only have good things to say. He was a hard taskmaster, but that's the way it has to be if you're to get the right discipline and enthusiasm from your players. Bill could always get the best out of us. It was a privilege to have had him as my manager."

MARTIN PETERS
"It was the thought of playing for Bill that made me decide to join Spurs from West Ham. Everybody in the game admired him and his achievements. He would encourage us to go out and play the way we

had been brought up to play, with the emphasis on pure football. This was good for me because I was used to a similar style at West Ham. Bill and Hammers manager Ron Greenwood were good friends and shared the same outlook on the game. It had to be played properly, with style and skill. Bill was a football man from the top of his head to the tip of his toes, and he could be considered 'the manager's manager'. He was a major servant to English football and a fantastic man. I always found him honest and fair and willing to listen if you had a point you wanted to put across. I honestly considered it an honour to serve under him. It was easy to see that he and Sir Alf Ramsey had played with each other for Tottenham, because they had the same perfectionist standards and believed in keeping the game simple yet positive. Bill's passing is a sad day for football and in particular for Tottenham, the club to which he was completely devoted and dedicated. He will be sadly missed but always warmly remembered by all those who had the privilege of playing for him. There is no doubt that he was one of the great English football managers and I felt so lucky to have become his captain at Spurs."

PHIL BEAL
"It used to be a joke among the lads that I was always the first name on Bill's teamsheet. Eddie Baily assured me it was true, and I was one of the few players who used to get a regular 'Well done' from Bill, who was famously mean with his praise. Of course, Greavsie got his own back on me for all the pranks I played on him by saying that the reason I was always the first name on Bill's teamsheet was because he wrote it in alphabetical order! I thought the world of him and always found him a fair man who made sense with his assessments of your performance. I can think of few people who could match his coaching knowledge. He could come up with tactics to suit any situation, and knew exactly how to exploit any team's weaknesses. How he did not get a knighthood is a disgrace. He was up there with the very best managers like Busby, Shankly, Ramsey and Clough. Those people who described him as dour did not really know him. He had a good sense of humour and liked to have laughter in the dressing room when the time was right. To him a good team spirit was vital, and he always demanded that we went out of our way to recognise the support of our fans. I was at the dinner where he was made the

first Life Member of the Hall of Fame, and I realised then that he was looking frail, but it still came as a shock when he died. It's difficult to imagine Spurs without Bill Nicholson. He was Mr Tottenham and gave his heart and soul to the club. I felt privileged to have played for him. He was a wonderful man."

JOHN PRATT
"I cried the day Martin Chivers rang me to tell me that Bill had died. He was such an important figure in my life. Bill WAS Tottenham Hotspur Football Club in my eyes. He treated us all like one big family. Bill had no favourites and rollocked us all equally! He demanded our very best efforts at all times and was quick to come down on anybody giving less than his best. Bill could forgive almost anything except lack of total commitment. I used to get quite a lot of stick from some sections of the Tottenham crowd and it would have been easy to get disheartened, but the fact that Bill had faith in me and kept selecting me did wonders for my confidence. He once selected me for a match against Manchester United at Old Trafford and I asked him what I could expect. 'Well, John,' he said with a straight face, 'put it this way – instead of getting 40,000 people hating you as here at White Hart Lane, you will get 50,000 fans hating you.' Yes, despite what people may say, he had a sense of humour! If I was satisfying Bill I knew I must have been doing something right because he was an out-and-out perfectionist. He was up there with Shankly for having a great relationship with the fans. He always found time to talk to them and was happy to listen to their point of view. He used to tell us in his team talks how important the supporters were. 'They pay your wages,' he'd say. 'They are entitled to criticise because they've paid to come in. Now go out and entertain them.' He not only wanted us to win matches, but to do it in what he called the Spurs style. The day Bill died a bit of Tottenham died with him. There will never be another Bill Nicholson."

DAVE MACKAY
"What I always admired about Bill was his blistering honesty. He was as straight as a die, in football and in his life away from the game. If he gave you his word, he meant it. Few managers could match him for putting the fans first. He continually told us that we had a duty to

give them value for their entrance money. I did not envisage playing for any other club than my boyhood favourites Hearts, but I am so pleased I allowed Bill to talk me into joining Tottenham Hotspur. How lucky am I to have played for two of the greatest clubs in the world, and then to have enjoyed the autumn of my career with the great Brian Clough at Derby County. Tommy Walker at Hearts, Bill Nick at Spurs and Cloughie at Derby. There have been no better managers, and Bill was probably the greatest of them all. When I broke my leg for a second time in a reserve match, I ordered our trainers not to let Bill know until his first-team game was over. I did not want to add to any pressure on him. That was the sort of loyalty and respect he inspired in his players. He was kind enough to say that I was his best signing. After I had collected the FA Cup as Spurs skipper in 1967, I could truthfully say the best thing I had done was sign for Bill back in 1959. What an adventure we had together."

*

Two and a half years after Bill's death, Darkie passed away, and in a private ceremony her ashes were placed alongside Bill's in a secret place beneath the White Hart Lane pitch. When the new ground was being built, their caskets were moved to a temporary spot and then – in 2018 – they were re-interred in a specifically selected place where the new pitch overlaps the boundaries of the old, as near as possible to the road that was named after him – Bill Nicholson Way.

The club held a private ceremony attended by Bill and Darkie's immediate family, and daughter Jean summed it up when she said: "Dad has been returned home and Mum is with him. My sister Linda and I are so grateful for the respect and affection that everyone at the club continues to show towards them. There is no more fitting memorial than for him to rest below the new pitch, and having Mum by his side makes it even more special.

"Dad's dream was always for his beloved Spurs to be the best in the world, and it is clear that this new stadium project is a giant step towards that aspiration. We are proud that Dad played a major role in developing the club's history and that his contribution is being remembered in this way. We're sure Dad would have enjoyed watching the current team play – in the way that he always advocated. The fact that the Spurs are taking him with them into the future means so much to us all."

Yes, not a dry eye in the house. COYS!

On the tenth anniversary of Bill's passing in 2014, three generations of the Nicholson family were invited guests at the home match with Newcastle United, when many of his former players joined in a minute's applause in his memory. T-shirts worn by the Tottenham players during their warm-up had 'Echo of Glory' written on the front. The phrase was made famous when Nicholson was reported to have said: "It is better to fail aiming high than to succeed aiming low. And we of Spurs have set our sights very high, so high in fact that even failure will have in it an echo of glory."

These words actually came from Danny Blanchflower and ghostwriter Ralph Finn, but over the years they have somehow been attributed to Bill. But he would not complain because they captured exactly what he felt about the Beautiful Game.

I must add my own heartfelt, personal tribute to Bill Nicholson. The way he treated me as an 18-year-old rookie writer back in 1958 spoke volumes of the man and the manager. Many people in the same situation would have found an excuse to avoid being interviewed by a kid reporter, but Bill had infinite patience and understanding. Forty years later Bill was still talking and I was still listening. It was a pleasure and a privilege listening to the Master.

*

Now for something completely different. As we were approaching the end of our Bill Nicholson odyssey, both Steve and I were conscious that we needed to get under the great man's skin as we were presenting him as a one-dimensional, football-obsessed man. Then, on reflection, we realised that is exactly what he was. In the 40-plus years that I conversed with Bill, I can remember very few occasions when the topic shifted from the Beautiful Game.

We wondered who we could turn to for another view of the great man, and then I had the brainwave of sitting and listening to John Fennelly talking about the manager he knew better than most during his 38 years of sterling service to Tottenham. John has served as the Spurs press officer and the club's distinguished and award-winning programme editor, as well as its head of publications and omniscient facts and figures man, taking over the latter role from the master statistician Andy Porter when Andy left this mortal coil all too early in 2014. In short, I was listening to the Spurs oracle on one of his favourite topics – the life and times of the unique Bill Nicholson.

"As a schoolboy Spurs supporter, I knew the great man by sight at games and on the occasional visit to the old Cheshunt training ground near where I was brought up. When I became a Fleet Street copyboy at 17, working for the famous Hayters Sports Agency, part of my beat was White Hart Lane. But I did not meet Bill until I finished my apprenticeship and started covering Spurs for the *Tottenham Weekly Herald*.

"That connection grew even stronger when I took on the role as the club's first-ever press officer in 1984. Bill, with a sense of humour that few people realised he possessed in spades, immediately nicknamed me 'Scoopy' due to my journalistic background. I was to discover that he delivered his 'jokes' in a deadpan, almost sarcastic way that continually wrong-footed people who were not sure if he was being serious.

"My first interview with Bill came when he was granted the freedom of the borough and I was looking to write a piece about it for the *Herald*. I found out as much as I could about his new entitlements and was particularly taken by one – did he plan to graze his sheep on the various greens throughout the district, as he was now permitted to do? He just stared at me in silence as he clearly illustrated that he did not suffer fools gladly and was only going to answer sensible questions! A cold-eyed stare from Bill matched anything even Muhammad Ali could produce to intimidate his opponents.

"On another occasion, I tried to wind him up by suggesting that the 1960/61 season was a poor campaign overall in terms of quality of opponent. At least this time he had the grace to smile!

"Oh, how he used to grumble about Tottenham's below-par performance when they completed the historic Double in the FA Cup final against Leicester. He so wanted Spurs to be at their best that day, when the eyes of the entire football world was on the 'Team that Bill Built'.

"There had been a rumour going around at the time that Bill had been offered a knighthood, so I thought I'd try that line. 'What would

I want a knighthood for?' was his only reply. He didn't deny it, he certainly deserved one... and I still wonder.

"Bill liked nothing better than getting together with former players of his generation who were now coaches – and there were certainly enough of them at Spurs in those days. It didn't matter what level they had played at, he just never switched off, talking tactics, games, personalities... it never ceased.

"When he returned from his brief spell at West Ham to link up with fellow Yorkshireman Keith Burkinshaw, Bill's scouting and advisory role left him more time for his favourite past time. I remember walking into his office one morning to see the club's schoolboy scout on his knees while Bill, sitting behind his desk, threw paper balls in his direction. As he rolled up another sheet, I asked what was going on.

"Bill looked at me incredulously. 'I am demonstrating the angle that the crosses were coming in,' he said. Yes, it was obvious really, I should have known!

"On another day, I went to the café just outside the main gates for a late lunch. It was empty apart from one table occupied by Bill and the crusty (okay, and trusty...) coaching crew.

"When my sausage, egg and chips arrived, I reached for the salt. There were no condiments on my table. Nor were there any on the remaining empty tables. I then noticed all of them scattered across the surface in front of the coaches. While they were all deep in conversation, I pinched the salt.

"Suddenly there was an exasperated shout from Bill: "Where's the centre-forward gone!?"

"Scoop's got it!" he was informed by one of his indignant disciples. Bill stood up, walked over and snatched back the salt. He was using the condiments to illustrate various tactical moves. I didn't dare ask for the ketchup!

"Bill was giving his customary manager's press conference in the cold carpark one wintry afternoon following a game at White Hart Lane. He was still fuming about the visitors' late equaliser, which he was convinced was offside.

"But he wasn't interfering with play, Bill," one seasoned hack insisted in those pre-VAR days.

"Well, if he's not interfering with play, he shouldn't be fucking out there," snarled Bill! He rarely swore, but when he did it landed like a hand grenade!

"Holding court in his office one day, Bill was talking to two players of a similar vintage to himself. They were discussing various opponents from the old days, including one pre-war centre-half who didn't seem particularly appreciated for his skills level. As was often the case in that era, he was clearly an old-fashioned stopper. Clear the ball, boot someone up in the air… and ignore questions later.

"Bill recalled that he was back in the penalty area preparing to defend a late corner when the opposition No.5 moved up to join what was clearly going to be a mad scramble.

Bill growled at him: "What are you doing here?"

"C'mon, Bill," came a nervous reply, "it's tactics. I've been told to come up."

"Sod off," said Bill. "What's the point of you being here? Get back." His opponent retreated! And Bill's audience weren't surprised either. I was, but then Bill seems to have dominated both ends of the field. I wish, like you Norman, I'd seen him play.

"I had interviewed veteran goalkeeper John 'Budgie' Burridge about his early days as a player. He recalled that he had such a late first-team call-up that he had to rush out to buy a suit to wear as the group set off for an away game.

"In between the players taking the pee out of his pristine shiny outfit, one veteran performer turned to the fledgling custodian to discuss tactics. "When we lose possession and come under pressure, we adopt the 'W' formation," he quietly advised.

"Budgie responded nervously, respectively calling his skipper 'Mister' before going on to say: "I am just a new trainee; I don't know what the 'W' formation is." Without looking up from his card game, the older man snarled: "Just welly it son, welly it!" It was probably the only piece I ever wrote that Bill appreciated!

"When the great man took over as manager in 1958, Spurs famously beat Everton 10-4 at home in his first game. Naturally it was one that I interviewed him about.

"Bill always walked home from the Lane to his house nearby. 'What did you think about as you strolled back alone in the dark after that great result?' I asked, like any trained interviewer. Without a flicker, he replied: 'I've got to sort that defence out!'

'SIR BILL'

"We were sitting in the Nicholson front room at the time, and his lovely wife, Darkie, chipped in: 'Do you know, Scoop, he didn't even tell me that he'd got the job. I didn't know until I read the papers the following morning!'

"'Why?' I asked in amazement.

"Bill chuckled as he replied: 'Well, you don't tell women things...' Old fashioned or what?

"Speaking of Darkie, Bill actually banned her from attending matches, claiming that she was unlucky. But she told me that she secretly went anyway and was a regular in the East Stand as her husband steered Spurs to the Double!

"In fact, when Bill got what was to be his only senior England cap, she was told to stay away from Goodison Park where England were to play Portugal. Naturally Darkie was not going to miss that one, but she was nearly spotted when Bill scored after 19 seconds and incredibly ran to exactly the same spot on the terraces where she was standing so he could celebrate with the fans. As Bill loomed over her, Darkie managed to hide behind a big man in the melee that followed!

"Another time, Bill was driving Darkie back to his Scarborough home to celebrate their 36th wedding anniversary when he turned westwards and started heading across the Moors in appalling weather.

"'I've got a surprise for you,' he smiled. The surprise turned out to be that he wanted to watch Goole Town and a young winger called Tony Galvin!

"On another occasion, he was on his way home from an unsuccessful scouting trip to the south coast. As he waited for his train, he was recognised by a fan on the other platform who called across and asked him where he was going. Bill explained his wasted journey.

"'You should go to Weymouth next and watch a lad called Graham Roberts.' Bill did – and Graham went on to become a Spurs legend, all because Bill was willing to listen to a fan.

"Similarly, when Gary Mabbutt decided that he needed a move from Bristol Rovers, he wrote to a number of clubs but received no replies – apart from Bill. When Gary nervously met him for the first time, one of the all-time great managers immediately put him at his ease by saying: 'Nice to meet you. Call me Bill.' As you can see from those stories, he never showed the 'big boss' attitude.

"Bill was so hands on in every area of the club that he would even

A FOND FINAL FAREWELL

be seen with his sleeves rolled up digging the pitch at White Hart Lane. But when it came to his own back garden – which looked out over Tottenham Cemetery – he would get Ron Henry to do it. Ron, our wonderful Double-winning full-back, was a nurseryman by trade after he retired from the game and would give Bill a lift to home matches. But often as 3pm approached, Ron was still out there mowing the lawn on which the Spurs boss practised his putting in his rare moments away from his football duties.

"'It had to be pristine,' Ron told me. 'He would stand there making sure that the lines were perfectly straight. It would have to be like Wembley before Bill was satisfied!' A perfectionist in every way.

"Bill was the worst back-seat driver you could imagine – as I found to my cost when I sometimes drove him around. One time, we were due to visit a Spurs employee at North Middlesex Hospital when I arrived at his home to collect him. The traffic was just a continual flow outside his house as I prepared to move off, driving the way I was facing.

"'What are you doing?' he demanded.

I replied: 'With all this traffic it's best that I go this way and turn around further up.'

"No, no, no," he insisted as he climbed out of the car and marched into the road with his hand up, ordering a speeding old-fashioned Routemaster style double-decker to stop.

"As the bus screeched to a halt, the driver's door flew back with such clear aggression that I expected a barney. But all I heard was a mild, respectful "Hello Bill, what's happening?" By now the whole street had come to a standstill, allowing me to do a U-turn and head back to the High Road.

"Sadly, once in the hospital, the usual thing happened. Entering the lift, we were continually greeted with "Hello Bill" while we went up and down for ages as a Spurs fan seemed to board at every floor – Bill chatted away to them all. We almost missed visiting time! He always found time to chat to supporters. 'They pay our wages,' he'd say. 'They have earned my time.'

"Unusually, Bill was quite emotional when he attended a pre-match ceremony outside the main gates to dedicate the road as Bill Nicholson Way. I had hoped to write a main piece as the two of us looked back on his great days at the club, but it clearly wasn't the time. All he could say to me was: 'It's been my life, Tottenham Hotspur. And I love the club.'

"On reflection, that was more than enough."

Thank you for that insight, John Fennelly, a man who continues to have Spurs in his soul. It underlines what Steve and I had concluded: Bill Nicholson – 'Sir Bill' – was totally dedicated to football in general and Tottenham Hotspur in particular. There was no room for outside influences. It was football, football, football. There has rarely been dedication to match it.

How on earth did the Establishment fail to give him the recognition of a knighthood? None so blind as those who will not see.

For us, he will always be 'Sir Bill'.

CHAPTER 23

TEAM OF TEAMS

Bill did not do trivia. While his squad busied themselves playing cards or listening on primitive headphones to music on tape recorders – and later compact discs – during long journeys to and from matches, he concentrated on writing tactical plans and lists of things to do at the training ground. He could never switch off.

During the years of the Nicholson reign, I wrote thousands of words about him and his teams, and I have the scrapbooks to prove it. We travelled to a dozen countries together, me as a member of the press brigade as we followed Spurs campaigning in Europe, and also when Bill was acting as manager of the England Under-23 side on their summer tours – an annual job he performed with great pride and total commitment. He was always a Three Lions patriot. What an England manager he would have made!

It became a ritual that on the Sunday after home matches my late pal Harry Miller of the *Daily Mirror* and I would drop in on Bill at his Lane office. "Here they come," he'd say with mock annoyance. "The terrible twins, Giller and Miller – songs at the piano. Got no time to talk, catching up with correspondence."

Then he would talk for an hour, and at the same time dragging any football gossip he could from Harry and me. People not in the game fail to realise that the English football scene is just a large village in which everybody knows everybody else and wants to hear their neighbours' and rivals' business.

We rarely got a story we could print out of Bill, because he would always discipline himself to say: "This is off the record."

But just to hear the wisest of men talking about the game he knew better than most was like sitting at the feet of an Attenborough of football. Strangely, Bill was happiest talking about defeats. He was never one to gloat about victories, but he would come out with all guns blazing against his players when he felt they were not giving of their best.

Bill was humble to a fault. It was also not in his nature to want the huge house and flashy car trappings that usually come with success. Throughout his time at Tottenham – and especially after the lifting of the maximum wage in 1961 – he earned a lot less than his players. He was never ever motivated by profit, only league points and pots.

One particular Sunday, Harry and I were standing listening to Bill on the edge of the pitch in a deserted stadium when we were interrupted by the tinkling of a bicycle bell. We looked up to find Bill's wife, Darkie, glowering at her husband, her bike alongside her and sporting a headscarf and tweed skirt, looking for all the world like a character out of the pages of an Agatha Christie novel.

She was a born smiler and I never ever found her less than friendly and charming, even when I was ringing Bill at home for late-night quotes on a breaking story. But this day she was clearly agitated.

"D'you know what the time is, Willie?" she called. "You're supposed to be taking the girls out."

Bill threw a hand to his head. "God, I completely forgot," he said. "Blame Giller and Miller. I'll be right home."

Darkie waved a friendly hand at Harry and me and then rode off, mission accomplished. This revealed the pre-occupational nature of Bill. He could only think of football, but to help us better understand him, I have excavated contrasting 'Tales of the Unexpected' about Bill that provided him with a mixture of amusement and bemusement.

First, we go back to the England Under-23 summer tour of 1967 that coincided with the Six-Day War, and at the height of hostilities the squad was briefly stranded in Bulgaria. Bill Nick was in charge of 16 players, trainer Wilf McGuinness of Manchester United, six members of the FA blazered brigade, and along for the ride were seven of Fleet Street's finest football writers. I would say that. I was one of them.

Along with Bill, the central character in this story is Peter Corrigan, sadly a no-longer-with-us columnist of the *Independent on Sunday*, a former sports editor of *The Observer* and certainly one of the finest and funniest journalists of my old-git generation. At that time Peter was reporting for the broadsheet *Sun* before it morphed into the soaraway tabloid toy of Murdoch.

As the war reached its peak, it suddenly became impossible to make telephone or telex contact with our London offices. I was earning my daily bread at the time with the *Express*, and along with my colleagues I sat fretting and frustrated in the team's hotel headquarters in Sofia as the edition deadlines approached and disappeared into the distance.

In those pre-internet days, you had to order your telephone calls through the hotel switchboard, and we were informed that all lines were down. You have to remember the mood at the time. There was wild rumour of Russia getting involved and nuclear weapons being used as Israeli tanks and jet fighters destroyed the combined forces of Egypt, Jordan and Syria. We agreed among us that if anybody should be lucky enough to get through, we would put over a shared story that could be distributed at the London end.

Bill Nick was aware of our communication problems because he too was unable to make contact with the UK, and he was wondering if the plug should be pulled on the tour. War was raging to the south of us and fears were that it could easily escalate and spread north to take us into the danger zone. There was even talk of the RAF sending a special flight to 'rescue' the squad of England's best young footballers. Oh yes, and the small, rag-tag army of journalists.

After two days of total silence, it was Peter Corrigan who suddenly got the desperately awaited call and found himself being put through to the *Sun* sports desk from the lobby of the hotel.

It was an appalling line and he was reduced to screaming, "Peter Corrigan!" into the mouthpiece in a bid to make himself heard at the other end.

Bill Nick joined the rest of us gathered around him, willing him to keep the precious line open. We couldn't believe it when he suddenly threw down the receiver without having dictated a word.

On the other end of the line had been a veteran sub-editor with a pronounced stutter. Peter, tearing out what little hair he had left, looked at us wild-eyed and said: "I've just been told that P-P-Peter C-C-Corrigan is in B-B-Bulgaria, and then he put the phone down and cut me off.'

'SIR BILL'

I seem to remember saying something like "F-f-f-fancy that" – or words to that effect.

It was Bill who was first to see the funny side of it, and as he told the FA officials what had happened he could hardly talk for laughing, his 'dour Yorkshireman' image under threat.

Back home the following season his sense of humour was challenged when giving a team meeting before a vital First Division match. He was interrupted by his top goalscorer Jimmy Greaves suddenly having a terrible sneezing fit.

Bill worried that he was going to lose his main marksman to flu but was relieved that Jimmy later made a full recovery and was fit to play. It was many months later when king of the pranksters Philip Beal owned up to having sprinkled sneezing powder on Greavsie's shoulders. You were never safe when Bealy was about, as I discovered to my cost when I once found my portable typewriter balanced on the crossbar at Cheshunt training ground after he'd spirited it away while I was interviewing Bill.

It got to the stage where Bill had to call Bealy and his accomplice Joe Kinnear to one side and warn them to control their appetite for crazy pranks (mind you, they were amateurs compared to Paul Gascoigne when he arrived to bring chaos to most training sessions, including once riding in on an ostrich, and another time firing airgun pellets at the golden cockerel on top of the main stand. Yes, daft as a brush.)

In the early 1960s, Bill's biggest headaches were caused by the inseparable 'terrible twins' John White and Cliff Jones, who were always up to mischief. The worst that Bill could remember was when police were called to their hotel on the eve of a match in Manchester. It had been reported that somebody was threatening to jump from one of the rooms. It turned out to be Whitey hanging from his bedroom window shouting, "Help!" He was not in danger because Jonesie was inside holding on to him.

The team once stayed pre-match in a stately, historic venue and the hotel manager had to plead with Bill to instruct his players to behave. Jonesie and Whitey were once again the culprits. They had found swords and were fighting a mock duel up and down the sweeping hotel staircase.

John was a bundle of fun, which added to the grief when he was taken from us by that bolt of lightning in the summer of '64. "The worst day of all our lives at Tottenham," said Bill.

*

It was in Tottenham's centenary year of 1982 that I sat Bill down for the challenging job of selecting the greatest Spurs team from his playing and managing days. Our trivia-hating hero considered it one of the most difficult tasks he had ever faced, but typical of him he did the exercise thoroughly and arrived with a sheaf of notes on every position. They were not scribbled notes, but beautifully written in the ornate handwriting of which he was justifiably proud. After much agonising, he came up with the following selection…

Goalkeeper: Pat Jennings

"Bill Brown was the only one who ran him close, but Pat had it over him because of his greater physical presence. People do not realise how near I came to not signing Pat from Watford. I offered him £38 a week, which I thought was reasonable for an 18-year-old novice. Pat turned it down flat! He said he was earning that already at Vicarage Road. Hard-up Watford were desperate for the transfer fee and their manager Bill McGarry talked me into upping the offer to £40 plus £5 appearance money every time he was selected for the first team. So we did the deal and, after a nervy start, Pat settled down to become one of the world's great goalkeepers.

"I remember Bill Shankly once saying to me that Pat should be outlawed because of the size of his hands after he had saved two penalties at Anfield. Even now I'm not sure if Shanks was joking!

"Pat never gave me a moment's problem, and even I was astonished when the club agreed to sell him to the Arsenal. It was after I had finished managing and I thought Pat would be at Spurs for life.

"He developed great positional sense to go with his natural ability to stop shots. I think it had something to do with him playing a lot of Gaelic football in his youth.

"Ted Ditchburn, our goalkeeper in the 'Push and Run' side, also made my shortlist, but he played in a different era when goalkeeping was much more of a physical challenge. Ted used to get battered black and blue by forwards who were allowed to barge goalies. That was when we used to have the saying 'all goalkeepers are mad'. They had to take their lives in their hands every time they went on the field.

"Pat would have been able to look after himself in that era. He was immensely strong, a natural athlete and brave beyond measure. We had to be patient with him at first, but once he conquered his nerves he became an extraordinary goalkeeper with a perfect temperament. He, Mike England and Philip Beal had a perfect understanding, and this spread confidence throughout the team, particularly to Pat, who became expert at knowing when to leave his line. That understanding between the triangle of players at the heart of your defence is absolutely vital."

Full-backs: Alf Ramsey and Cyril Knowles
"Alf was a supreme right-back. I should know because I played in front of him for hundreds of matches. He was very stylish, had a cultured right foot and never ever panicked. He was not so strong with his left, but good enough to convince people he was two-footed.

"His speciality was jockeying his wingers into no man's land so that they could not get their crosses over. His tackle was firm and decisive and delivered in textbook style. Alf was a deadly accurate passer of the ball and would take most of our penalties and free-kicks.

"As you can imagine, he was a thinking man's player and such a student of tactics that we used to call him 'The General'. We spent every waking hour – when we weren't playing – talking tactics and theories, always trying to dream up different approaches to the game. Tottenham back then was like being at a university of football.

"Alf was not the fastest of runners, but we had a great understanding and I would be his cover if there was a winger who was particularly quick. I used to joke with him that he got rid of wingers as revenge for those who had been too quick and clever for him. There were not many of those, I promise you. He was a master at marking. It was once wrongly suggested that Alf and I disliked each other. It was just that circumstances meant we were often fierce but friendly rivals. We always wanted to get one over on each other. I had enormous respect for his knowledge of the game.

"Knowlesy would have been a perfect partner for Alf, although completely contrasting in personality and attitude. While Alf was totally wrapped up in every game, Cyril was sometimes a daydreamer and also a joker who would be trying to amuse the crowd rather than concentrate on doing the right things properly.

"He had started out as a winger and had all the tricks of a clever player, like his brother Peter at Wolves, and he used to drive me mad with his habit of casually dribbling the ball out of defence. Cyril could unleash an extremely mean tackle when necessary and used that educated left foot of his to launch swift counter attacks.

"He had a devil-may-care temperament, and I was very fond of him. If he had a fault it was his casualness, but when it really mattered you could count on him to do his job. He gets his place in my defence just ahead of that loyal man Ron Henry, who had to hold off a strong challenge from Mel Hopkins in the Double days."

Central Defenders: Mike England and Ron Burgess
"Two great Welshmen at the heart of my defence. Mike was a magnificent centre-half, who gets the nod ahead of my 'Push and Run' mate Harry Clarke and just edges out Maurice Norman from the Double side. He was a more classical player than Big Mo, who was enormously strong but Mike had the edge in all-round skill. Mike and the hugely underrated Philip Beal had a great understanding and were almost impassable when both were on top of their game. If Mike didn't get you, then Phil did.

"Both Mike and Maurice were commanding in the air. Beal, who had a fine temperament, would have had a lot of England caps to his name but for the presence of the immaculate Bobby Moore – who I tried to sign before the 1966 World Cup finals. However, once England had won under his captaincy there was no chance of West Ham daring to let him go until he was past his best.

"Alongside Mike is the man I always call the greatest of all players to pull on a Lilywhite shirt – Ron Burgess. He was a phenomenal player, whether helping out in defence of driving the team forward from midfield. Ron was a real powerhouse with astonishing energy and the complete all-rounder. Defending or attacking, he was an unstoppable force and a fantastic captain who you would follow over the top – as dear old Eddie Baily would say. A great man to have alongside you in the trenches. We were close friends and joined Spurs on the very same day back in 1936. What a player!"

Midfield: Danny Blanchflower, John White and Dave Mackay

"How could I choose any other midfield trio? They were the engine room of the team that created history by winning the Double and then drove us – with Tony Marchi in for the injured Mackay – to the first major European trophy victory.

"Danny was one of the most intelligent and imaginative of all players, who used brain power rather than muscle to dominate matches. He was very neat and precise, and a brilliant reader of a game. If he had a fault it was not giving enough attention to his defensive duties, but Peter Baker usually provided sound cover.

"John White was fittingly nicknamed 'The Ghost' because defences could never work out where he was coming from with his clever runs and beautifully weighted passes. He had great stamina and could run all day, and he had a real footballer's brain and could outthink and outwit opponents.

"Then there was the thundering tackling and giant heart of Dave Mackay, the best buy I ever made. He was the equivalent of two men on the pitch and had subtle skill to go with his driving power.

"I could not consider Glenn Hoddle because he did not make it into the first team while I was manager; even so I don't think I would have selected him ahead of Danny and John White. Others who just missed out were Martin Peters, Eddie Baily, Alan Mullery and that big-hearted competitor Steve Perryman. I loved Ossie Ardiles but he came after my management."

Forwards: Cliff Jones, Alan Gilzean and Jimmy Greaves

"Cliff Jones was an easy one. Though mainly a right-footed player, he could operate on either wing and would give the team important width. He had the speed to trouble any defence, was as brave as a lion and, for a small man, was quite amazing in the air. It was like being able to call on two wingers, because Cliff could be a handful whether coming from right or left. His fast diagonal runs used to cause panic in so many defences. As he often used to tell me, he was a world-class winger.

"Other wingers who came into the frame were the two Terrys, Medwin and Dyson, and 'Push and Run' pair Sonny Walters and Les Medley. But Cliff was comfortably the best of them.

"Of course, the simplest selection of all was Jimmy Greaves, the greatest British goalscorer of my lifetime. He made the job of putting the ball into the net look easy, and let's face it goals are what the game is all about, whether scoring them or stopping them. Jimmy was a born goalscorer, and I considered myself very lucky to have signed him... even though we should have had him straight from school for nothing!

"My hardest job was picking who should partner Greavsie. I got my shortlist down to Len Duquemin, Bobby Smith, Alan Gilzean and Martin Chivers, who for three seasons was probably the best No.9 in Europe. Any one of them would have done the job, but I finally settled for the artistic Gilly because I read a quote from Jimmy saying that is what he preferred, just ahead of the battering-ram Smithy. If that is what Jimmy wants, that is what he gets. He is the main man."

So there we have Bill Nicholson's team of teams, in a flexible 4-3-3 formation:

'SIR BILL'

                    Jennings
Ramsey   England   Burgess   Knowles
    Blanchflower   White   Mackay
      Jones   Gilzean   Greaves

It's interesting to see that Bill selected only three English players – Ramsey, Knowles and Greaves. Under pressure from this diligent, persistent reporter, Bill chose this shadow side:

                    Brown
Baker   Norman   Beal   Henry
   Mullery   Perryman   Peters
     Chivers   Smith   Dyson

Ten Englishmen and one Scot – Bill Brown – in Bill's second-best line-up of Tottenham players. What a game it would have been between those two sides! Of course, 'Skip' Perryman had to have his say:

"I could not resist joining in the selecting game when I saw Bill's two teams. Any side that includes Pat Jennings, Mike England, Cliff Jones and the 'G-Men' – Greavsie and Gilly – has to have utmost respect, and the inclusion of the Double trio of Blanchflower, White and Mackay is a no-brainer. From everything I've been told about them, there has rarely been a midfield combination to touch them.

"All the old-timers assured me that Alf Ramsey was the best right-back the club ever had. I've only seen old black and white film of him but you can see he was a class player, with good balance and excellent distribution. Like so many, he lost his best years to the war, and I'm told he knocked two years off his age when reporting back for playing duty after peace had been declared. So he was in his late twenties before he joined Spurs. No wonder he'd slowed down. Cyril Knowles was still operating when I got into the team and he was one of the club's great characters. He had a winger's ball control and could be lethal with the sort of no-holds-barred tackling that would get him sent to

the Tower in today's much softer game. He was always cheerful and good company. Nice one, Cyril!

"I would have had to make out a case for Glenn Hoddle and Ossie Ardiles from my generation to be included, but I have to bow to Bill's superior knowledge and understanding of the game. He was out on his own, and it was my privilege to play for him."

While we're in selecting game mood, I must throw in a contribution I once got from my dear old friend and work colleague Danny Blanchflower. Danny tried hard to hide his disappointment when Tottenham's great North London rivals Arsenal repeated the Double feat 10 years after he had led Spurs to the League Championship and the FA Cup.

Privately he told me: "We did it with style and guile, while they were more smash and grab. Surely anybody with any judgement at all will admit we were the better side in every way. We were not only easy on the eye, but had the Championship wrapped up with weeks to go, while Arsenal did not clinch it until beating Tottenham at White Hart Lane in the last week of the season."

I sat Danny down in the summer of 1971 and got him to compare the Tottenham and Arsenal Double-winning sides. These were his considered man-by-man ratings:

Bill Brown v Bob Wilson
"Not a lot to choose between them. Bill used to give me grey hairs with some of his positioning, but he had a good, safe pair of hands and never let the side down. Wilson has made enormous improvements and is now just a fingertip ahead of Bill. So I select Bob, but he is not in the same class as Pat Jennings."

Peter Baker v Pat Rice
"I often felt guilty about taking my wages because Peter did so much covering behind me! I had a dodgy knee in my last three seasons at Tottenham, and I would not have been nearly as effective without Peter working so hard. Pat is a good, solid and reliable right-back, but my conscience insists I give the nod to Peter."

Ron Henry v Bob McNab
"Ron was greatly underestimated and deserved more than his solitary cap for England. He had good ball control and could tackle with venom. Bobby McNab is a tigerish player who uses the ball intelligently, and just edges out Ron in my opinion."

Danny Blanchflower v Peter Storey
"As if I'm not going to select myself! Accuse me of many things, but not false modesty. With respect to Peter, he doesn't have my experience which meant I could dictate matches not only with my passing but with my thinking. It strikes me Peter is played mainly in a destructive role. He does it efficiently but it's too negative for my taste."

Maurice Norman v Frank McLintock
"Frank and I had the captain's responsibility in common, and I think it fair to say we were both key players for our team. Of course, Frank was right-half in the Leicester team we beat to clinch the Double in the FA Cup final. He has switched to centre-half with impressive skill and determination, and – while Maurice had a distinct edge in the air – I would have to pick Frank to fill the No.5 shirt."

Dave Mackay v Peter Simpson
"Sorry, but this is no race. Peter is one of the most consistent defenders in the country, but he is not in the same league as Dave Mackay. If I was picking a World XI, Dave would be one of my first choices. He energised the team, frightened the life out of the opposition and had exceptional skill to go with his strength."

Cliff Jones v George Armstrong
"We are talking world-class – Cliff – against a good-quality domestic player. Cliff had the speed, the skill and the courage to take apart the tightest defence. His bravery was beyond belief and he used to make me shudder the way he would dive in where others feared to tread. George is a fine creative winger but not in the same class as Jones. We are talking one of the greatest wingers the UK has ever produced."

John White v George Graham
"Again, this is no race. John was the hidden ace in our team, making it tick with his measured passes and opening the way to goal with clever blindside running. George has good skills and is a player of vision, but John was a class above him. He was a joy to play with and always popping up in the right place to collect a pass. But for his tragically early death, I am convinced John would have written himself much larger into football's hall of fame."

Bobby Smith v John Radford
"At his peak in that Double year, Bobby broke down the best defences in the land with his battering-ram strength and explosive finishing. He was not all raw power: he had deceptive changes of pace and excellent close control. People used to find it hard to believe that he stood only 5ft 9in tall. John is a determined player with good positional sense and a deft touch in front of goal, but you ask any centre-half whom he would least like to mark out of Smith and Radford and I guarantee they would all go for the Tottenham man."

Les Allen v Ray Kennedy
"Les was the perfect partner for Bobby Smith in that Double season, playing with subtlety and skill that balanced Bobby's strength. He was unlucky to lose his place the following season to the one and only Jimmy Greaves (we are talking genius with Jimmy, so it is no reflection on Les). Ray Kennedy is a strong, willing and promising player but has some way to go before he can be considered as effective as Allen."

Terry Dyson v Charlie George
"Our Mr Dependable, Terry could be counted on to run himself into the ground for the team. But going on potential and promise, I am giving Charlie George the final place. He is an outstanding prospect and has natural finishing skills that you cannot teach. He has that natural ability to be able to do the unexpected. In football, that is a priceless gift."

'SIR BILL'

So Danny Boy's combined 'Doubles' team lined up like this (in 4-2-4 formation):

Wilson

Baker McLintock Mackay McNab

Blanchflower White

Jones Smith Allen George

Inevitably, I asked Danny who he would have managing the team out of Bill Nicholson or Bertie Mee, and his response is the reason for giving this side such prominence in this book:

"That is the easiest choice of all. Bertie Mee is a master organiser, excellent at man management and supreme at delegation, but he is not in the same street as Bill Nicholson when it comes to football management. Yes, Mee's Arsenal have just become the second team after Spurs to win the league and FA Cup Double this century, but come on – I know I'm biased, but they were not fit to tie the boot laces of Bill's Double team. I would put Bill up there with managers of the highest calibre, along with the likes of Matt Busby, Bill Shankly and Jock Stein of Celtic fame. Bill has a vast knowledge of the game at all levels, is a genius of a tactician and is the most honest man I have ever met. An absolute diamond.

"We had a shaky start to our relationship because Jimmy Anderson stuck his oar in and stirred it up between us. But once we started acting like adults – and Jimmy was off the scene – we found common ground in that we both loved the Beautiful Game and wanted it presented in full, brilliant technicolour, not the black and white of so many mean teams.

"He used to get somewhat jumpy when I kept talking openly about doing the Double. Bill was quite a superstitious man and thought it was challenging the gods of football to talk about what at the time was considered the impossible dream. I used to tell that delightful wife of his, Grace, that she should prepare herself to welcome home the most famous manager in the country. But, of course, the strength of their union is that she did not allow the fortunes of football – often the outrageous slings and arrows of the game – to dictate his moods at home.

TEAM OF TEAMS

"It was in Grace and their wonderful daughters that Bill found sanctuary from the pressures of football management. That we managed to actually win the Double as we had dared prophecy made us the 'Cocks of the Football Walk'. There has not been a team to match us at our peak, so please don't be impertinent and mention that other club from North London!"

I showed Danny's selection to Bill, and he gave an exaggerated shudder: "No, sorry. Too many Reds for my taste. The Tottenham Double side was untouchable."

I looked for a hint of a smile. But 'Sir Bill' was deadly serious. And for Danny Boy, the victory pipes were calling.

Now, over to the other great skipper, Steve Perryman...

CHAPTER 24

FINAL SHOTS

Steve Perryman MBE

We are coming towards the climax of our journey through the life and times of Bill Nicholson, but for me it is one that will never end, because 'Sir Bill' will always be with me. He more than anybody gave me the code of conduct by which I have lived my life, and it is only now – working on this tribute book – that I realise just what an impact the great man had on me.

Norman and I have done our best to capture the real Bill Nick. If you have a picture in your head of a perfectionist of a man in every aspect of his life, sincere, very serious, direct, meticulous, motivational, a family man married to Darkie *and* to Tottenham Hotspur, above all honest and totally trustworthy, then we have done our job.

In this final chapter, I have pushed Norman to one side and am giving it to you straight about the Bill Nicholson I knew, respected and loved – yes, loved. Let me start by taking one of my early games as an example of Bill's integrity and his demand for things to be done properly.

I was still an unknown when I was selected for a league match at Leeds. They were one of the most famed and feared teams in the land at the time, with a reputation for not just playing brilliant football but playing it with a win-at-all-costs competitive attitude that made them hated outside Yorkshire.

There I was, a kid barely out of the football pram and battling for midfield supremacy with the likes of Billy Bremner, Johnny Giles and Norman Hunter, of 'Bites Yer Legs' notoriety. This 'Southern Softie' decided I was going to fight fire with fire and took them on at their own don't-give-an-inch game.

We had been playing a few minutes when – whack. Giles had caught me and sent me tumbling. Welcome to the big boys' game.

A few minutes later Giles and I went for a 50-50 ball and this time he went over as I threw myself into the tackle with a determination that surprised him. Everybody thought it was me getting my own back for the first challenge, but I was just being competitive and had no thought of revenge in my head. From that moment on I was a marked man, and the Leeds players took turns trying to rough up this young whippersnapper. Steve Who?

We won the match 2-1 thanks to two cracking goals from Big Chiv, and as we came off at the end Giles offered me his hand but I brushed it aside. He had just spent 90 minutes trying to hurt me, break my leg even. I was not going to be two-faced and pretend all was forgotten.

Sharp-eyed reporters picked up on the little altercation and the talking point in the Monday newspapers was that I had refused to shake hands with Giles. Oh yes, and I may have made a less than friendly gesture. I was just pleased to get off the pitch in one piece.

Bill Nick called me to one side, having read the newspapers.

"Is this true, young man?" he asked. "Did you refuse to shake his hand?"

"Dead right," I said, possibly puffing out my chest. "He'd been kicking me all game and could have broken my leg."

"Well," said Bill, "let me tell you that when you're representing Spurs you must be sporting and return a handshake at the end of a match. If you don't you will never wear a Spurs shirt again."

There you have Bill Nicholson. Everything had to be done properly and by the book and good sportsmanship reigned.

Many years later Johnny Giles apologised to me for his behaviour in that match. He was a magnificent footballer, but when he joined Leeds from Manchester United he came under Don Revie's influence and suddenly became devious – what we called in the game 'a crafty tackler'. Players like Norman Hunter, Jack Charlton and Billy Bremner were open with their aggressive play, but the likes of Giles and Allan Clarke got their kicks in sneakily. The irony was that the defeat cost Leeds the league title and virtually handed it to that other lot down the road.

I never ever knew Bill Nicholson to ask his players to cross the line and hurt an opponent. Tell a lie – there was just once I recall when even he was moved to want to kick the opposition. It was a UEFA Cup match against Setubal in Portugal and we had been kicked black and blue by one aggressive individual. At half-time he was moved to say: "For goodness sake somebody take out their No.6 before he puts you all in hospital." That was the one and only time I ever heard him want us to resort to physical violence. Bill was a footballing pacifist. He liked us to play hard but fair.

In fact he used to go out of his way to praise the opposition to their faces. I remember the second leg of the UEFA Cup final against Wolves at the Lane in 1972, when we scrambled through thanks to Chiv scoring two great goals in the first leg at Molineux before Mullers got the goal that settled it for us at the Lane. That was the night that Alan made a one-man lap of honour while we were all stuck in the dressing room because of a crowd invasion of the pitch. The only person missing was Bill Nick. He had gone into the Wolves dressing room where he spent 10 minutes telling them how great they had been and how unlucky they were not to have won the trophy!

That was typical – Bill being Bill and giving all the plaudits to the opponents. It upset a few of my team-mates but I was not bothered. As long as we had the trophy to show off, Bill could shower the praise wherever he liked. It revealed how gracious he was in victory or defeat.

He had a real poker face, so you did not really know what he was thinking. The one time he could not hide his feelings was in the UEFA Cup final against Feyenoord in Rotterdam in 1974. Their supporters had dished out a lot of punishment in the first leg in London, and some of our fans were set on revenge in the Netherlands.

Events got completely out of hand, and because of the rioting and fighting in the stands Bill was unable to give his half-time tactics talk. I was in the dressing room and so it was not possible for me to see Bill address the crowd, pleading for them to behave. Apparently he was in tears of anger and frustration. That, I remember, was the breaking point for Bill and the beginning of the end of his managing days.

The following season he was a shell of the man who had led Tottenham to so many 'Glory Glory' nights. It got to the point where he and Eddie Baily had lost it and were making daft decisions. All good things come to an end, and Bill knew he had overcooked it and was just about burned out. Coventry had asked for me in return for two of their players, and the fact that Bill was even considering it was proof to me – conceited if you like, but fact – that he had lost his judgement.

Nobody could believe it when the directors ignored his advice and named Terry Neill as his successor rather than Bill's nomination of Danny Blanchflower and my nemesis, Johnny Giles.

But thank goodness the Bill Nicholson era was not completely over. He was invited to return to the club when Keith Burkinshaw took over as manager and became an important influence in the background.

I thought back to when I first joined the club as a 15-year-old straight from school. I had not been there five minutes when Bill put me forward for a television interview about the challenges of being a football apprentice. "You're a grammar school boy," he said. "You can be the spokesperson."

This was completely against how I had wanted to conduct myself. My idea was to keep a low profile while I learned about the game. There were 15 other apprentices at the club, all of them older and more experienced than me, and I knew I was letting myself in for a lot of ridicule and mickey-taking if I gave the interview after such a small taste of my new life.

After losing sleep for two nights, I plucked up the courage to go to Bill's office and tell him I didn't want to do the interview.

His response: "I've told the TV people that you're doing it, and you're doing it. Young man, you can do anything you put your mind to."

So in my first few weeks in football I had discovered the real Bill Nicholson. When he had made up his mind on something, nothing would shift him. And that was how he managed Spurs for 16 years – from the boot room to the boardroom.

You can do anything you put your mind to. Thanks, Bill.

My lasting impression of Bill is of a meticulous man, thorough in all that he did and tunnel-visioned about football. Everything had to be just so. He never sought the searchlight of personal glory and was the consummate team man. Bill was always smartly dressed in an old-fashioned way and the one permanent feature was a biro pen stuck in his top jacket pocket. He was an inveterate note taker, particularly during matches, rarely scribbling but writing clearly and precisely. Just so.

FINAL SHOTS

I am sure that if he could have started from scratch, he would have loosened up a bit and squeezed a little more enjoyment from life. But as his devoted wife Darkie used to say, he was not only married to her but to Spurs. Bill gave it all he'd got and it was a never-ending source of disbelief that others did not share his all-consuming enthusiasm and desire for getting things right.

Yes, everything had to be just so. I count myself lucky to have come under his spell early in my career. He passed on only good habits.

I always look back on him as like a second father and I was fiercely proud to be a member of his Spurs family.

My co-author Norman Giller and I wondered how we could close this tribute to 'Sir Bill' in suitable style. We decided to turn to an interview – more of a conversation – Jimmy Greaves had with him for *A Centenary Celebration* video that Norman scripted in 1982. Bill and Jim were two of our favourite people in the world. I had the privilege of playing with Jim in his last few months as a Spurs goal master, and was a regular on his Terry Baker-promoted chatshow circuit in the autumn of his life. Norman was his best mate for 64 years and delivered his eulogy, so it is fitting the last word in our 'Sir Bill' journey goes to two White Hart Lane legends…

Jim: "Well, Bill, it's 20 years since you came and rescued me from my prison in Italy…"

Bill: "Best bit of business I ever did. But we should have had you straight from school for nowt."

Jim: "That was down to my Dad. He got sweet-talked by that rascal of a scout Jimmy Thompson, who whisked me off to Chelsea. I'll be honest, I loved my days at the Bridge and had a good rapport with the fans there. But when I joined Spurs I knew I was with the best club in the world, and that's down to you."

Bill: "Don't embarrass me, Jim. I had a great team around me. I couldn't have done it on my own. It was all because of teamwork."

Jim: "I knew it wouldn't take you long to talk about team work. That was always your mantra: 'There's no "I" in team.'"

Bill: "But it's true. You can't win things with a bunch of individualists.

You have to sing from the same song sheet, and that was what my job was as a coach – getting everybody in harmony. It's not rocket science. Just play for each other. It worked a treat with our Double team."

Jim: "You can say that again. I played against them twice that season with Chelsea and they were the best club side I ever faced. That's why I jumped at the chance to play with them when you bought me from Milan. I've still not seen an English side to match them, particularly the midfield trio of Danny, dear John White and the untouchable Dave Mackay."

Bill: "I wanted you, Jim, from the moment you scored that fantastic goal against us in your Chelsea debut in 1957."

Jim: "Yes, I got lucky and managed to nip past three or four tackles, including from the man who became my close friend, Danny Blanchflower. I've never known anybody to match his reading of a game."

Bill: "You and me both. He was a great thinker but could come up with some weird ideas. I remember that he once wanted us to play with our goalkeeper Bill Brown at centre-half. We tried it once in training and gave up after, I think, Jim Iley had twice lobbed the ball into an empty net."

Jim: "He was always looking to do something different. He once challenged me to a game of golf in which we had to play one-handed. He sulked because as somebody who is ambidextrous I was able to keep switching hands..."

Bill: "Danny was on the transfer list when I first took over as manager. Thank goodness we got that sorted out because it was his burning belief that we could do the Double that motivated the whole team."

Jim: "I joined the following season and was petrified that I was going to upset the rhythm of the team. But thank goodness I got off to a great start with that hat-trick against Blackpool, and from then on I was accepted by the other players and the supporters."

FINAL SHOTS

Bill: "You scored that excellent goal after just three minutes in the 1962 FA Cup final against Burnley. It was just like a putting shot from the edge of the green, and nobody could believe it when it went all the way into the net past half a dozen players."

Jim: "You know me, Bill, I didn't boast about goals, but I was particularly pleased with that one because I'd predicted I would score early and that shot was as accurate as any I'd ever hit."

Bill: "You scored some fantastic goals. There was that one against Manchester United when you beat four men in the space of a hall carpet, and then that cracker against Leicester. You went past at least five players before selling a dummy to Peter Shilton and then passing the ball into the net – your trademark way of finishing."

Jim: "Funniest goal was that one Pat Jennings scored up at Old Trafford in the '67 Charity Shield. The wind got the ball and took it first bounce over the head of Alex Stepney and into the United net. Gilly and I had no idea who'd scored it until we looked back to see Pat dancing in the penalty area. It was the week before the season started and Pat was able to boast that he was the club's joint top scorer!"

Bill: "Pat was one of my best signings. My old Spurs buddy Ron Burgess tipped me off that he'd signed this young goalkeeper when he was at Watford. By the time I wanted to buy him Bill McGarry had taken over as manager and it took several weeks to persuade Pat that Spurs was the right club for him."

Jim: "He was a bag of nerves when he arrived and you had to bring Bill Brown back for a few matches. I told Pat that he was going to become one of the world's greatest goalkeepers. He certainly proved me a good judge. I couldn't believe it when Spurs allowed him to move to Highbury. I don't think the fans ever forgave them. Who was your best buy, Bill?"

Bill: "No question, Dave Mackay. It was like buying two men. He tackled like a tank and had the sweetest of left feet. Most of all, he was a driver who could lift the players around him by both example and exhortation. When Mackay was raging and waving his fist, his team-mates could not help but respond by raising their game. And the bravery of the man. Most footballers would have given up the ghost when he broke a leg for a second time, but it just made him more determined to play again. I never liked the hyperbole that the press went in for, but to call him the 'Miracle Man' was accurate and justified."

Jim: "I would name him top of my list of the great motivators. He was just a born leader of men. You could almost hear the bagpipes as he went into battle. There's something they put into the water in Scotland. My favourite partner was Alan Gilzean. That was a great bit of transfer business when you bought him from Dundee."

Bill: "Yes, you two together as 'The G-Men' were something special. The pair of you were poetry in motion. I also enjoyed your partnership with Bobby Smith. He was a completely different player to Gilly, using a lot of muscle power, but the end product was just as impressive."

Jim: "I loved playing with them both. Bobby was much more than just a physical force. He had excellent skill and good positional sense. Gilly could do things I'd never seen before. Defenders never quite knew how to mark him because he could completely deceive them by a simple flick of the ball. What was your most satisfying match as manager, Bill?"

Bill: "That's a pretty easy question to answer. You scored two goals in the match but the best player on the night was Terry Dyson – yes, of course, the European Cup Winners' Cup final victory over Atletico Madrid. We became the first British club to win a major trophy in Europe. Nobody will ever be able to take that record away from us."

Jim: "We might have beaten Jock Stein's Celtic to the European Cup if we had not been robbed in the semi-final against Benfica. I scored a perfectly good goal in the second leg that was criminally ruled offside."

Bill: "That's football, Jim. If the gods are against you, there's nothing you can do about it."

FINAL SHOTS

Jim: "This had nothing to do with the gods. This was an appalling refereeing decision. I was always able to shrug off the calls that went against me, but this one continues to hurt and haunt me all these years later. We could have gone on to win the trophy that year because Real Madrid were a shadow of their great side of the 1950s."

Bill: "That's football, Jim. Some you win, some you lose."

And that was how the conversation ended, with Bill being philosophical and Jim angry over that disallowed goal in the 1962 European Cup semi-final.

If Bill had won that he would surely, surely have become SIR BILL.

Thank you from Steve and I for your company. And thank you 'Sir Bill'. COYS!

EXTRA-TIME

During my 14 years as a member of the *This Is Your Life* scriptwriting team, I was continually trying to get Bill Nicholson booked. One of my roles was to prepare dossiers for the show's producer, Malcolm Morris, who would run them past Eamonn Andrews and – for the later series – Michael Aspel.

Sadly, a much-deserved tribute never got past the programme planning stage. But at least this book gives me the chance to take a microscope to Bill's life and times. One of the reasons the programme producers were nervous about featuring Bill was that his close confidante, Danny Blanchflower, had famously turned down Eamonn and told him politely where to stick his red book. It cost thousands to scrap the planned show, because relatives, club-mates and friends had been brought from all parts of the globe to join in a tribute to Danny Boy that never ever took place. The fear was that Bill – a shy, private man – might be tempted to do a Danny.

As I'd learned over the years from our first face-to-face meeting in 1958, Bill was very much a tracksuit manager, and only really content when at the Cheshunt training ground working on tactics and theories with his other family – the players.

I have fished out the dossier I compiled for the eyes of Eamonn Andrews in 1981, and here it is in the original note form (the quotes were put in to give Eamonn a taste of what the guests might say). We had to give each proposed subject a codeword, because if ever it leaked out that a *Life* show was being planned it would be instantly shelved. These are my notes, exactly as they dropped on to the desk of that legendary broadcaster:

'SIR BILL'

THIS IS YOUR LIFE BILL NICHOLSON DOSSIER

SUGGESTED CODEWORD: COCKEREL

Submitted by Norman Giller for the confidential attention of Eamonn Andrews

SUMMARY: William Edward Nicholson, ex-footballer and later football manager; born Scarborough, North Yorkshire, 26 January 1919; played for Tottenham Hotspur 1936-55, coach 1956-58, manager 1958-74, managerial consultant West Ham 1975-76; currently chief scout and consultant at White Hart Lane; capped once for England in 1951; OBE 1975

PERSONAL: Married to Grace (known as 'Darkie'). They have two daughters (Linda and Jean), and throughout his managerial career with Tottenham he and the family lived in an end-of-terrace house within walking distance of White Hart Lane. Darkie famously cycled to the local shops on a push bike. He banned her from watching them play because he considered her a jinx.

Quote (circa 1970) from Darkie, a charming and bubbly lady: "I accept that Bill has two marriages – one to me, the other to football in general and Tottenham Hotspur in particular. Even when we are on summer holiday in Scarborough his mind is eaten up with ideas for the following season. Sometimes I wonder if he should have a bed put in his office at White Hart Lane!"

EARLY LIFE: Born and raised between the wars in Scarborough, the second youngest of a hansom cab driver's nine children. Grew up during the Depression, and on leaving school at the age of 16, he took

EXTRA-TIME

a job as a laundry boy and played his football for Scarborough Young Liberals and Scarborough Working Men's Club. In 1936, aged 17, he was spotted by Spurs and moved south to join their nursery club, Gravesend & Northfleet, before turning professional in 1938. Served an apprenticeship at £2 a week. Best person to cover this part of his footballing life is Ronnie Burgess, who captained Spurs and Wales in the 1950s and was Bill's close pal; they joined Spurs on the same day. Worth a close-up of a pencil-written letter from Spurs scout Ben Ives offering Bill a month's trial. It's now a family heirloom. Quote (circa 1961) from Ron Burgess: "Bill was the most conscientious footballer I ever played with. He gave 100 per cent in everything that he did and would always put the team first. In those early days at Gravesend and then in the first team he unselfishly agreed to play at left-back, even though he was essentially right-footed. He lost his best years to the war, otherwise he would have won a load of England caps."

WAR YEARS: Bill had just started to establish himself in the first team when war was declared in September 1939. He served in the Durham Light Infantry, stationed mainly in England first as an infantry corporal, then a physical training instructor sergeant. He also found time for Saturday guest appearances with Middlesbrough, Sunderland, Newcastle United and Darlington.

When he reported back to Spurs in 1945 he first of all played at centre-half and then switched to right-half – the position in which he was to establish himself as one of the most reliable and industrious players in the league. He became a key man in the Spurs 'Push and Run' team that in back-to-back seasons of 1949 to 1951 won the Second Division and First Division titles. Note to Eamonn: Ideally we should bring in Alf Ramsey here, but he always refuses to do the show. I think he's in fear that he will be the subject. Instead, we can go for 'Push and Run' schemer Eddie Baily, who was Bill's right-hand man at Tottenham. Quote (circa 1967) from Eddie Baily, England and Tottenham inside-left and later coach, who was nicknamed the 'Cheeky Chappie' after comedian Max Miller: "Bill was a player's player. He did not hunt personal glory but gave everything he had to the team. You could count his bad games on the fingers of 'One Arm Lou' [a notorious ticket spiv of the time]. The 'Push and Run' side would not have functioned nearly so well without Billy's energy and enthusiasm. He covered for Alf behind him and prompted the forwards with neat rather than spectacular passes. He left those to me! He learned a lot from our great manager Arthur Rowe, and when he retired it was obvious he would make an outstanding coach and manager. He was a born tactician and he and Alf Ramsey were trying to introduce new attacking ideas."

PLAYING CAREER: Bill played 314 league games for Spurs as a defensive, anchorman midfield player, and scored six goals. He won one England cap for England as stand-in for the injured Billy Wright against Portugal at Goodison in May 1951, when he was 32. Remarkably, he scored with his first kick in international football, netting from 20 yards with a drive in the first minute. He never got another call-up because of the consistency of Billy Wright.

Quote (circa 1980) from Billy Wright, England and Wolves captain, former Arsenal manager and now Head of Sport at ATV: "Typical of Bill, when I told him he had deserved another chance with England he said, 'No, you are the better player and the No.4 England shirt belongs to you.' I have rarely known such a modest man, and he is the perfect role model for young players coming into the game and also young managers. I may have been a better player, but it was no race as to which of us was the better manager! He was one of the top three in the game. His coaching ability was second to none."

THE COACH: In 1954, Bill was honest enough to admit that his troublesome knee would not allow him to play at full power anymore and he voluntarily stood down from the team, and after helping the reserves for a while retired to concentrate on his great love – coaching. He gained his FA coaching badge at the first attempt and worked with the Tottenham youth squad as well as the Cambridge University team. In 1957 he became assistant to Spurs manager Jimmy Anderson, who had replaced the unwell Arthur Rowe. In 1958 he was a member of the England coaching staff that travelled to Sweden for the World Cup finals.

Quote (circa 1968) from Sir Walter Winterbottom, England manager 1947-1962 and later chairman of the Central Council for Physical Recreation: "I assigned Bill to watch the Brazilians during the 1958 games in readiness for our match. He came back with his head full of tactical plans, and we sat down and worked out how we could stop a team that was beating everybody in sight. It was largely due to Bill's creative input that we held Brazil to a goalless draw. It was an extraordinary performance against a team that became arguably the greatest world champions ever. Bill has proved beyond question that he is one of the most astute managers and coaches our game has ever produced."

Bill juggled his Tottenham manager's role with taking charge of the England Under-23 summer tours for many years and was the choice of a lot of good judges to take over the England job before his old Tottenham team-mate Alf Ramsey was appointed manager in 1962.

THE CLUB MANAGER: In October 1958, Bill was appointed manager in place of Jimmy Anderson and on the very day that he took charge Spurs beat Everton 10-4! The star of the match was 'Tom Thumb' Tommy Harmer, who scored one goal and helped create seven others.

Quote (circa 1980) from Tommy Harmer, Tottenham's 'tiny tot' midfield schemer, a chain-smoker and now a messenger in the City: "It was one of those matches when everything we touched turned to goals. It could easily have been 15-8. When we came off at the end I said to Bill: 'Don' t expect this every week, Boss.'"

The greatest feat with which Bill will always be associated was the league and FA Cup Double of 1960/61, the first time it had been achieved in the 20th century and considered the 'Impossible Dream'. Bill and his captain Danny Blanchflower were the driving force that lifted Tottenham into the land of legend. Many experts rate that Double team the greatest British club side of all time.

Note to Eamonn: The perfect person to produce here would be Danny, but after your previous experience I am sure you will not second that opinion! So I suggest Dave Mackay, the heart of the Spurs...

Quote (circa 1980) from Dave Mackay: "Bill was a master tactician who could see a game in his mind before it was played. He had a photographic memory when it came to footballers and could recall instantly the strengths and weaknesses of almost any player he had ever seen. I considered myself fortunate to play under him and tried to take his attitude and application into management."

'SIR BILL'

The summer after completing the Double, Bill went to Italy and bought Jimmy Greaves from AC Milan for £99,999 (not wanting to give Jimmy the pressure of being the first £100,000 footballer). That following season Spurs won the FA Cup and reached the semi-finals of the European Cup, going out in controversial circumstances to eventual champions Benfica. This should be when we spring Jimmy Greaves (with whom I am currently writing our sixth book together).

Quote (1981) from Jimmy Greaves: "Bill would not be my choice as company for a night out on the town, but he would be first on my list of managers. He can be dour and tunnel-visioned where football is concerned, but he does not see his job to be a comedian. His teams always entertain on the pitch, and that is because he gives them free rein. He never tried to put any restrictions on me, and I enjoyed the freedom. We won the FA Cup for Bill in 1962, which was consolation for not beating Benfica in the European Cup semi-final. I had a perfectly good goal ruled offside, which would have given us a chance of reaching the final."

The following season Tottenham created history by becoming the first British team to win a major European trophy, with a 5-1 victory over Atletico Madrid in the European Cup Winners' Cup final in Rotterdam. We could have fun here by bringing on Bill's big pal Bill Shankly...

Quote (circa 1973) from Bill Shankly, legendary Liverpool manager: "Bill's the canniest manager in the business and always comes up with tactical thoughts that make the difference between winning and losing. He showed us all the way to win in Europe and has set standards that we are all trying to match. I have enormous respect for him as a manager and as a man."

In less than a year Nicholson lost the engine room of his dream team. Skipper Danny Blanchflower retired with a knee injury, the swashbuckling Dave Mackay suffered a twice-broken leg, and John White was tragically killed when struck by lightning on a golf course. Bill set about rebuilding his side and brought in Pat Jennings from Watford, Cyril Knowles from Middlesbrough, Alan Mullery from Fulham, Mike England from Blackburn, Alan Gilzean from Dundee and Terry Venables from Chelsea.

Quote (circa 1980) from Terry Venables: "It was close to an impossible job to follow in the footsteps of that great Double side. That is the sort of team that comes along only once in a lifetime. But we did our best and managed to win the FA Cup in 1967. Bill set the benchmarks for all future Tottenham managers. with a historic victory over Atletico Madrid in the European Cup Winners' Cup final in Rotterdam."

To give the programme a splash of show business celebrity, we could spring comedian/satirist Peter Cook, who is a Spurs fanatic ...

Quote (circa 1977) from Peter Cook: "The sainted Bill Nicholson is the Almighty of football management. He more than anybody gave Spurs the cloak of greatness by winning the Football League Championship and FA Cup in the same season. I have tried to explain to the piano player Dudley Moore that it's the equivalent of getting a Double First at Cambridge, but as he went to the dark side at Oxford he has no idea what I'm talking about. I am just surprised that Bill has not asked for you to present him with a Tottenham blue rather than Arsenal red book..."

There were victories in the League Cup (1971 and 1973) and the UEFA Cup (1972), but Nicholson set his targets high and – disillusioned by the pay demands of several of his players and hooliganism among a section of the supporters – he resigned in 1974 but was coaxed back to Spurs in a consultancy capacity by manager Keith Burkinshaw after a brief interlude at West Ham. Keith would be a welcome guest...

Quote (circa 1980) from Keith Burkinshaw: "Bill is rightly revered throughout the world of football as not only an outstanding coach and manager but for the dignified way he has always represented our game."

This could trigger a walk-on of all the current first-team squad, with skipper Steve Perryman and Argentine Osvaldo Ardiles acting as spokesmen for the players.

Bill was rewarded with an OBE in 1975 for his services to football, while most in the game and certainly the Tottenham supporters feel he should have been given a knighthood. As a surprise guest at the end of the show, I suggest we spring Arthur Rowe, manager of the 'Push and Run' Spurs who was a huge influence on Bill both as a player and as a coach. Bill will be thrilled to see him.

That was my dossier for the eyes only of Eamonn Andrews, but the show producers decided that Bill had led a too one-dimensional football-football-football life, and the risk of him saying 'no' was too great. So 'Bill Nicholson, This Is Your Life' got no closer to realisation than this memo.

THE NUMBERS GAME

Collated by Michael Giller, sports historian and statistician (who as a starry-eyed boy used to sleep in Steve Perryman's Spurs shirt).

Full name: William Edward Nicholson
Born: 26 January 1919
Birthplace: Scarborough, North Riding of Yorkshire
Died: Aged 85, 23 October 2004 (Potters Bar, Hertfordshire)
Height: 5ft 8in (1.73 metres)
Peak playing weight: 10st 12lbs (68.95kg)

THE PLAYER
16/3/1936: Joined Tottenham Hotspur as an amateur
3/8/1938: Signed professional forms with Spurs
League games: 314; Goals: 6
FA Cup ties: 27; Goals: 0

League debut
22/10/1938: Blackburn Rovers (a) Lost 3-1
Hooper, Ward, Nicholson, Spelman, Page, Buckingham, Sargent, Morrison, Ludford, Hall (GW), Lyman

Final appearance
4/12/1954: Everton (h) Lost 3-1
Reynolds, Ramsey (c), Hopkins, Nicholson, Clarke, Marchi, Gavin, Brooks, Dunmore, Baily (1), Robb

Guest appearances: Newcastle Utd, Darlington, Hartlepool Utd, Sunderland, Middlesbrough, Fulham whilst serving with the Durham Light Infantry during the Second World War. He also played one match for Spurs on home leave in 1945

249

'SIR BILL'

INTERNATIONAL RECORD
England caps: 1; Goals: 1
19/5/1951: Portugal (h) Won 5-2; international friendly
Williams, Ramsey (c), Eckersley, Nicholson (1), Taylor, Cockburn, Finney (1), Pearson, Milburn (2), Hassall (1), Metcalfe

HONOURS
1949/50 Second Division Champions
1950/51 First Division Champions

1949/50 Second Division Champions
20/8/1949: Brentford (a) Won 4-1
Ditchburn, Ramsey, Withers, Nicholson, Clarke, Burgess (c), Walters, Bennett (1), Duquemin (1), Baily, Medley (2)

22/8/1949: Plymouth Argyle (h) Won 4-1
Ditchburn, Ramsey (1 pen), Withers, Nicholson, Clarke, Burgess (c), Walters, Bennett (1), Duquemin, Baily (1), Medley (1)

27/8/1949: Blackburn Rovers (h) Lost 3-2
Ditchburn, Ramsey, Withers, Nicholson, Clarke, Burgess (c), Walters (2), Bennett, Duquemin, Baily, Medley

31/8/1949: Plymouth Argyle (a) Won 2-0
Ditchburn, Ramsey, Withers, Nicholson, Clarke, Burgess (c), Walters, Bennett (1), Duquemin, Baily (1), Medley

3/9/1949: Cardiff City (a) Won 1-0
Ditchburn, Ramsey, Withers, Nicholson, Clarke, Burgess (c), Walters, Bennett, Duquemin, Baily, Medley (1)

5/9/1949: Sheffield Wednesday (h) Won 1-0
Ditchburn, Ramsey, Withers, Nicholson, Clarke, Burgess (c), Walters, Bennett, Duquemin (1), Baily, Medley

10/9/1949: Leeds United (h) Won 2-0
Ditchburn, Ramsey, Withers, Nicholson, Clarke, Burgess (c), Walters, Bennett (1), Duquemin, Baily (1), Medley

17/9/1949: Bury (h) Won 3-1
Ditchburn, Ramsey, Withers, Nicholson (1), Clarke, Burgess (c), Walters, Bennett, Duquemin (1), Baily (1), Medley

24/9/1949: Leicester City (a) Won 2-1
Ditchburn, Ramsey, Withers, Nicholson, Clarke, Burgess (c), Walters (1), Bennett, Duquemin (1), Baily, Medley

THE NUMBERS GAME

1/10/1949: Bradford Park Avenue (h) Won 5-0
Ditchburn, Ramsey (1 pen), Withers, Nicholson, Clarke, Burgess (c), Walters (1), Bennett (1), Duquemin, Baily, Medley (2)

8/10/1949: Southampton (a) Drew 1-1
Ditchburn, Ramsey, Withers, Nicholson, Clarke, Burgess (c), Walters (1), Bennett, Duquemin, Baily, Medley

15/10/1949: Coventry City (h) Won 3-1
Ditchburn, Ramsey (c), Withers, Nicholson, Clarke, Ludford, Walters, Bennett (1), Duquemin (2), Baily, Medley

22/10/1949: Luton Town (a) Drew 1-1
Ditchburn, Ramsey, Withers, Nicholson, Clarke, Burgess (c), Walters (1), Bennett, Duquemin, Baily, Medley

29/10/1949: Barnsley (h) Won 2-0
Ditchburn, Ramsey, Withers, Nicholson, Clarke, Burgess (c), Walters, Bennett, Duquemin (1), Baily (1), Medley

5/11/1949: West Ham United (a) Won 1-0
Ditchburn, Ramsey, Withers, Nicholson, Clarke, Burgess (c), Walters (1), Bennett, Duquemin, Baily, Medley

12/11/1949: Sheffield United (h) Won 7-0
Ditchburn, Ramsey, Withers, Nicholson, Clarke, Burgess (c), Walters (3), Bennett, Duquemin (2), Baily, Medley (2)

19/11/1949: Grimsby Town (a) Won 3-2
Ditchburn, Ramsey (1), Withers, Nicholson, Clarke, Burgess (c), Walters, Bennett (1), Duquemin, Baily, Medley (1)

26/11/1949: Queens Park Rangers (h) Won 3-0
Ditchburn, Ramsey, Withers, Nicholson (1), Clarke, Burgess (c), Cook, Bennett (2), Duquemin, Baily, Medley

3/12/1949: Preston North End (a) Won 3-1
Ditchburn, Ramsey, Withers, Nicholson, Clarke, Burgess (c), Cook, Bennett (1), Duquemin (1), Baily, Medley (1)

10/12/1949: Swansea Town (h) Won 3-1
Ditchburn, Ramsey, Withers, Nicholson, Clarke, Burgess (c), Cook, Bennett (1), Duquemin (2), Baily, Medley

17/12/1949: Brentford (h) Drew 1-1
Ditchburn, Ramsey, Withers, Nicholson, Clarke, Burgess (c), Scarth, Bennett, Duquemin, Baily (1), Medley

'SIR BILL'

24/12/1949: Blackburn Rovers (a) Won 2-1
Ditchburn, Ramsey, Withers, Nicholson, Clarke, Burgess (c), Scarth (1), Bennett, Duquemin, Baily, Medley (1)

26/12/1949: Chesterfield (h) Won 1-0
Ditchburn, Ramsey (1 pen), Withers, Nicholson, Clarke, Burgess (c), Walters, Bennett, Duquemin, Baily, Medley

27/12/1949: Chesterfield (a) Drew 1-1
Ditchburn, Ramsey, Withers, Nicholson, Clarke, Burgess (c), Rees, Scarth (1), Duquemin, Baily, Medley

31/12/1949: Cardiff City (h) Won 2-0
Ditchburn, Ramsey (c), Withers, Nicholson, Clarke, Ludford, Walters, Rees (1), Duquemin, Baily (1), Medley

14/1/1950: Leeds United (a) Lost 3-0
Ditchburn, Ramsey, Withers, Nicholson, Clarke, Burgess (c), Walters, Rees, Duquemin, Baily, Medley

21/1/1950: Bury (a) Won 2-1
Ditchburn, Ramsey, Withers, Nicholson, Clarke, Burgess (c), Walters (1), Rees, Bennett (1), Baily, Medley

4/2/1950: Leicester City (h) Lost 2-0
Ditchburn, Ramsey, Withers, Nicholson, Clarke, Burgess (c), Walters, Rees, Bennett, Baily, Medley

18/2/1950: Bradford Park Avenue (a) Won 3-1
Ditchburn, Ramsey, Withers, Nicholson, Clarke, Burgess (c), Ludford, Walters, Bennett, Duquemin (2), Rees (1), Medley

25/2/1950: Southampton (h) Won 4-0
Ditchburn, Ramsey (c), Withers, Nicholson, Clarke, Ludford, Walters, Rees (1), Duquemin (1), Baily, Medley (2)

4/3/1950: Coventry City (a) Won 1-0
Ditchburn, Ramsey, Withers, Nicholson, Clarke, Burgess (c), Walters, Rees, Duquemin, Baily, Medley (1)

11/3/1950: Luton Town (h) Drew 0-0
Ditchburn, Ramsey, Withers, Nicholson, Clarke, Burgess (c), Walters, Rees, Duquemin, Baily, Medley

18/3/1950: Barnsley (a) Lost 2-0
Ditchburn, Ramsey, Withers, Nicholson, Clarke, Burgess (c), Walters, Bennett, Duquemin, Baily, Medley

25/3/1950: West Ham United (h) Won 4-1
Ditchburn, Ramsey, Withers, Nicholson, Clarke, Burgess (c), Walters (2), Bennett (1), Duquemin, Baily, Medley (1)

THE NUMBERS GAME

1/4/1950: Queens Park Rangers (a) Won 2-0
Ditchburn, Ramsey, Withers, Nicholson, Clarke, Burgess (c), Walters, Bennett, Duquemin, Baily (1), Medley (1)

7/4/1950: Hull City (h) Drew 0-0
Ditchburn, Ramsey, Withers, Nicholson, Clarke, Burgess (c), Walters, Bennett, Duquemin, Baily, Medley

8/4/1950: Preston North End (h) Won 3-2
Ditchburn, Ramsey, Withers, Nicholson, Clarke, Burgess (c), Walters (1), Bennett (1), Duquemin, Baily, Medley (1)

10/4/1950: Hull City (a) Lost 1-0
Ditchburn, Ramsey, Withers, Nicholson, Clarke, Burgess (c), Scarth, Bennett, Duquemin, Baily, Medley

15/4/1950: Sheffield United (a) Lost 2-1
Ditchburn, Tickridge, Withers, Nicholson, Clarke, Burgess (c), Walters, Bennett, Duquemin, Baily, Medley (1)

22/4/1950: Grimsby Town (h) Lost 2-1
Ditchburn, Ramsey, Withers, Clarke, Marchi, Burgess (c), Walters, Rees, Duquemin (1), Baily, Medley

29/4/1950: Swansea Town (a) Lost 1-0
Ditchburn, Ramsey, Willis, Clarke, Marchi, Burgess (c), Walters, Bennett, Duquemin, Rees, Medley

6/5/1950: Sheffield Wednesday (a) Drew 0-0
Ditchburn, Ramsey, Willis, Clarke, Burgess (c), Nicholson, Walters, Bennett, Duquemin, Baily, Medley

1949/50 League Summary
Played: 42; Won: 27; Drew: 7; Lost: 8; Goals For: 81; Goals Against: 35; Points: 61
Appearances: Ted Ditchburn (42); Alf Ramsey (41); Charlie Withers (40); Harry Clarke (42); Ron Burgess (39); Bill Nicholson (39); Sonny Walters (35); Les Bennett (35); Len Duquemin (40); Eddie Baily (40); Les Medley (42); Billy Rees (11); George Ludford (4); Jimmy Scarth (4); Bobby Cook (3); Tony Marchi (2); Arthur Willis (2); Sid Tickridge (1)
Goalscorers: Les Medley (18); Len Duquemin (16); Les Bennett (14); Sonny Walters (14); Eddie Baily (8); Alf Ramsey (4, 3 pens); Billy Rees (3); Bill Nicholson (2); Jimmy Scarth (2)

'SIR BILL'

1950/51 First Division Champions
19/8/1950: Blackpool (h) Lost 4-1
Ditchburn, Ramsey, Withers, Nicholson, Clarke, Burgess (c), Walters, Bennett, Duquemin, Baily (1), Medley

23/8/1950: Bolton Wanderers (a) Won 4-1
Ditchburn, Ramsey, Withers, Nicholson, Clarke, Burgess (c), Walters (1), Murphy (1), Duquemin (1), Baily, Medley (1)

26/8/1950: Arsenal (a) Drew 2-2
Ditchburn, Ramsey, Willis, Clarke, Nicholson, Burgess (c) (1), Walters (1), Murphy, Duquemin, Baily, Medley

28/8/1950: Bolton Wanderers (h) Won 4-2
Ditchburn, Ramsey, Willis, Clarke, Nicholson, Burgess (c), Walters, Duquemin (2), Bennett, Baily (1), Medley, 1 own goal

2/9/1950: Charlton Athletic (a) Drew 1-1
Ditchburn, Ramsey (1 pen), Willis, Nicholson, Clarke, Burgess (c), Walters, Bennett, Duquemin, Baily, Medley

6/9/1950: Liverpool (a) Lost 2-1
Ditchburn, Ramsey, Willis, Nicholson, Clarke, Burgess (c), Walters, Murphy, Duquemin, Baily, Medley (1)

9/9/1950: Manchester United (h) Won 1-0
Ditchburn, Ramsey, Willis, Nicholson, Clarke, Burgess (c), Duquemin, Murphy, Walters (1), Bennett, Baily

16/9/1950: Wolverhampton Wanderers (a) Lost 2-1
Ditchburn, Ramsey, Willis, Nicholson, Clarke, Burgess (c), Walters, Bennett, Duquemin, Baily, Medley, 1 own goal

23/9/1950: Sunderland (h) Drew 1-1
Ditchburn, Ramsey, Willis, Nicholson, Clarke, Burgess (c), Walters, McClellan, Uphill, Baily (1), Medley

30/9/1950: Aston Villa (a) Won 3-2
Ditchburn, Ramsey, Willis, Nicholson, Clarke, Burgess (c), Walters, Murphy (1), Duquemin (1), Baily, Medley (1)

7/10/1950: Burnley (h) Won 1-0
Ditchburn, Tickridge, Willis (c), Nicholson, Clarke, Brittan, Walters, Murphy, Duquemin, Bennett, Medley (1)

14/10/1950: Chelsea (a) Won 2-0
Ditchburn, Ramsey, Willis, Nicholson, Clarke, Burgess (c), Walters (1), Bennett, Duquemin (1), Baily, Medley

21/10/1950: Stoke City (h) Won 6-1
Ditchburn, Ramsey (c), Willis, Nicholson, Clarke, Brittan, Walters (1), Bennett (2), Duquemin (2), Baily, Medley (1)

28/10/1950: West Bromwich Albion (a) Won 2-1
Ditchburn, Ramsey, Willis, Nicholson, Clarke, Burgess (c), Walters (1), Bennett, Duquemin, Baily, Medley (1)

4/11/1950: Portsmouth (h) Won 5-1
Ditchburn, Ramsey, Willis, Nicholson, Clarke, Burgess (c), Walters (1), Bennett, Duquemin (1), Baily (3), Medley

11/11/1950: Everton (a) Won 2-1
Ditchburn, Ramsey, Willis, Nicholson, Clarke, Burgess (c), Walters, Bennett, Duquemin, Baily (1), Medley (1)

18/11/1950: Newcastle United (h) Won 7-0
Ditchburn, Ramsey (c) (1 pen), Willis, Nicholson, Clarke, Brittan, Walters (1), Bennett (1), Duquemin, Baily (1), Medley (3)

25/11/1950: Huddersfield Town (a) Lost 3-2
Ditchburn, Ramsey (c), Willis, Nicholson (1), Clarke, Brittan, Walters (1), Bennett, Duquemin, Baily, Medley

2/12/1950: Middlesbrough (h) Drew 3-3
Ditchburn, Ramsey (1 pen), Willis, Nicholson, Clarke, Burgess (c), Walters (1), Bennett, Duquemin (1), Baily, Medley

9/12/1950: Sheffield Wednesday (a) Drew 1-1
Ditchburn, Ramsey, Willis, Nicholson, Clarke, Burgess (c), Walters, Bennett (1), Duquemin, Baily, Medley

16/12/1950: Blackpool (a) Won 1-0
Ditchburn, Ramsey (c), Willis, Nicholson, Clarke, Brittan, Walters, Bennett, Duquemin (1), Baily, Medley

23/12/1950: Arsenal (h) Won 1-0
Ditchburn, Ramsey, Willis, Clarke, Nicholson, Burgess (c), Walters, Bennett, Duquemin, Baily (1), Medley

25/12/1950: Derby County (a) Drew 1-1
Ditchburn, Ramsey (c), Willis, Nicholson, Clarke, Brittan, Walters, Murphy (1), Duquemin, Bennett, Medley

26/12/1950: Derby County (h) Won 2-1
Ditchburn, Ramsey, Willis, Nicholson, Clarke, Burgess (c), Scarth, McClellan (2), Murphy, Baily, Medley

'SIR BILL'

30/12/1950: Charlton Athletic (h) Won 1-0
Ditchburn, Ramsey, Willis, Nicholson, Clarke, Burgess (c), Walters (1), Bennett, Duquemin, Baily, Medley

13/1/1951: Manchester United (a) Lost 2-1
Ditchburn, Ramsey (c), Willis, Nicholson, Clarke, Brittan, Walters, McClellan, Murphy, Baily (1), Medley

20/1/1951: Wolverhampton Wanderers (h) Won 2-1
Ditchburn, Ramsey, Willis, Nicholson, Clarke, Burgess (c), Walters (1), McClellan (1), Murphy, Baily, Medley

3/2/1951: Sunderland (a) Drew 0-0
Ditchburn, Ramsey, Willis, Clarke, Nicholson, Burgess (c), Walters, McClellan, Murphy, Baily, Medley

17/2/1951: Aston Villa (h) Won 3-2
Ditchburn, Ramsey (1 pen), Willis, Clarke, Brittan, Burgess (c), Walters, McClellan, Murphy, Baily (1), Medley (1)

24/2/1951: Burnley (a) Lost 2-0
Ditchburn, Ramsey, Willis, Nicholson, Clarke, Burgess (c), Walters, McClellan, Murphy, Baily, Medley

3/3/1951: Chelsea (h) Won 2-1
Ditchburn, Ramsey, Willis, Nicholson, Clarke, Burgess (c) (1), Walters, Wright (1), Murphy, Baily, Medley

10/3/1951: Stoke City (a) Drew 0-0
Ditchburn, Ramsey, Willis, Nicholson, Clarke, Burgess (c), Walters, Wright, Murphy, Baily, Medley

17/3/1951: West Bromwich Albion (h) Won 5-0
Ditchburn, Ramsey, Willis, Nicholson, Clarke, Burgess (c), Walters, Bennett (1), Duquemin (3), Baily (1), Murphy

23/3/1951: Fulham (a) Won 1-0
Ditchburn, Ramsey, Willis, Nicholson, Clarke, Burgess (c), Walters, Bennett, Duquemin, Baily, Murphy (1)

24/3/1951: Portsmouth (a) Drew 1-1
Ditchburn, Ramsey, Willis, Nicholson, Clarke, Burgess (c), Walters, Uphill (1), Duquemin, Baily, Murphy

26/3/1951: Fulham (h) Won 2-1
Ditchburn, Ramsey, Withers, Nicholson, Clarke, Burgess (c), Murphy (1), Bennett (1), Duquemin, Baily, Medley

THE NUMBERS GAME

31/3/1951: Everton (h) Won 3-0
Ditchburn, Ramsey, Willis, Nicholson, Clarke, Burgess (c), Walters (1), Bennett (1), Duquemin, Baily, Murphy (1)

7/4/1951: Newcastle United (a) Won 1-0
Ditchburn, Ramsey, Willis, Nicholson, Clarke, Burgess (c), Walters (1), Bennett, Duquemin, Baily, Murphy

14/4/1951: Huddersfield Town (h) Lost 2-0
Ditchburn, Willis, Withers, Nicholson, Clarke, Burgess (c), Walters, Bennett, Duquemin, Baily, Murphy

21/4/1951: Middlesbrough (a) Drew 1-1
Ditchburn, Ramsey, Willis, Nicholson, Clarke, Burgess (c), Walters, Murphy (1), Duquemin, Baily, Medley

28/4/1951: Sheffield Wednesday (h) Won 1-0
Ditchburn, Ramsey, Willis, Nicholson, Clarke, Burgess (c), Walters Murphy, Duquemin (1), Baily, Medley

5/5/1951: Liverpool (h) Won 3-1
Ditchburn, Ramsey, Willis, Nicholson, Clarke, Burgess (c), Walters (1), Murphy (2), Duquemin, Baily, Medley

1950/51 League Summary

Played: 42; Won: 25; Drew: 10; Lost: 7; Goals For: 82; Goals Against: 44; Points: 60

Appearances: Ted Ditchburn (42); Alf Ramsey (40); Arthur Willis (39); Harry Clarke (42); Ron Burgess (35); Bill Nicholson (41); Sonny Walters (40); Peter Murphy (25); Len Duquemin (33); Eddie Baily (40); Les Medley (35); Les Bennett (25); Colin Brittan (8); Sid McClellan (7); Charlie Withers (4); Dennis Uphill (2); Alex Wright (2); Jimmy Scarth (1); Sid Tickridge (1)

Goalscorers: Sonny Walters (15); Len Duquemin (14); Eddie Baily (12); Les Medley (11); Peter Murphy (9); Les Bennett (7); Alf Ramsey (4 pens); Sid McClellan (3); Ron Burgess (2); Bill Nicholson (1); Dennis Uphill (1); Alex Wright (1), 2 own goals

'SIR BILL'

THE MANAGER AND THE TEAMS HE SELECTED

December 1954: Joined Tottenham coaching staff after retirement
July 1955: Became first-team coach; coached Cambridge University and England Under-23s
August 1957: Appointed assistant manager at White Hart Lane
June 1958: Assistant manager to Walter Winterbottom at the 1958 World Cup in Sweden
11/10/1958: Succeeded Jimmy Anderson as Spurs manager
First match as manager:
11/10/1958: Everton (h) Won 10-4
Hollowbread, Hopkins, Baker, Ryden (1), Blanchflower (c), Iley, Medwin (1), Harmer (1), Smith (4), Stokes (2), Robb (1)

Final match in charge:
11/9/1974: Middlesbrough (h) Lost 4-0; League Cup, second round
Jennings, Evans, Beal, Naylor, Osgood (Conn), Perryman (c), Neighbour, Pratt, Chivers, Coates, McGrath

Total games as Spurs boss: 832; Won: 408; Drew: 196; Lost: 228
Honours: 1960/61 First Division and FA Cup Double winners; 1962 FA Cup; 1963 European Cup Winners' Cup; 1967 FA Cup; 1971 League Cup; 1972 UEFA Cup; 1973 League Cup

THE 1960/61 DOUBLE SEASON
The League Campaign
20/8/1960: Everton (h) Won 2-0
Brown, Baker, Henry, Blanchflower (c), Norman, Mackay, Jones, White, Smith (1), Allen (1), Dyson

22/8/1960: Blackpool (a) Won 3-1
Brown, Baker, Henry, Blanchflower (c), Norman, Mackay, Medwin (1), White, Smith, Allen, Dyson (2)

27/8/1960: Blackburn Rovers (a) Won 4-1
Brown, Baker, Henry, Blanchflower (c), Norman, Mackay, Medwin, White, Smith (2), Allen (1), Dyson (1)

31/8/1960: Blackpool (h) Won 3-1
Brown, Baker, Henry, Blanchflower (c), Norman, Mackay, Medwin, White, Smith (3), Allen, Dyson

THE NUMBERS GAME

3/9/1960: Manchester United (h) Won 4-1
Brown, Baker, Henry, Blanchflower (c), Norman, Mackay, Medwin, White, Smith (2), Allen (2), Dyson

7/9/1960: Bolton Wanderers (a) Won 2-1
Brown, Baker, Henry, Blanchflower (c), Norman, Mackay, Medwin, White (1), Saul, Allen (1), Dyson

10/9/1960: Arsenal (a) Won 3-2
Brown, Baker, Henry, Blanchflower (c), Norman, Mackay, Medwin, White, Saul (1), Allen (1), Dyson (1)

14/9/1960: Bolton Wanderers (h) Won 3-1
Brown, Baker, Henry, Blanchflower (c) (1 pen), Norman, Mackay, Jones, White, Smith (2), Allen, Dyson

17/9/1960: Leicester City (a) Won 2-1
Brown, Baker, Henry, Blanchflower (c), Norman, Mackay, Jones, White, Smith (2), Allen, Dyson

24/9/1960: Aston Villa (h) Won 6-2
Brown, Baker, Henry, Blanchflower (c), Norman, Mackay (1), Jones, White (2), Smith (1), Allen (1), Dyson (1)

1/10/1960: Wolverhampton Wanderers (a) Won 4-0
Brown, Baker, Henry, Blanchflower (c) (1), Norman, Marchi, Jones (1), White, Smith, Allen (1), Dyson (1)

10/10/1960: Manchester City (h) Drew 1-1
Brown, Baker, Henry, Blanchflower (c), Norman, Mackay, Jones, White, Smith (1), Allen, Dyson

15/10/1960: Nottingham Forest (a) Won 4-0
Brown, Baker, Henry, Blanchflower (c), Norman, Mackay (1), Jones (2), White (1), Smith, Allen, Dyson

29/10/1960: Newcastle United (a) Won 4-3
Brown, Baker, Henry, Blanchflower (c), Norman (1), Mackay, Jones (1), White (1), Smith (1), Allen, Dyson

2/11/1960: Cardiff City (h) Won 3-2
Brown, Baker, Henry, Blanchflower (c) (1 pen), Norman, Mackay, Medwin (1), White, Smith, Allen, Dyson (1)

5/11/1960: Fulham (h) Won 5-1
Brown, Baker, Henry, Blanchflower (c), Norman, Mackay, Jones (2), White (1), Smith, Allen (2), Dyson

12/11/1960: Sheffield Wednesday (a) Lost 2-1
Brown, Baker, Henry, Blanchflower (c), Norman (1), Mackay, Jones, White, Smith, Allen, Dyson

'SIR BILL'

19/11/1960: Birmingham City (h) Won 6-0
Brown, Baker, Henry, Blanchflower (c), Norman, Mackay, Jones (2), White (1), Smith (1 pen), Allen, Dyson (2)

26/11/1960: West Bromwich Albion (a) Won 3-1
Brown, Baker, Henry, Blanchflower (c), Norman, Mackay, Jones, White, Smith (2), Allen (1), Dyson

3/12/1960: Burnley (h) Drew 4-4
Brown, Baker, Henry, Blanchflower (c), Norman (1), Mackay (1), Jones (2), White, Smith, Allen, Dyson

10/12/1960: Preston North End (a) Won 1-0
Brown, Baker, Henry, Blanchflower (c), Norman, Mackay, Jones, White (1), Saul, Allen, Dyson

17/12/1960: Everton (a) Won 3-1
Brown, Baker, Henry, Blanchflower (c), Norman, Mackay (1), Jones, White (1), Smith, Allen (1), Dyson

24/12/1960: West Ham United (h) Won 2-0
Brown, Baker, Henry, Blanchflower (c), Norman, Mackay, Jones, White (1), Smith, Allen, Dyson (1)

26/12/1960: West Ham United (a) Won 3-0
Hollowbread, Baker, Henry, Blanchflower (c), Norman, Mackay, Medwin, White (1), Smith, Allen (1), Dyson, 1 own goal

31/12/1960: Blackburn Rovers (h) Won 5-2
Brown, Baker, Henry, Blanchflower (c) (1), Norman, Marchi, Medwin, White, Smith (2), Allen (2), Dyson

16/1/1961: Manchester United (a) Lost 2-0
Brown, Barton, Henry, Blanchflower (c), Norman, Mackay, J. Smith, White, B. Smith, Allen, Dyson

21/1/1961: Arsenal (h) Won 4-2
Brown, Baker, Henry, Blanchflower (c) (1 pen), Norman, Mackay, Jones, White, Smith (1), Allen (2), Dyson

4/2/1961: Leicester City (h) Lost 3-2
Brown, Baker, Henry, Blanchflower (c) (1 pen), Norman, Mackay, Jones, White, Smith, Allen (1), Dyson

11/2/1961: Aston Villa (a) Won 2-1
Brown, Baker, Henry, Blanchflower (c), Norman, Mackay, Jones, White, Smith (1), Allen, Dyson (1)

22/2/1961: Wolverhampton Wanderers (h) Drew 1-1
Brown, Baker, Henry, Blanchflower (c), Norman, Mackay, Jones, White, Smith (1), Allen, Dyson

THE NUMBERS GAME

25/2/1961: Manchester City (a) Won 1-0
Brown, Baker, Henry, Blanchflower (c), Mackay, Marchi, Medwin (1), White, Smith, Allen, Dyson

11/3/1961: Cardiff City (a) Lost 3-2
Brown, Baker, Henry, Blanchflower (c), Norman, Mackay, Jones, White, Smith, Allen (1), Dyson (1)

22/3/1961: Newcastle United (h) Lost 2-1
Brown, Baker, Henry, Blanchflower (c), Norman, Mackay, Jones, White, Smith, Allen (1), Dyson

25/3/1961: Fulham (a) Drew 0-0
Brown, Baker, Henry, Blanchflower (c), Norman, Marchi, Jones, White, Saul, Allen, Dyson

31/3/1961: Chelsea (h) Won 4-2
Brown, Baker, Henry, Blanchflower (c), Norman, Marchi, Jones (2), White, Saul (1), Allen (1), Dyson

1/4/1961: Preston North End (h) Won 5-0
Brown, Baker, Henry, Blanchflower (c), Norman, Marchi, Medwin, White (1), Saul (1), Allen, Jones (3)

3/4/1961: Chelsea (a) Won 3-2
Brown, Baker, Henry, Blanchflower (c), Norman (1), Mackay, Medwin (1), White, Smith (1), Allen, Jones

8/4/1961: Birmingham City (a) Won 3-2
Brown, Baker, Henry, Blanchflower (c), Norman, Mackay, Jones, White (1), Smith (1), Allen (1), Dyson

17/4/1961: Sheffield Wednesday (h) Won 2-1
Brown, Baker, Henry, Blanchflower (c), Norman, Mackay, Jones, White, Smith (1), Allen (1), Dyson

22/4/1961: Burnley (a) Lost 4-2
Brown, Baker (1), Henry, Blanchflower (c), Norman, Mackay, Medwin, White, Smith (1), Allen, Dyson

26/4/1961: Nottingham Forest (h) Won 1-0
Brown, Baker, Henry, Blanchflower (c), Norman, Mackay, Medwin (1), White, Smith, Allen, Dyson

29/4/1961: West Bromwich Albion (h) Lost 2-1
Brown, Baker, Henry, Blanchflower (c), Norman, Mackay, Jones, White, Smith (1), Allen, Dyson

'SIR BILL'

1960/61 League Summary
Played: 42; Won: 31; Drew: 4; Lost: 7; Goals For: 115; Goals Against: 55; Points: 66
Appearances: Bill Brown (41); Peter Baker (41); Ron Henry (42); Danny Blanchflower (42); Maurice Norman (41); Dave Mackay (37); Cliff Jones (29); John White (42); Bobby Smith (36); Les Allen (42); Terry Dyson (40); Terry Medwin (14); Tony Marchi (6); Frank Saul (6); John Hollowbread (1); John Smith (1); Ken Barton (1)
Goalscorers: Bobby Smith (28, 1 pen); Les Allen (22); Cliff Jones (15); John White (13); Terry Dyson (12); Danny Blanchflower (6, 4 pens); Terry Medwin (5); Dave Mackay (4); Maurice Norman (4); Frank Saul (3); Peter Baker (1); 1 own goal

1960/61 FA Cup
7/1/1961: Third round; Charlton Athletic (h) Won 3-2
Brown, Baker, Henry, Blanchflower (c), Norman, Mackay, Medwin, White, Smith, Allen (2), Dyson (1)

28/1/1961: Fourth round; Crewe Alexandra (h) Won 5-1
Brown, Baker, Henry, Blanchflower (c), Norman, Mackay (1), Jones (1), White, Smith (1), Allen (1), Dyson (1)

18/2/1961: Fifth round; Aston Villa (a) Won 2-0
Brown, Baker, Henry, Blanchflower (c), Norman, Mackay, Jones (1), White, Smith, Allen, Dyson, 1 own goal

4/3/1961: Quarter-final; Sunderland (a) Drew 1-1
Brown, Baker, Henry, Blanchflower (c), Norman, Mackay, Jones (1), White, Smith, Allen, Dyson

8/3/1961: Quarter-final replay; Sunderland (h) Won 5-0
Brown, Baker, Henry, Blanchflower (c), Norman, Mackay (1), Jones, White, Smith (1), Allen (1), Dyson (2)

18/3/1961: Semi-final, Villa Park; Burnley, Won 3-0
Brown, Baker, Henry, Blanchflower (c), Norman, Mackay, Jones (1), White, Smith (2), Allen, Dyson

6/5/1961: FA Cup final, Wembley: Leicester City, Won 2-0
Brown, Baker, Henry, Blanchflower (c), Norman, Mackay, Jones, White, Smith (1), Allen, Dyson (1)

1960/61 FA Cup Summary
Played: 7; Won: 6; Drew: 1; Lost: 0; Goals for: 21; Goals against: 4

Appearances: Bill Brown (7); Peter Baker (7); Ron Henry (7); Danny Blanchflower (7); Maurice Norman (7); Dave Mackay (7); Cliff Jones (6); John White (7); Bobby Smith (7); Les Allen (7); Terry Dyson (7); Terry Medwin (1)
Goalscorers: Bobby Smith (5); Terry Dyson (5); Les Allen (4); Cliff Jones (4); Dave Mackay (2); 1 own goal

1961/62 FA Cup

6/1/1962: Third round; Birmingham City (a) Drew 3-3
Brown, Baker, Henry, Blanchflower (c), Norman, Mackay, Jones (1), White, Smith, Greaves (2), Allen

10/1/1962: Third round replay; Birmingham City (h) Won 4-2
Brown, Baker, Henry, Blanchflower (c), Norman, Mackay, Medwin (2), White, Allen (1), Greaves (1), Jones

27/1/1962: Fourth round; Plymouth Argyle (a) Won 5-1
Brown, Baker, Henry, Blanchflower (c), Norman, Mackay, Medwin (1), White (1), Allen, Greaves (2), Jones (1)

17/2/1962: Fifth round; West Bromwich Albion (a) Won 4-2
Brown, Baker, Henry, Blanchflower (c), Norman, Mackay, Medwin, White, Smith (2), Greaves (2), Jones

10/3/1962: Quarter-final; Aston Villa (h) Won 2-0
Brown, Baker, Henry, Blanchflower (c) (1), Norman, Mackay, Medwin, White, Smith, Greaves, Jones (1)

31/3/1962: Semi-final, Hillsborough; Manchester United, Won 3-1
Brown, Baker, Henry, Blanchflower (c), Norman, Mackay, Medwin (1), White, Smith, Greaves (1), Jones (1)

5/5/1962: FA Cup final; Wembley; Burnley, Won 3-1
Brown, Baker, Henry, Blanchflower (c) (1 pen), Norman, Mackay, Medwin, White, Smith (1), Greaves (1), Jones

1961/62 FA Cup Summary
Played: 7; Won: 6; Drew: 1; Lost: 0; Goals for: 24; Goals against: 10
Appearances: Bill Brown (7); Peter Baker (7); Ron Henry (7); Danny Blanchflower (7); Maurice Norman (7); Dave Mackay (7); Terry Medwin (7); John White (7); Bobby Smith (4); Jimmy Greaves (7); Cliff Jones (7); Les Allen (3)
Goalscorers: Jimmy Greaves (9); Terry Medwin (4); Cliff Jones (4); Bobby Smith (3); Danny Blanchflower (2, 1 pen); Les Allen (1); John White (1)

'SIR BILL'

1962/63 European Cup Winners' Cup

31/10/1962: First round, first leg; Rangers (h) Won 5-2
Brown, Baker, Henry, Blanchflower (c), Norman (1), Mackay, Medwin, White (2), Allen (1), Greaves, Jones, 1 own goal

11/12/1962: First round, second leg; Rangers (a) Won 3-2
Brown, Baker, Henry, Blanchflower (c), Norman, Mackay, Medwin, White, Smith (2), Greaves (1), Jones

Won 8-4 on aggregate

5/3/1963: Quarter-final, first leg; Slovan Bratislava (a) Lost 2-0
Brown, Baker, Henry, Marchi (c), Norman, Mackay, Saul, White, Smith, Greaves, Jones

14/3/1963: Quarter-final, second leg; Slovan Bratislava (h) Won 6-0
Brown, Hopkins, Henry, Marchi (c), Norman, Mackay (1), Saul, White (1), Smith (1), Greaves (2), Jones (1)

Won 6-2 on aggregate

24/4/1963: Semi-final, first leg; OFK Belgrade (a) Won 2-1
Brown, Baker, Henry, Marchi (c), Norman, Mackay, J. Smith, White (1), B. Smith, Greaves, Dyson (1)

1/5/1963: Semi-final, second leg; OFK Belgrade (h) Won 3-1
Brown, Baker, Henry, Blanchflower (c), Norman, Marchi, Jones (1), White, Smith (1), Mackay (1), Dyson

Won 5-2 on aggregate

15/5/1963: The Final, Rotterdam: Atletico Madrid, Won 5-1
Brown, Baker, Henry, Blanchflower (c), Norman, Marchi, Jones, White (1), Smith, Greaves (2), Dyson (2)

1962/63 European Cup Winners' Cup Summary

Played: 7; Won: 6; Drew: 0; Lost: 1; Goals for: 24; Goals against: 9
Appearances: Bill Brown (7); Peter Baker (6); Ron Henry (7); Danny Blanchflower (4); Maurice Norman (7); Dave Mackay (6); Cliff Jones (6); John White (7); Bobby Smith (6); Jimmy Greaves (6); Tony Marchi (5); Terry Dyson (3); Terry Medwin (2); Frank Saul (2); Les Allen (1); Mel Hopkins (1); John Smith (1)
Goalscorers: Jimmy Greaves (5); John White (5); Bobby Smith (4); Terry Dyson (3); Cliff Jones (2); Dave Mackay (2); Les Allen (1); Maurice Norman (1); 1 own goal

THE NUMBERS GAME

1966/67 FA Cup

28/1/1967: Third round; Millwall (a) Drew 0-0
Jennings, Kinnear, Knowles, Mullery, England, Mackay (c), Robertson, Greaves, Gilzean, Venables, Jones

1/2/1967: Third round replay; Millwall (h) Won 1-0
Jennings, Kinnear, Knowles, Mullery, England, Mackay (c), Robertson, Greaves, Gilzean (1), Venables, Jones

18/2/1967: Fourth round; Portsmouth (h) Won 3-1
Jennings, Beal, Knowles, Mullery, England, Mackay (c), Robertson, Greaves (1), Gilzean (2), Venables, Jones

11/3/1967: Fifth round; Bristol City (h) Won 2-0
Jennings, Kinnear, Knowles, Mullery, England, Mackay (c), Robertson, Greaves (2), Gilzean, Venables, Jones

8/4/1967: Quarter-final; Birmingham City (a) Drew 0-0
Jennings, Kinnear, Knowles, Mullery, England, Mackay (c), Robertson, Greaves, Gilzean, Venables, Saul

12/4/1967: Quarter-final replay; Birmingham City (h) Won 6-0
Jennings, Kinnear, Knowles, Mullery, England, Mackay (c), Robertson, Greaves (2), Gilzean (1), Venables (2), Saul (1)

29/4/1967: Semi-final, Hillsborough; Nottingham Forest Won 2-1
Jennings, Kinnear, Knowles, Mullery, England, Mackay (c) (Jones), Robertson, Greaves (1), Gilzean, Venables, Saul (1)

20/5/1967: FA Cup Final, Wembley: Chelsea, Won 2-1
Jennings, Kinnear, Knowles, Mullery, England, Mackay (c), Robertson (1), Greaves, Gilzean, Venables, Saul (1)

1966/67 FA Cup Summary

Played: 8; Won: 6; Drew: 2; Lost: 0; Goals for: 16; Goals against: 3

Appearances: Pat Jennings (8); Joe Kinnear (7); Cyril Knowles (8); Alan Mullery (8); Mike England (8); Dave Mackay (8); Jimmy Robertson (8); Jimmy Greaves (8); Alan Gilzean (8); Terry Venables (8); Cliff Jones (5); Frank Saul (4); Phil Beal (1)

Goalscorers: Jimmy Greaves (6); Alan Gilzean (4); Frank Saul (3); Terry Venables (2); Jimmy Robertson (1)

1970/71 League Cup

9/9/1970: Second round; Swansea City (h) Won 3-0
Hancock, Kinnear, Want, Mullery (c) (Pearce), England, Beal, Morgan (1), Perryman (1), Chivers, Gilzean, Peters (1)

7/10/1970: Third round; Sheffield United (h) Won 2-1
Jennings, Kinnear, Knowles, Mullery (c), England, Beal, Morgan (Pearce 1), Perryman, Chivers (1), Gilzean, Peters

28/10/1970: Fourth round; West Bromwich Albion (h) Won 5-0
Jennings, Kinnear, Knowles, Mullery (c), England, Beal, Pearce, Perryman, Chivers, Gilzean (2), Peters (3)

18/11/1970: Quarter-final; Coventry City (h) Won 4-1
Jennings, Kinnear, Knowles, Mullery (c), England, Beal (Neighbour), Pearce, Pratt, Chivers (3), Gilzean (1), Peters

16/12/1970: Semi-final, first leg; Bristol City (a) Drew 1-1
Jennings, Kinnear, Knowles, Mullery (c), England, Beal, Pearce, Perryman, Chivers, Gilzean (1), Peters

23/12/1970: Semi-final, second leg; Bristol City (h) Won 2-0
Jennings, Kinnear, Knowles, Mullery (c), England (Pearce 1), Beal, Neighbour, Perryman, Chivers (1), Gilzean, Peters

Won 3-1 on aggregate

27/2/1971: League Cup final, Wembley: Aston Villa, Won 2-0
Jennings, Kinnear, Knowles, Mullery (c), Collins, Beal, Neighbour, Perryman, Chivers (2), Gilzean, Peters

1970/71 League Cup Summary

Played: 7; Won: 6; Drew: 1; Lost: 0; Goals for: 19; Goals against: 3
Appearances: Pat Jennings (6); Joe Kinnear (7); Cyril Knowles (6); Alan Mullery (7); Mike England (6); Phil Beal (7); Jimmy Neighbour (3); Steve Perryman (6); Martin Chivers (7); Alan Gilzean (8); Martin Peters (7); Jimmy Pearce (6); Roger Morgan (2); Peter Collins (1); Ken Hancock (1); John Pratt (1); Tony Want (1)
Goalscorers: Martin Chivers (7); Alan Gilzean (4); Martin Peters (4); Jimmy Pearce (2); Steve Perryman (1); Roger Morgan (1)

THE NUMBERS GAME

1971/72 UEFA Cup

14/9/1971: First round, first leg; Keflavik (a) Won 6-1
Jennings, Kinnear, Knowles, Mullery (c) (2) (Souness), England, Beal, Gilzean (3), Perryman, Chivers, Peters, Coates (1) (Pearce)

28/9/1971: First round, second leg; Keflavik (h) Won 9-0
Jennings, Evans, Knowles (1), Mullery (c) (Pearce), England, Beal, Gilzean (2), Perryman (1), Chivers (3), Peters (Holder 1), Coates (1)

Won 15-1 on aggregate

20/10/1971: Second round, first leg; Nantes (a) Drew 0-0
Jennings, Kinnear, Knowles, Mullery (c), England, Beal, Neighbour, Perryman, Chivers, Gilzean (Morgan), Peters

2/11/1971: Second round, second leg; Nantes (h) Won 1-0
Jennings, Evans, Knowles, Pratt, England, Beal, Neighbour, Perryman, Chivers, Gilzean (Pearce), Peters (c) (1)

Won 1-0 on aggregate

8/12/1971: Third round, first leg; Rapid Bucharest (h) Won 3-0
Jennings, Evans, Knowles, Perryman, England, Beal, Neighbour, Gilzean, Chivers (2), Peters (c) (1), Coates (Pearce)

15/12/1971: Third round, second leg; Rapid Bucharest (a) Won 2-0
Jennings, Evans, Knowles, Pratt, Collins, Beal, Gilzean, Perryman (Naylor), Chivers (1), Peters (c), Coates (Pearce 1)

Won 5-0 on aggregate

7/3/1972: Quarter-final, first leg; UTA Arad (a) Won 2-0
Jennings, Evans, Knowles, Pratt, England (1), Beal, Morgan (1), Perryman, Chivers, Gilzean (Collins), Peters (c)

21/3/1972: Quarter-final, second leg; UTA Arad (h) Drew 1-1
Jennings, Evans, Knowles, Pratt, England, Naylor, Morgan, Perryman, Gilzean (1), Peters (c), Coates

Won 3-1 on aggregate

5/4/1972: Semi-final, first leg; AC Milan (h) Won 2-1
Jennings, Kinnear, Knowles, Mullery (c), England, Naylor, Gilzean, Perryman (2), Chivers, Peters, Coates (Neighbour)

'SIR BILL'

19/4/1972: Semi-final, second leg; AC Milan (a) Drew 1-1
Jennings, Kinnear, Knowles, Mullery (c) (1), England, Beal, Pratt (Naylor), Perryman, Chivers, Peters, Coates

Won 3-2 on aggregate

3/5/1972: UEFA Cup final, first leg:
Wolverhampton Wanderers (a) Won 2-1
Jennings, Kinnear, Knowles, Mullery (c), England, Beal, Gilzean, Perryman, Chivers (2), Peters, Coates (Pratt)

17/5/1972: UEFA Cup final, second leg:
Wolverhampton Wanderers (h) Drew 1-1
Jennings, Kinnear, Knowles, Mullery (c) (1), England, Beal, Gilzean, Perryman, Chivers, Peters, Coates

Won 3-2 on aggregate

1971/72 UEFA Cup Summary

Played: 12; Won: 8; Drew: 4; Lost: 0; Goals for: 30; Goals against: 6
Appearances: Pat Jennings (12); Joe Kinnear (6); Cyril Knowles (12); Alan Mullery (7); Mike England (11); Phil Beal (10); Alan Gilzean (11); Steve Perryman (12); Martin Chivers (11); Martin Peters (12); Ralph Coates (9); Ray Evans (6); John Pratt (6); Jimmy Pearce (5); Terry Naylor (4); Jimmy Neighbour (4); Roger Morgan (3); Peter Collins (2); Phil Holder (1); Graeme Souness (1)
Goalscorers: Martin Chivers (8); Alan Gilzean (6); Alan Mullery (4); Steve Perryman (3); Martin Peters (2); Ralph Coates (2); Mike England (1); Cyril Knowles (1); Phil Holder (1); Jimmy Pearce (1); Roger Morgan (1)

1972/73 League Cup

6/9/1972: Second round; Huddersfield Town (h) Won 2-1
Jennings, Kinnear, Knowles, Pratt, England (c), Beal (Naylor), Pearce, Perryman, Chivers (1), Gilzean (1), Coates

3/10/1972: Third round; Middlesbrough (a) Drew 1-1
Jennings, Kinnear, Knowles, Naylor, England (c), Beal, Pearce (1), Perryman, Chivers, Pratt, Coates

11/10/1972: Third round replay; Middlesbrough (h) Drew 0-0
Jennings, Kinnear, Knowles, Pratt (Pearce), England, Naylor, Gilzean, Perryman, Chivers, Peters (c), Coates

30/10/1972: Third round second replay; Middlesbrough (h) Won 2-1
Jennings, Evans, Knowles, Pratt (Gilzean 1), England, Dillon, Pearce, Perryman, Chivers, Peters (c) (1), Coates

1/11/1972: Fourth round; Millwall (h) Won 2-0
Jennings, Evans, Knowles, Pratt, England, Naylor, Pearce, Perryman (1), Chivers, Gilzean (Coates), Peters (c) (1)

4/12/1972: Quarter-final; Liverpool (a) Drew 1-1
Jennings, Evans, Knowles, Pratt, England, Naylor, Pearce, Perryman, Chivers, Gilzean, Peters (c) (1)

6/12/1972: Quarter-final replay; Liverpool (h) Won 3-1
Jennings, Evans, Knowles, Pratt (1), England, Naylor, Pearce, Perryman, Chivers (2), Gilzean (Neighbour), Peters (c)

20/12/1972: Semi-final, first leg; Wolverhampton Wanderers (a) Won 2-1
Jennings, Evans, Knowles, Pratt (1), England, Naylor, Pearce, Perryman, Chivers, Gilzean, Peters (c) (1)

30/12/1972: Semi-final, second leg; Wolverhampton Wanderers (h) Drew 2-2
Jennings, Evans, Knowles, Pratt, England, Naylor, Pearce, Perryman, Chivers (1), Gilzean (Coates), Peters (c) (1)

Won 4-3 on aggregate

3/3/1973: League Cup final, Wembley: Norwich City, Won 1-0
Jennings, Kinnear, Knowles, Pratt (Coates 1), England, Beal, Pearce, Perryman, Chivers, Gilzean, Peters (c)

1972/73 League Cup Summary

Played: 10; Won: 6; Drew: 4; Lost: 0; Goals for: 16; Goals against: 8

Appearances: Pat Jennings (10); Ray Evans (6); Cyril Knowles (10); John Pratt (10); Mike England (10); Terry Naylor (8); Jimmy Pearce (10); Steve Perryman (10); Martin Chivers (10); Alan Gilzean (9); Martin Peters (8); Ralph Coates (7); Joe Kinnear (4); Phil Beal (3); Mike Dillon (1); Jimmy Neighbour (1).

Goalscorers: Martin Peters (5); Martin Chivers (4); Alan Gilzean (2); John Pratt (2); Ralph Coates (1); Steve Perryman (1); Jimmy Pearce (1).

MAJOR SIGNINGS

Dave Mackay (1959–1968), Hearts, £32,000
"My first and best signing. Hearts manager Tommy Walker turned me down at first and I then tried to buy Mel Charles from Swansea. Thank goodness, he preferred to join Arsenal, and so I went back for Mackay. It was like getting three players in one... skillful, astonishing strength and stamina, and a born leader of men with a never-give-up competitive spirit."

Bill Brown (1959–1966), Dundee, £16,500
"I watched Brown playing for Scotland against England at Wembley. The Scots were beaten 1-0 but I was impressed by Bill's handling and positioning. I caught the overnight train to Dundee, did the business and was heading back to London by lunchtime, feeling very happy with myself. Bill proved an excellent buy and gave us much-needed stability at the back."

Tony Marchi (1959–1965), Torino, £20,000
"Tony Marchi was an Edmonton boy who came back to us from Italy to take over as first-team cover from Jim Iley, a fine midfield player who we allowed to move on to Nottingham Forest. I saw Tony as a utility midfielder who could fill in wherever he was needed. A solid, reliable player who had been taught all the right things as a lad growing up with Spurs."

John White (1959–1964), Falkirk, £20,000
"John had played for Scotland against Northern Ireland, so I was able to get first-hand scouting reports from Danny Blanchflower, Dave Mackay and Bill Brown. They were unanimous in their opinion that I should sign him. He was still doing his Army national service, and when I found out that he was a Scottish Command cross-country runner, that clinched it and I snapped him up. What a buy!"

Les Allen (1959–1965), Chelsea, £20,000
"Chelsea manager Ted Drake was desperate to sign Johnny Brooks. I'd had my eye on Les Allen ever since he'd lost his place in the Chelsea attack to a young Jimmy Greaves. We agreed on a straight swap,

and the Double season proved that I had got the better of the deal. Les was a very capable player and just unlucky to have been around at the same time as the phenomenal Greavsie."

John Smith (1960–1964), West Ham, £20,000
"John Smith had been prominent in West Ham's promotion season back to the First Division. Their manager Ted Fenton thought his team was short of firepower and I talked him into letting me have the very capable midfielder Smith for our stylish but unpredictable striker Dave Dunmore. We did a straight swap, which again was a good bit of business for Tottenham."

Jimmy Greaves (1961–1970), AC Milan, £99,999
"This was the most wearing yet ultimately satisfying transfer deal I was ever involved in. The Italians messed us about and tried to get Chelsea and Spurs involved in an auction. We outmanoeuvred them, and we finished up getting the greatest British goalscorer I've ever seen. The frustrating thing is that we should have had him for nothing straight from school!"

Laurie Brown (1964–1966), Arsenal, £40,000
"This was one of my more controversial signings. Bobby Smith had gone off the boil, mainly because of his off-field gambling problems. I replaced him with Laurie Brown from Arsenal because I thought he could do a job alongside Jimmy Greaves, but it did not work out and I quickly had to switch him back into a defensive role that he had played with Arsenal."

Jimmy Robertson (1964–1968), St Mirren, £25,500
"I signed Jimmy from St Mirren on Transfer Deadline Day in 1964 and he lived up to expectations as a direct winger, particularly with his crucial goal against Chelsea in the 1967 FA Cup final. He was not the easiest person to get along with and I admit to a mistake in swapping him for Arsenal winger David Jenkins, who our supporters just refused to accept. It was all rather messy."

Pat Jennings (1964–1977), Watford, £27,000
"It took Pat quite a while to settle down after I signed him from Watford, but once he conquered his nerves he became one of the world's

great goalkeepers. He showed a perfect temperament after his early settling-in period, and those large hands of his broke the hearts of many forwards both for Tottenham and Northern Ireland. I could not believe it when Spurs sold him to Arsenal."

Alan Gilzean (1964–1974), Dundee, £72,500

"Alan Gilzean was one of my most satisfying signings. I had to be at my most persuasive to get him, with Sunderland making great efforts to beat me. They had offered him a £20 win bonus on top of his basic pay and I told him that was illegal. He took my word for it and signed for Spurs. I later discovered I'd given him bum information but he shrugged it off and gave us great service."

Cyril Knowles (1964–1975), Middlesbrough, £45,000

"I had a soft spot for Cyril. I signed him from Middlesbrough and watched him develop into a top-flight left-back. He'd have got many more England caps but for the superb Ray Wilson. Cyril had the terrible tragedy of losing his child in a freak accident and I don't think he was ever quite the same after that. He went into management and I was only too pleased to give him advice."

Alan Mullery (1964–1974), Fulham, £72,500

"I initially wanted Alan to play right-back in place of Peter Baker, but he flatly refused. For a while I toyed with the idea of buying Mike Bailey from Charlton, but finally signed Mullery. He had a torturous time winning over the fans but his midfield drive and enthusiasm eventually got him accepted as an exceptional player who gave Spurs great service."

Dennis Bond (1967–1973), Watford, £20,000

"I remember that Dennis went down with chicken pox just as he signed for us from Watford, and this delayed his progress. We signed him as a squad player, covering for our forwards and he did not quite live up to his promise. On his day he had lots of talent but could not force himself into the first team on a regular basis and we allowed him to move on to Charlton, and he finished up back at Watford."

Terry Venables (1966–1969), Chelsea, £80,000

"Terry was unfortunate to follow in the footsteps of midfield masters Danny Blanchflower and John White, and our supporters never fully warmed to him. They continually compared him with two exceptional players, and he did not enjoy the rapport with the crowd that he had at Chelsea. His one major highlight was helping us win the FA Cup against his old club at Wembley in 1967."

Mike England (1966–1975), Blackburn, £95,00

"I missed a tempting club trip to Vancouver and the United States to make sure I clinched Mike's transfer from Blackburn, and it was worth every moment of my time. He was a thoroughbred centre-half who was commanding in the air and efficient with his footwork. At last I had found the right man to fill the gap left by the magnificent Maurice Norman."

Roger Morgan (1968–1973), QPR, £110,000

"Roger joined us from Queens Park Rangers at just about the time clubs were copying Alf Ramsey's 4-3-3 formation and getting rid of wingers. I didn't hold with this negative tactic and was continually looking for players who could attack down the flanks. Roger had his moments but sadly he was handicapped by a series of injuries and could not live up to his promise."

Martin Chivers (1968–1976), Southampton, £125,00

"No player gave me and coach Eddie Baily more sleepless nights than Martin, who was mean, moody and, yes, also magnificent at times. We had lots of differences about his attitude and approach, but I have to say that when firing on all cylinders there were few more explosive centre-forwards in the world. He could be so infuriating, yet we finished up the best of friends!"

Peter Collins (1968–1972), Chelmsford, £10,000

"Peter joined us from Chelmsford on the same day that Chivers arrived in a British record deal, club loyalist Frank Saul going to Southampton as a £25,000 makeweight. The contrast in their transfers was vast, but the £10,000 we invested in Collins was repaid many times over. He proved to be one of my best bargain buys and provided excellent cover at centre-half for Mike England."

Martin Peters (1970–1975), West Ham, £200,000

"Martin was sheer class and I jumped at the chance of signing him from West Ham. Ron Greenwood said he needed Jimmy Greaves as a makeweight to save himself from a backlash from his supporters. I knew in confidence that Jimmy was a shadow of the player who had scored some of the greatest goals ever seen, but I was on the receiving end of a lot of criticism from some of our supporters."

Ralph Coates (1971–1977), Burnley, £192,000

"Thank goodness Ralph scored the winning goal against Norwich in the 1973 League Cup final at Wembley. At last the Spurs supporters saw what I knew he could do when I signed him from Burnley. He really struggled to settle and the transfer fee sat on his shoulders like a sack of coal. But eventually he won the fans over with his 100 per cent effort and considerable talent."

Neil McNab (1974–1978), Morton, £40,000

"I was backing a hunch when I bought 16-year-old Neil McNab from Morton. He showed tremendous potential and I was confident he was going to make it. He never quite lived up to my expectations but had sufficient skill to please spectators. I had left by the time he established himself and he had all the talent to be able to play football the Spurs way."

Alfie Conn (1974–1977), Rangers, £150,000

"Alfie was my last signing for Spurs, and I remember being upset when he turned up with his hair far too long. One of my pet hates has always been long hair! He was a clever ball player, reminding me of the tricks his Dad used to get up to when starring with Hearts in the 1950s. Alfie Jnr never really settled at Spurs and later became famous as the first footballer to play for both Rangers and Celtic."

Frank Saul, Phil Beal, Derek Possee, Jimmy Pearce, Keith Weller, Ray Evans, Roger Hoy, John Pratt, Steve Perryman, Phil Holder, Graeme Souness, Jimmy Neighbour, Tony Want, Terry Naylor, Barry Daines, Keith Osgood, and Chris Jones all joined direct from school, while Joe Kinnear signed as a 17-year-old amateur from St Albans in 1963.

TIMELINE

1919
Born 15 Vine Street, Scarborough, North Yorkshire on 26 January, William Edward Nicholson is the second youngest of nine children born to Joe and Edith Nicholson. Joe, who has a limp because of a permanent lame leg, is a hansom cab driver; Edith is a char cleaner and the family organiser.

1926
An uncle gives Bill his first tanner rubber ball and he becomes a fanatic, with the ball always at his feet.

1930
Wins a scholarship to the Scarborough High School for Boys, playing in the school Under-15s team at centre-half at the age of 11.

1935
Leaves school to work in a laundry supervising the machines, and in his spare time plays for the Young Liberals football team in a local league. He is a utility defender, playing mostly at centre-half.

1936
Spurs chief scout Ben Ives writes a letter in pencil to Bill's parents on 29 February – Leap Year Day – inviting Bill to Tottenham for a month's trial. The *Tottenham Herald* publishes a report of his debut on 21 March, playing for Tottenham's 'A' team in a 5-3 defeat by Guildford City. He scores a hat-trick in his second appearance, a 7-1 victory over Brentwood Mental Hospital on 19 November and is offered a groundstaff boy's role. He and an ex-miner from Swansea called Ron Burgess sign apprentice professional contracts on the same day. Their wage: £2 a week.

1937
Features for Northfleet Amateurs, switching from playing at inside-forward to left-back.

1938
Promoted to London Combination reserves team in a 3-0 home win over Bournemouth & Boscombe Athletic on 1 January and is rewarded with a professional contract with senior nursery club Northfleet United at £7 a week. Wins his first silverware on 18 April, a Kent Senior Cup winners' medal in the final against Dover. Makes his Football League debut at Blackburn Rovers on 22 October. He finishes the game limping on the wing with a thigh injury as Spurs lose 3-1. Moves into digs with the Lawrence family at Farningham Road, Tottenham, a few doors away from the twin Power sisters. He falls in love with Grace, known to everybody as 'Darkie' to differentiate between her and her blonde twin.

1939-45
War is declared on 3 September, and he serves with the Durham Light Infantry and becomes a lance corporal and is subsequently promoted to sergeant, acting as a physical training instructor. Plays wartime guest football for Newcastle, Darlington, Hartlepool United, Middlesbrough, Sunderland, Fulham and one match at Spurs. Gets posted to Italy for the last six months of the war where he comes under the influence of future Amateur Athletics Association coach Geoff Dyson. Coaching is now Bill's major interest.

1942
Marries Grace at St Mary's Church, Lambsdown Road, Tottenham, on 1 March. Bill is 23, Darkie 21. The marriage lasts 62 years. They have two daughters, Linda and Jean.

1946
Resumes his playing career with Tottenham Hotspur, who are ground-sharing with Arsenal while Highbury is being repaired after being used as an Air Raid Precautions Centre during the war. Joe Hulme, the former Arsenal and England winger, is the manager. Attends an FA-organised coaching course at Birmingham University,

the idea of England manager Walter Winterbottom, and gets a full badge at the first attempt.

1948
Plays in the FA Cup semi-final against Blackpool at Villa Park, going down to a 3-1 defeat after extra-time. The £18,815 gate receipts are a ground record. Scores the first of his six league goals in 314 appearances at Fulham on 4 December 1948.

1949
Arthur Rowe takes over from Joe Hulme as Spurs manager on 4 May, and right-back Alf Ramsey joins from Southampton the next day. The 'Push and Run' era is about to start.

1949-51
Bill misses only four matches as over the course of back-to-back seasons Spurs win the Second and First Division Championships. A permanent travelling reserve, he wins his only England cap against Portugal at Goodison Park on 19 May 1951, and scores with his first kick in international football, after just 20 seconds. He is a non-playing England understudy to Billy Wright in 22 international matches.

1953
A mistimed back-pass by Alf Ramsey gifts Blackpool a winning goal in the 1953 FA Cup semi-final at Villa Park. "The hardest defeat to take in all my playing career," says Bill.

1954
Because of a recurring knee injury, Bill retires and switches to the Spurs coaching staff as the right-hand man to new manager Jimmy Anderson, who has taken over from the unwell Arthur Rowe. Walter Winterbottom appoints him part-time manager of England Under-23s.

1958
Watches Brazil in the 1958 World Cup and hatches the plan that inspires England to get a goalless draw in the World Cup finals – the only team to hold the eventual world champions. Winterbottom goes on record to state that it was all down to Bill's tactical genius.

'SIR BILL'

1958–59
Bill's first match as Tottenham manager (in place of the unwell Jimmy Anderson) comes on 11 October – a famous 10-4 victory over Everton. Bill takes the job without a contract. Just three defeats in the last 12 games of the season sees Tottenham scramble clear of relegation and they finish 18th of 22 clubs. Bill signs Dave Mackay, Bill Brown, John White and Les Allen, and they join Danny Blanchflower, Bobby Smith, Cliff Jones, Terry Dyson, Terry Medwin, Maurice Norman, Peter Baker and Ron Henry as the Double team takes shape.

1959–60
Spurs kick-off the 1959/60 season with a 12-match unbeaten run on the way to third place in the First Division. Skipper Danny Blanchflower starts to talk about doing "the Impossible Double".

1960–61
Tottenham win their first 11 league matches to set up the Double, and clinch it by beating Leicester City 2-0 in the FA Cup final at Wembley. Bill becomes one of the few men to win the League Championship as a player and manager.

1961
Buys Jimmy Greaves from AC Milan for a record £99,999, deliberately dropping a pound short of making Greavsie the world's first £100,000 player.

1962
Retains the FA Cup, beating Burnley 3-1 after the disappointment of a European Cup semi-final defeat by Benfica. Finish third in the First Division title race following two defeats by Alf Ramsey's eventual champions Ipswich Town.

1963
Spurs become the first British team to win a major European trophy, capturing the European Cup Winners' Cup with a scintillating 5-1 victory over holders Atletico Madrid in the final in Rotterdam.

TIMELINE

1967
A hat-trick of 1960s FA Cup triumphs at Wembley, with goals from Jimmy Robertson and Frank Saul lifting Tottenham to a 2-1 victory over Chelsea in the first all-London FA Cup final.

1971
On transfer deadline day, he makes Martin Peters the first £200,000 player, with Jimmy Greaves going to West Ham in part exchange. Two goals in the last 10 minutes by Martin Chivers give Spurs a 2-0 League Cup final victory over Third Division Aston Villa at Wembley.

1972
Another two goals by Martin Chivers in the first leg at Wolves give Spurs a stranglehold on the UEFA Cup, and skipper Alan Mullery clinches victory with Spurs' goal in a 1-1 draw in the second leg of the final at White Hart Lane.

1973
Substitute Ralph Coates scores with a spectacular shot to give Spurs a League Cup final victory over Norwich City at Wembley.

1974
Rioting fans scar Tottenham's feat of reaching the UEFA Cup final in Rotterdam – a match eventually won by Feyenoord. On 29 August Bill announces his retirement after 16 years in the Spurs hot seat. He leaves the club on 13 September, taking a scouting role at West Ham after a short break from the game.

1976
In July, Bill returns to Tottenham as consultant and chief scout. Among his signings are Gary Mabbutt, Graham Roberts and Tony Galvin.

1977
Awarded an OBE that he collects at Buckingham Palace.

1991
Appointed President of Tottenham Hotspur.

1998
Receives Freedom of the Borough of Haringey.

1999
Bill attends a ceremony to see an approach road to White Hart Lane re-named Bill Nicholson Way in his honour.

2003
Inducted into the English Football Hall of Fame.

2004
First to be inducted into the Tottenham Hall of Fame. Moves with Darkie into a warden-assisted flat in Potters Bar and dies in a nearby Hertfordshire hospital on 23 October 2004, aged 85.

Darkie, Bill's wife for 62 years, dies three years later, on 31 July 2007. Bill and Darkie's ashes were placed side by side in caskets hidden beneath the perimeter of the White Hart Lane pitch, and later were moved to a similar position at the new Tottenham Hotspur Stadium. RIP.

INDEX

AC Milan, 78-79, 81, 86, 96, 126, 236, 270, 278
Alexander Laundry, 7
Alf Garnett, 16, 116
Ajax, 10, 86
Allen, Bradley, 72
Allen, Clive, 72
Allen, Dennis, 72
Allen, Les, 61, 62, 71, 72, 7, 88, 179, 181, 227, 228, 269, 277
Allen, Martin, 72
Allen, Paul, 72
Allison, Malcolm, 173, 196
Alloa Athletic, 70
Amateur Athletic Association, 14
Amsterdam, 88
Anderson, Jimmy, 9, 37, 38-39, 40-41, 42-43, 48, 52, 102, 201, 228, 245, 277
Andrews, Eamonn, 241
Anfield, 114, 175, 219
Arbroath, 65
Arce, Oscar, 165
Ardiles, Osvaldo, 164, 166, 223, 225, 247
Argentina, 165
Armstrong, George, 226
Army Physical Training Corps, 13

Arsenal, 7, 8, 9, 17, sharing ground 21, 32, 64, 65, 70, 73, 99, 100, 102, 109, 118, 139, 153, 157, 158, 159, 165, 195, 219, 225, 228, 247, 270
Aspel, Michael, 241
Aston Villa, 31-34, 64, 67, 109, 279
Athens, 11
Atletico Madrid, 70, 93-94, 174, 238, 246, 247, 279
Austria, 45
Baily, Eddie, 14, 15-16, 22, 23, 24-26, 42, 48, 83, 115, 118, 123, 150, 151, 155-156, 162, 164, 175, 178, 181, 182-183, 188, 201, 205, 222, 223, 233, 243
Baker, Peter, 53, 62, 66, 88, 93, 181, 222, 224, 225, 228
Baker, Terry, 84, 95, 235
Baldwin, Tommy, 109
Ball, Alan, 63
Banks, Gordon, 64
Bannister, Sir Roger, 59
Barcelona, 10
Barnsley, 67, 161
Battersby, John, 78
Baseball Ground, 111

Beal, Phil, 61, 108, 130, 140, 141, 142, 151, 158, 181, 218, 220, 221-222, 224
Bearman, Fred, 55
Belfast, 67
Belo Horizonte, 29
Benfica, 79, 86, 88, 89, 238, 246, 278
Bennett, Les, 23, 41
Berlin Olympics, 8
Best, George, 63, 73
Bill Nicholson Way, 114, 207, 280
Blackburn Rovers, 10, 99, 246, 272, 276
Blackpool, 21, 26, 236, 277
Blanchflower, Danny, 14, 30, leaves Aston Villa for Spurs 30-35, 48, 53, 55-57, 62, 64, 67-68, 70, 71, 78, 79, 88, 91, 92, 93, 97, 98, 99, 104, 151-154, 156, 164, 171, 173, 208, 222, 223, 224, 225, 226, 228, 234, 236, 241, 245, 246, 278
Blanchflower, Jackie, 33, 67
Bobroff, Paul, 166
Bolshoi Ballet, 60
Bolton Wanderers, 163, 185
Bond, Dennis, 61, 271
Bonetti, Peter, 108, 110
Book, Tony, 69
Bowles, Stan, 105
Boyle, John, 109
Brabrook, Peter, 77
Brancepeth, 13
Brazil 41, 45-46, 244-45, 278
Brazil, Alan, 179
Bremner, Billy, 63, 231, 232
Brentford, 74

Brentwood Mental Hospital, 275
Brighton & Hove Albion, 71, 163
BBC, First TV broadcast, 8
Bristol Rovers, 163, 203-204
Brookmans Park, Herts, 183
Brooks, Johnny, 72
Brown, Bill, 62, 65, 68, 87, 88, 92, 94, 181, 195, 219, 224, 225, 236, 237, 269, 278
Brown, Laurie, 99, 270
Buckingham, Vic, 10, 14
Buckle, Bobby, 2, 8
Buenos Aires, 165
Bulgaria, 216
Burgess, Ron, 8, 9, 10, 22, 23, 41, 156, 164, 197, 222, 224, 237, 243, 275
Burkinshaw, Keith, 159, 161, 171, 201, 210, 234, 247
Burnley, 35, 55. 88, 91, 103, 142, 174, 236, 237, 273, 278
Busby, Sir Matt, 22, 113, 114, 182, 195, 203, 205, 228
Café Royal, 78
Cambridge University, 14, 244
Cameron, John, 2
Canada, 65, 181
Cantwell, Noel, 97, 108
Carter, Raich, 115
Catterick, Harry, 49, 177, 197
Chalmers, Len, 64, 74
Channon, Mike, 130
Channel Islands, 23
Chapman, Herbert, 7, 64
Charity Shield, 89, 110, 237
Charlton Athletic, 163
Charlton, Sir Bobby, 63, 140, 142
Charlton, Jack, 68, 232

INDEX

Chelmsford, 272
Chelsea, 15, 67, 71, 72, 77, 78, 83, 99, 100, 102, 107-112, 139, 173, 197, 235, 236, 246, 269, 272, 279
Cheshunt training ground, 2, 4, 98, 185, 186, 203, 209, 218, 241
Chivers, Martin, 42, 79, 106, 116, 124, 130, 137, 140, 141, 143, 155, 172, 175-176, 178, 180, 181, 183, 190, 202-203, 206, 223, 224, 232, 272, 279
Chorzow, 85
Chuzo, Alvarez, 94
Clarke, Allan 'Sniffer', 196
Clarke, Harry 68, 221
Clayton, Eddie, 181
Coates, Ralph, 130, 139-143, 179, 273, 279
Clough, Brian, 46, 111, 139, 176, 205, 207
Colchester United, 70
Collar, Enrique, 94
Collins, Bobby, 53, 54
Collins, Peter, 61, 181, 272
Coluna, Mario, 87
Conn, Alfie, 163, 273
Cooke, Charlie, 108, 109, 110
Corrigan, Peter, 216-218
Coventry City, 149, 150, 155, 233
Creighton Road, 16, 121, 177
Crewe Alexandra, 55, 106
Crews Hill golf course, 70
Cruyff, Johan, 10, 157
Crystal Palace, 123
Cullis, Stan, 182
Cyprus, 72

Daily Express, 1, 2, 3, 21, 107, 110, 119, 217
Daily Mirror, 33
Daines, Barry, 273
Dalglish, Kenny, 169
Dalyell, Tam, MP, 120
Darlington, 13, 243
Davis, Joe, 11
De Jong, Theo, 147
Derby County, 68, 111, 139, 207
Ditchburn, Ted, 16, 41, 65, 220
Dixon, Wilf, 158, 161
Docherty, Tommy, 109, 110, 111, 173-174, 194
Dukla Prague, 86
Duncan, John, 155
Dundee, 65, 99, 246, 269, 271
Dunfermline, 195
Dunlop, Albert, 53
Duquemin, Len, 23, 156, 188, 223
Durban City, 65
Durham Light Infantry, 13, 243, 276
Dyson, Geoff, 13, 14, 15, 37, 62, 275
Dyson, Ginger, 70
Dyson, Terry, 61, 64, 70, 85, 88, 93, 95, 174, 181, 223, 224, 227, 238

Edinburgh, 69, 119
Edmonton, 22, 104
Edward VIII abdication, 8
Edwards, Duncan, 201
Egypt, 217
Enfield, 65, 71, 181
England cap, 27-30, 242, 244, 277
England, Mike, 61, 99, 108, 118-119, 140, 141, 147, 158, 220, 224, 246, 272

England Under-23s, 141, 196, 197, 215, 216, 245, 277
English Football Hall of Fame, 280
Eric Morecambe, 165
Eriksson, Sven-Goran, 198
Essex, 72
European Cup semi-final, 79, 89, 172, 246
European Cup Winners' Cup 70, 71, 91-96, 97, 174, 193, 238, 279
Eusebio, 87
Evans, Harry, 98, 116
Evans, Ray, 273
Everton, 51-54, 186, 245, 275
FA Cup, 2, 10, 21, 26, 34, 35, 37, 39, 41, 55, 59, 62, 64, 69, 71, 74, 88, 96, 100-102, 106, 107-112, 112, 113, 123, 139, 166, 167, 170, 173, 193, 197, 207, 236, 277
FA Coaches Association, 168
Falkirk, 70, 269
Faulkner, Charlie, 49, 150
Fennelly, John, 208-214
Ferguson, Sir Alex, 195
Feyenoord, 86, 147, 233, 279
Finn, Ralph, 208
Finney, Sir Tom, 28, 29, 73
Fiorentina, 178
Fleet Street, 33, 216
Football Association, 22, 70, 77
Football Hall of Fame, 21
Franklin, Neil, 15
Fulham, 13, 70, 98, 103, 271, 275, 277
Freedom of the Borough of Haringey, 280

Galvin, Tony, 167, 279
Gardner, Maureen, 14
Garrincha, 189
Gascoigne, Paul, 218
George, Charlie, 227, 228
George V, 8
George VI, 8
Giles, Johnny, 63, 153, 231-232, 234
Gilzean, Alan, 61, 79, 83-84, 99, 105, 108, 110-111, 140, 141, 163, 164, 172, 174, 180, 195, 223, 224, 236, 238, 246, 271
Glasgow Celtic, 79, 114, 172, 228, 238
Glasgow Rangers, 70, 92, 273
Glentoran, 67
Goodison Park, 197, 277
Gornik Zabrze, 85-86
Gosforth Park Hotel, 117
Graham, George, 109, 195, 227
Gravesend and Northfleet, 8, 9, 23, 41, 164, 243, 276
Greaves, Jimmy, 8, 34, 71, 72, 75, 77-84, 86-87, 88, 91, 92, 93, 95, 98, 99, 101, 102, 104, 107, 108, 110-111, 113-126, 156, 164, 169, 171-172, 174, 176, 180, 190, 200-201, 218, 223, 224, 234-239, 246, 270, 278
Greaves, Jim Snr (Dad), 77
Greaves, Danny, 35
Greenwood, Ron, 49, 125-126, 156, 195, 198, 205
Guildford City, 70, 275
Hagan, Jimmy, 9
Hammond, Richard, 177
Hampden Park, 33

INDEX

Harpenden, 66
Harris, Allan, 109
Harris, Ron, 109, 197
Harris, Jimmy, 53
Hartlepool United, 13, 276
Harmer, Tommy, 52-54, 181, 245
Haslam, Harry, 165-166
Harvey, Colin, 63
Hastings, 71
Hateley, Mark, 110
Hateley, Tony, 109
Haynes, Johnny, 103
Hayters Sports Agency, 209
Hearts, 68, 207, 269
Henry, Ron, 62, 66-67, 88, 93, 94, 179, 181, 213, 221, 224, 226
Hickson, Dave, 53
Highbury 21, 28, 33, 118, 157, 159, 195
Hill, Jimmy, 198
Hillary, Sir Edmund, 59
Hillsborough, 49
Hinton, Marvin, 109, 174
Hitler, 8, 11, 19, 23
Holder, Phil, 142, 273
Hoddle, Glenn, 157, 159, 163, 164, 190, 202, 222
Hollins, John, 109, 225
Hollowbread, Johnny, 53
Hopkins, Mel, 53, 67, 179, 181, 221
Houghton, Eric, 33
Howe, Don, 196
Hoy, Roger, 273
Hulme, Joe, 21, 23, 277
Hungary, 22, 41, 68, 98
Hunter, Norman, 63, 231, 232
Hurst, Sir Geoff, 49, 63, 125, 198-199

Iceland, 29, 122
Independent on Sunday, 216
Ipswich Town, 48, 88, 89, 278
Italy, 13, 29, 78, 96, 235, 275
Iley, Jim, 53, 236
Ives, Ben, 7, 243, 275
Japan, 179
Jarrow Hunger March, 8
Jennings, Pat, 61, 65, 99, 107, 108, 110, 117-118, 130, 140, 143, 155, 158, 179, 180, 181, 197, 199-200, 219, 224, 225, 237, 246, 271
Jezzard, Bedford, 103
Jol, Martin, 198
Jones, Bryn, 73
Jones, Chris, 273
Jones, Cliff 3, 55, 61, 62, 73, 85, 86, 88. 91, 92, 93, 107, 108, 113-114, 130. 144, 155, 179, 180, 181, 190, 192, 201, 218, 223, 224, 226, 228, 278
Jones, Herbert, 7
Jones, Ivor, 73
Jones, Ken, 73
Jones, Lesley-Ann, 73
Jordan, 217
Kane, Harry, 42, 123
Keelan, Kevin, 140
Keegan, Kevin, 143, 197
Kendall, Howard, 63, 197
Kenilworth Road, 165
Kennedy, Ray, 227
Kingswood Secondary Modern School, 77
Kinnear, Joe, 108, 130, 140, 203, 218, 273
Kirkup, Joe, 108, 109

Knowles, Cyril, 61, 65, 99, 107, 108, 130, 140, 158, 180, 220-221, 224, 246, 272
Knowles, Peter, 221
Law, Denis, 63, 176
Lawton, Tommy, 15, 29, 109
Leadbetter, Jimmy, 88, 89
League Cup, 69, 72, 133, 138, 139, 141, 143, 247, 273, 279
Lee, Colin, 163
Leeds United, 155, 231-232
Leicester City, 64, 73, 74, 174, 209, 236, 237
Leyton Orient, 116
Lilleshall coaching school, 193
Lingdale, North Yorkshire, 71
Liverpool, 59, 107, 122, 139, 143, 161
Liverpool Street Station, 124
Lofthouse, Nat, 15
Loftus Road, 72
London Evening News, 40, 186
Louis Armstrong, 115
Luton Town, 165
Lyall, John, 156, 195
Lyn Oslo, 143
Lyons, Tom, 32
Mabbutt, Gary, 167, 179, 203-204, 279
Mackay, Dave, 35, 55, 62, 69, 70, 71, 85, 86, 87, 88, 92, 93, 94, 95, 97, 98, 99, 107, 108, 110, 112, 119, 141, 155, 164, 179, 180, 181, 195, 206-207, 222, 224, 226, 228, 236, 237, 245, 246, 269, 277, 278
Madinabeytia, Edgardo, 94
Malton, North Yorkshire, 70

Manchester City, 39, 166, 167
Manchester United, 22, 45, 64, 67, 97, 110, 206, 216, 232, 236
Mannion, Wilf, 29, 115
Marchi, Tony, 64, 91, 93, 94, 179, 181, 222, 269
Matthews, Stanley, 21, 26, 28, 73
Maximum football wage, 8, 23
Max Miller, 116, 243
McGarry, Bill, 196, 219, 237
McCreadie, Eddie, 109
McGrath, Chris, 148
McGuinness, Wilf, 216
McIlroy, Jimmy, 35
McLintock, Frank, 226, 228
McNab, Bob, 226, 228
McNab, Neil, 273
McWilliam, Peter, 2, 9, 10, 11, 60
Medley, Les, 22, 23, 41, 223
Medwin, Terry, 53, 62, 64, 88, 97, 181, 203, 223, 278
Mee, Bertie, 228
Memorial Service, 190-193, 198
Mendonca, Jorge, 94
Merson, Paul, 105
Michels, Rinus, 10, 42
Middlesborough, 13, 46, 70, 99, 122, 243, 246, 271
Miller, Harry, 186, 215, 275
Minter, Billy, 42
Molineux, 55, 64, 233
Moore, Bobby, 49, 63, 68, 125, 222
Moores, Ian, 163
Morgan, Roger, 130, 272
Morris, Malcolm, 241
Mortensen, Stan, 29
Morton FC, 273

INDEX

Moscow, 60
Motson, John, 181
Muhammad Ali, 209
Mullery, Alan, 61, 98, 104-105, 108, 110, 118, 123, 130, 137, 190, 199, 223, 224, 233, 246, 271, 279
Munich air crash, 45, 67, 201
Musselburgh, Lothian, 70
Naylor, Terry, 151, 163, 179, 181, 273
Neighbour, Jimmy, 130, 181, 273
Neill, Terry, 152, 155, 157-159, 161, 165, 234
Newcastle United, 9, 13, 117, 208, 243, 276
Newry, 118
Nicholson, Bill
 Last of the Victorians 5-11, trial for Spurs 8, ground staff boy 9, Tottenham debut 10, Farningham Road lodgings 10, Second World War 13-19, marries Grace 13, first married home 16, first car 16, moves to Creighton Road 16, bans wife from watching him play 17, dislike of Arsenal red 17, resumes playing career after War 19, playing for the Push and Run Spurs 21-26, views on players' wages 24, only England cap, 27-30, knee injury forces retirement 30, rivalry with Alf Ramsey 37-43; coaching England, 1958 World Cup 45-48; turning down Sheffield Wednesday 49, the astonishing 10-4 start 51-54, The Double 59-75, signing Jimmy Greaves, 77-84, European Cup challenge 85-89, capturing the European Cup Winners' Cup 91-96, demise of the double team, 97-106, completing the FA Cup hat-trick 107-112 , the departure of Greavsie, 113-126, the tale of Gilzean and Chivers 127-137, Hair-raising League Cup final for Ralph Coates 139-145, nightmare in Rotterdam and the last days in charge 147-154, signing on the dole and an OBE, 155-160, back from the wilderness, 161, at home with The Master, 169-177, testimonial match and becomes first member of the Tottenham Hall of Fame, 178-183, a fond final farewell to The Master and the first interview 185-190, memorial service 190-193, tributes from the world of football 193-208, Bill and Darkie's ashes 207, This Is Your Life 241-247, major transfer signings 269-273
Nicholson, Edith (mother), 7, 275
Nicholson, Grace, aka Darkie (wife), 3, 10, 16-17, 'perfect manager's wife' 17, 19, 49, 160, 162, 170, 175, 176, 178, 185, 187, 194, 201, 207, 212, 216, 228, 231, 235, 242, 276

Nicholson, Jean (daughter), 16, 18, 19, 185, 188, 207, 242, 280
Nicholson, Joe (father), 6, 275
Nicholson, Linda, (daughter), 16, 19, 185, 187, 207, 242
Nicklin, Frank, 166
Ninian Park, 10
Norfolk, 68
Norman, Maurice, 35, 41, 62, 65, 68, 88, 93, 98, 181, 221, 224, 226
Normansell, Fred, 33
Northern Command, 15
Northern Ireland, 33, 67, 103, 118, 158
Northolt, Middlesex, 50
Norwich City, 68, 139, 142, 279
Notts County, 109
Nottingham, 69
Nottingham Forest, 69
Numbers Game, 249-268
OBE, 170, 242, 247, 280
OFK Belgrade, 92
Old Trafford, 97, 107, 110, 114, 206
Olympiakos, 143
O'Neill, Jimmy, 53
Ontario, 65
Orange, J.G. (Jack), 40
Osgood, Keith, 273
Osgood, Peter, 109
Oxford University, 14
Paisley, Bob, 122
Paxton Road, 180
Pearce, Jimmy, 61, 130, 140, 273
Pelé, 45, 189
Perryman, Ted, 49, 74, 144

Peters, Martin, 49, 63, 79, 83, 122, 125-126, 130, 140, 143, 151, 158, 173, 179, 180, 203, 204-205, 222, 224, 273, 279
Petrolheads, 177
Pleat, David, 180, 194
Plymouth Argyle, 125
Poland, 11, 85
Porter, Andy, 209
Portugal, 27, 143, 212, 244, 275, 277
Port Vale, 48
Postecoglou, Ange, 9
Possee, Derek, 273
Potters Bar, Herts, 185, 280
Poynton, Cecil, 60, 89, 91-92, 98, 117, 189
Pratt, John, 61, 140, 141, 163-164, 179, 181, 206, 273
Premier League, 38, 167
President of Tottenham, 280
Prince of Wales Hospital, Tottenham, 98
Professional Footballers' Association 24, 166, 204
'Push and Run' Spurs, 2, 10, 21-26, 115, 151, 164, 181, 182, 187, 188, 220, 221, 243, 247, 277
Puskas, Ferenc, 9
Queen's Park Rangers, 72, 74, 105, 167, 272
Radford, John, 227
Railton, Vic, 40, 186, 187
Ramiro, Ruiz, 94
Ramsey, Sir Alf, 14, 22, 24, 29, 37-43, 48, 79, 81, 83, 88, 89, 99, 114, 130, 173, 182, 194, 203, 205, 220-221, 224, 242, 243, 245, 277, 278

INDEX

Real Madrid, 86, 88, 239
Redbourn, Hertfordshire, 67
Red Star Belgrade, 143
Ressel, Peter, 149
Revie, Don, 39, 232
Rice, Pat, 225
Robb, George, 53
Roberts, Graham, 167, 212, 279
Robertson, Jimmy, 99, 108, 110, 111, 270, 279
Rodger, Jim, 119-120
Rotterdam, 92, 96, 147, 149, 233, 279
Rowe, Arthur, 2, 9, 14, 21-22, 23-24, 31, 37, 38, 40, 48, 60, 65, 77, 78, 89, 182, 243, 247, 277
Royal Scots Fusiliers, 15
Rupert Murdoch, 217
Rush, Ian, 171
Russia, 45
Ryden, John, 53, 54, 180
Saint & Greavsie, 173
St Albans, 273
St George's Park, Staffs, 193
St James' Park, 118
St Mirren, 99
Saul, Frank, 64, 72, 86, 108, 110, 111, 273, 279
Saunders, Ron, 139
Salonica, Greece, 72
Scarborough, 5, 13, 15, 242
Scarborough High School, 6, 275
Scarborough Young Liberals, 7, 243, 275
Scarborough Working Men's Club, 243
Schwarzenegger, Arnold, 60
Scholar, Irving, 104, 166

Scotland, 33, 70, 103
Scunthorpe, 161
Sexton, Dave, 193, 195
Shackleton, Len, 115
Shankly, Bill, 107, 114, 175, 176, 182, 195, 197, 203, 205, 206, 219, 228, 246
Sheffield United, 165
Sheffield Wednesday, 64, 177
Shellito, Ken, 77
Sherpa Tenzing, 59
Shilton, Peter, 236
Shoreditch, 66
Simpson, Peter, 226
Slovan Bratislava, 92
Smith, Bobby, 42, 53, 55, 61, 62, 64, 71-72, 79, 86, 87, 88, 93, 94, 95, 99-104, 105, 175, 179, 181, 223, 224, 227, 228, 238
Smith, John, 64, 270
Smith, Tommy, 142
Souness, Graeme, 119-121, 273
South Africa, 65
Southampton, 37, 42, 124, 130, 163, 272, 277
Southgate, 65
Stamford Bridge, 71, 102, 173, 195, 235
Stein, Jock, 79, 114, 172, 195, 228, 238
Stepney, Alex, 110, 236
Stock Exchange, 166
Stokes, Alfie, 53, 189
Storey, Peter, 226
Sugar, Sir Alan, 171, 181
Sunderland, 1, 2, 13, 64, 243, 275
Swansea, 73, 275
Sweden, 45, 49, 189

Swindon Town, 69, 72
Syria, 217
Tanner ball players, 6, 275
Tagg, Ernie, 106
Tambling, Bobby, 109, 110
Taunton's Grammar School, 124
Taylor, Eric, 49
Taylor, Ernie, 115
Taylor, Peter, 163
Testimonial match, 81, 124, 169, 175, 177-178, 181
Thompson, Jimmy, 77, 235
The Double, 23, 179, 193, 199, 202, 209, 221, 222, 225-229, 236, 278
The Ghost of White Hart Lane, 70
The G-Men, 105
The Observer, 216
The Sun, 151, 166, 216
The Times, 124
This Is Your Life, 169, 241-247
Timeline, 275-280
Top Gear, 177
Torino, 269
Toronto Falcons, 65
Torquay United, 163
Tottenham Angels, 86
Tottenham Centenary Video, 8
Tottenham Hall of Fame, 180, 185, 280
Tottenham High Road, 186
Tottenham Tribute Trust, 179
Tottenham Weekly Herald, 209, 275
Tresadern, Jack, 8, 9
Turf Moor, 103, 142
Turin, 29
Turkey, 196

UEFA Cup 137, 143, 147, 233, 279
United States, 29
Upton Park, 190
Van Daele, Joop, 147
Van Hanegem, Willem, 147
VAR, 87-88
Venables, Terry, 77, 99, 104, 108, 109, 181, 193-194, 246, 272
Vicarage Road, 219
Villa, Ricardo, 166
Villa Park, 21, 32, 39
Vittoria Setubal, 143, 233
Wale, Frederick, 104, 166
Wales, 73, 201
Walker, Dickie, 49
Walker, Tommy, 207
Wallace, Barbara, 115, 186, 187
Wallis, Johnny, 60, 114
Walsall, 69
Walters, Sonny 22, 23, 223
Walthamstow Greyhound Stadium, 125
Want, Tony, 273
Warren Mitchell, 116
Waterloo Station, 124
Watford Football Club, 99, 197, 200, 219, 237, 271
Watson, Bill, 60
Welch, Julie, 98
Weller, Keith, 273
Welton, Pat, 162
Wembley, 103, 107, 112, 139, 140, 279
West Ham United, 49, 77, 79, 116, 124, 125, 155, 160, 179, 186, 187, 190, 195, 200, 210, 220, 242, 247, 270, 273, 279

INDEX

White, John, 55, 62, 67, 70-71, 79, 88, 92, 93, 94, 97-98, 99, 104, 116-117, 164, 173, 195, 218, 222, 224, 227, 228, 236, 246, 269, 277
White, Mandy, 98
White, Rob, 98
White, Sandra, 98
White Hart Lane, 2, 7, 8, 9, 17, 21, 61, 64, 70, 77, 85, 97, 104, 108, 113, 125, 139, 141, 143, 147, 151, 155, 157, 163, 166, 172, 178, 179, 180, 181, 186, 198, 199, 204, 207, 209, 212, 215, 233, 242, 279, 280
Whittaker, Tom, 33
Wilson, Bob, 225, 228
Winterbottom, Walter, 27, 28-29, 37, 45, 60, 168, 244, 277, 278
Who's the Greatest? (TV series), 169, 171, 177
Wolverhampton Wanderers, 27, 32, 45-46, 55, 64, 137, 139, 221, 233, 279
World Cup, 34, 45, 99, 102, 107, 165, 189, 189, 222, 275
World Cup Rally, 124
Wright, Billy, 24, 26, 27-28, 30, 157, 244, 277

'Sir' Bill Nicholson
(1919–2004)